C000171671

International Strategic Alliances

Joint Ventures Between Asian and U.S. Companies

BY

FREDERICK D. LIPMAN

WITH

PROFESSOR LARRY D. QIU

Published by Daniel Publishing LLC.

Library of Congress Cataloging-in-Publication Data:

Lipman, Frederick D. with Professor Larry D. Qiu

ISBN 0615680879
EAN 9780615680873

Printed in the United States of America

10 9 8 7 6 5 4 3 2 1

To Joyce Lipman, wife of my deceased brother,
Harold Lipman, and their family.

Other Works By Frederick D. Lipman

Whistleblowers: Incentives, Disincentives and Protection Strategies

The Family Business Guide: Everything You Need to Know to Manage Your Business from Legal Planning to Business Strategies

International and U.S. IPO Planning: A Business Strategy Guide

Executive Compensation Best Practices

Corporate Governance Best Practices: Strategies for Public, Private, and Not-for-Profit Organizations

Valuing Your Business: Strategies to Maximize the Sale Price

Audit Committees

The Complete Guide to Employee Stock Options

The Complete Guide to Valuing and Selling Your Business

The Complete Going Public Handbook

Financing Your Business with Venture Capital

How Much Is Your Business Worth

Going Public

Venture Capital and Junk Bond Financing

Table of Contents

Acknowledgements

The author wishes to thank Professor Larry D. Qiu, an Associate Dean at the University of Hong Kong, for his contribution to this book. The author located Professor Qiu because of an article dated August, 2006 which he wrote entitled "Cross-Border Strategic Alliances and Foreign Market Entry".

The author also wishes to acknowledge the assistance of the following attorneys at Blank Rome LLP in its New York, Philadelphia, Hong Kong and Shanghai offices in preparing this book: Jennifer L. Bell, Esq., Jennifer Hale Eagland, Esq., Fang Felton, Esq., Barry H. Genkin, Esq., Feige M. Grundman, Esq., Joseph T. Gulant, Esq., Anthony B. Haller, Eq., Shawn Li, Esq., Manuela M. Morais, Esq., William H. Roberts, Esq. and Shawn Wright, Esq.

I would also like to thank Victor Zhang, Esq., an attorney with a Beijing law firm, who was interning at Blank Rome LLP, for assisting me in obtaining English translations of Chinese government documents and in helping to edit several sections of this book.

The author would also like to thank Cheryl Halvorsen, a Blank Rome LLP librarian for her research assistance.

As with all my recent books, I acknowledge the help of Barbara Helverson who serves as the initial editor as well as the typist for the book.

Preface

This book is intended for middle-market and smaller companies that wish to grow their business internationally. Although great emphasis is placed upon Chinese-based and U.S.-based joint ventures, the business principles in this book apply to all cross-border strategic alliances, and include such diverse arrangements as simple distributorship arrangements, patent licenses and exclusive manufacturing contracts. Moreover, many of the examples of past successful international U.S. joint ventures contained in this book were based in Japan, India and the Republic of Korea and not in the Peoples Republic of China.

Chinese-based companies have also expressed an interest in forming U.S.-based strategic alliances in order to grow their business internationally. This book is also intended to help them navigate the formation of such strategic alliances in the U.S.

Throughout this book we use actual case studies of the experiences of Fortune 500 companies in their Asian international joint ventures. Their documented experiences, both positive and negative, are instructive for middle-market and smaller companies. Fortune 500 companies have, for many years, profited from strategic international alliances and have developed substantial expertise in creating and operating such alliances. Despite their expertise, many of these joint ventures have failed.

Middle-market and smaller companies, including so-called "born global" companies, lack the expertise of these Fortune 500 companies and need to study both the successes and the failures of these Fortune 500 global alliances as well as learn from their mistakes. This book is intended to help analyze these cross-border transactions in order to illustrate the mistakes to avoid and the elements of success.

Middle-market and smaller companies will also learn that
an Asian-based joint venture may be a good defensive move to
protect themselves from future competition from low cost Asian
competitors. The author uses the term "middle-market" companies to refer to companies with less than $1 billion in revenues
and which may be privately owned or publicly traded.

What is remarkable in studying the growth of Fortune 500
companies is the extent to which that growth has been international, particularly in Asia. Much of the growth of these large
companies occurred during the last 30 years, initially in the
Japanese markets and currently in the Chinese market. For
example, the net sales and income of Apple Inc in the Asia-Pacific
area each rose over 200% during the second quarter of fiscal 2012,
compared to the second quarter of fiscal 2011, making it the second-largest area in the world for Apple products.[1]

Although the older alliances with Japanese companies initially were based in Japan, many Japanese investors have now
invested elsewhere, including the U.S. (e.g. Toyota and Honda
U.S. plants). It is expected that Chinese companies that have
profited from joint ventures with U.S. companies will likewise,
in the future, begin investing in the U.S., including U.S.-based
joint ventures.

The U.S. currently has high labor costs compared to China.
Some believe that by 2015 the gap will have narrowed to the
point that the savings in transportation and other distribution
costs may make it economical for both Asian and U.S. companies to manufacture in the U.S. for U.S. consumption.[2] Moreover,
the U.S. possesses cheap natural gas. Indeed, the price of natural gas in the U.S. and Canada is currently the lowest in the
world.[3] The expansion of U.S. shale gas production in the future
may once again make manufacturing feasible in the U.S. for U.S.

---

[1] Form 10-Q for Apple, Inc. for Quarterly Period Ended March 31, 2012.

[2] David Conrads, "As Chinese wages rise, US manufacturers heard back
home", The Christian Science Monitor, May 10, 2012, http://www.
csmonitor.com/Business/new-economy/2012/0510/As-Chinese-
wages-rise-US-manufacturers-head-back-home

[3] "Igniting a Renaissance" PNC Investment Outlook, May 2012

consumption and encourage Asian companies to locate in the U.S.

Some believe that the 21st Century will be the Asian century. The population of China alone is approximately 20% of the world's population.[4] By 2040, India's population is expected to exceed that of China.[5] Businesses will want to take advantage of the huge potential growth in the Asian economies.

Organization of Book

The book consists of three parts:

- Part I is a general description of international strategic alliances with an emphasis on the lessons learned from prior successes and failures.

- Part II is a discussion intended for U.S. companies of what is involved in creating a Chinese-based joint venture.

- Part III is intended for Chinese companies who are interested in a joint venture based in the United States.

Chapter 1 contains a general discussion of joint ventures and includes a specific discussion of the Wahaha Mikado Joint Venture Company in the Peoples Republic of China, the Corning – Samsung joint venture in the Republic of Korea, and the recent growth of international and Chinese alliances, including QVC, Inc., Starbucks and Honeywell International. This chapter also analyzes the alternative of a merger to a joint venture and current Chinese direct U.S. investment.

Chapter 2 is entitled "Selecting the Right Partners" and contains a discussion of both the Yahoo! Inc. alliance with Alibaba Group Holding Ltd. in China as well as the Kentucky Fried Chicken – Mitsubishi joint venture in Japan and attempts to draw lessons from this last example. This chapter also reviews

---

[4] Matt Rosenberg, "China Population: The Population Growth of the World's Largest Country", About.Com, January 1, 2011, http://geography.about.com/od/populationgeography/a/chinapopulation.htm

[5] Id.

the Goodyear Tire and Rubber Company global alliance with Sumitomo Rubber Industries, Ltd. in Japan and the General Motors joint venture with Shanghai Automotive Industry Corp. in China. The chapter also mentions the so-called "Born Global" Phenomena and how the Xerox Corporation joint venture with Fuji Photo Film Co. Ltd. may have saved Xerox. Similarly to Xerox, middle-market companies may find that creating a China – based joint venture ultimately can save them from future competition from low-cost Asian competitors.

Chapter 3 provides an analysis of why joint ventures fail and gives specific examples of what works and what doesn't, including the Groupon joint venture with Tencent Holdings LTD in China.

This concludes Part I of the book.

In Part II of the book, Chapter 4 contains an overview of the current Chinese economy by Professor Larry Dongxiao Qiu of Hong Kong University, Hong Kong.

Chapter 5 explains how to negotiate a joint venture based in China and gives specific examples of the Chinese negotiating strategy. This chapter also contains an analysis of the negotiation between Ericsson, a Swedish multi-national corporation, and different Chinese projects in the telecommunication industry.

Chapter 6 reviews the business and legal issues of a Chinese-based joint venture. This chapter should be read in conjunction with Chapter 8 which contains a more detailed discussion of legal issues of U.S.-based joint ventures, many of which are also applicable in China. The chapter starts with an analysis of the investment restrictions imposed by the Chinese government on U.S. and other foreign companies and examines key provisions of a Chinese-based joint venture. The chapter concludes with a discussion of the U.S. Foreign Corrupt Practices Act, antitrust laws and similar international laws which will impact a Chinese joint venture.

Chapter 7 is entitled "Operating the Joint Venture in China and Terminating It." In this chapter we discuss four significant operational issues, including dealing with Chinese government officials, protecting intellectual property, Chinese employment law and relations, and Chinese business taxes. There is also an analysis of some of the difficult business issues in terminating a Chinese–based joint venture. This concludes Part II of the book.

Part III begins with Chapter 8 which is intended to advise Chinese companies that wish to create a U.S.-based joint venture. There are major differences between U.S. laws and Chinese laws affecting employees and these distinctions are reviewed in this chapter. This chapter also contains a discussion of what industries may be off-limits to Chinese companies.

Chapter 9 contains a detailed discussion of business and legal issues of U.S.-based joint ventures. This chapter should be read in conjunction with Chapter 6, which deals with the same subject for Chinese-based joint ventures.

One of the motivations for Chinese and other Asian entrepreneurs to make investments in the U.S. is to be able to obtain permanent U.S. residency for themselves and their families. Chapter 10 explains the requirements to obtain what is called the EB-5 visa for persons investing at least $1 million ($500,000 for certain areas) in the U.S. and creating a minimum of 10 full-time jobs for qualified U.S. workers.

Appendix 1 contains a detailed discussion of the case study of the Xerox and Fuji Xerox joint venture which is used at the Harvard Business School.

Appendix 2 contains the Catalogue, effective January 30, 2012, of encouraged, restricted and prohibited foreign investment industries published by the Peoples Republic of China. Appendix 2 will permit readers to determine in which industry category their proposed joint venture or other investment falls, which is extremely important in determining the difficulty in obtaining approvals from the Chinese government.

Appendix 3 contains a recent joint venture agreement for a start-up U.S. public company with its Chinese partners for a joint venture based in China. This Appendix is not intended to be a model to be followed since it is a bare-bones agreement which does not cover certain important topics.

PART I

Cross-Border Strategic Alliances

Chapter 1

Introduction

Many companies have grown their businesses by cross-border strategic alliances. Such large companies as Corning Incorporated, General Electric, General Motors, Motorola, Honeywell, Xerox, Cisco Systems, Goodyear, Starbucks and QVC have been able to spur their growth through transnational strategic alliances, particularly in Asia. However, even middle-market and smaller companies have become interested in international strategic alliances as a method of growing their revenues and income and protecting themselves from low-cost foreign competitors, many of which are in Asia.

The successes and mistakes of these Fortune 500 companies in their international strategic alliances provide an important learning tool for middle-market and smaller companies seeking international partners. Academic scholars have provided detailed analyses of the Asian joint ventures of these Fortune 500 companies. The stories in this chapter about Fortune 500 companies can be used as lessons for what works and what doesn't in Asian joint ventures for middle-market and smaller companies.

In some countries a strategic alliance is essential to penetrating their market since their laws may limit or prohibit foreign ownership or control. Even when there are no legal restrictions, few companies can enter new markets alone. For example, Motorola needed Toshiba's distribution capacity to access the Japanese semi-conductor market.[6]

These alliances take many forms. Some may be as simple as a contract to act as a licensee or distributor in a particular country or an exclusive manufacturing agreement. Other alliances take the form of enhanced buyer-seller partnerships, joint bidding, joint marketing or joint production arrangements, cooperative research, code-sharing (as in the airline industry), minority equity alliances, and formal joint ventures in which a separate entity is formed.[7] Some joint ventures have highly-structured governance; others use relatively informal governance mechanisms.

Another way of classifying strategic alliances is by those which require equity, such as an equity contribution to a new entity or a minority equity investment in an existing entity, and those which do not require equity, such as a license or distribution agreement.

An example of an equity joint venture in China is the very successful joint venture of General Motors with Shanghai Automotive Industry Corporation, which in both 2010 and 2011 sold more GM cars in China than in the U.S.

There are many other successful Asian joint ventures discussed in this chapter and subsequent chapters. However, it is well to begin the book with an international Chinese joint venture which reflects both the importance of aligning the interests of both partners to the joint venture as well as the cultural problems that must be overcome.

Wahaha Mikado Joint Venture Company

The Wahaha Mikado Joint Venture Company ("Joint Venture") is a food and beverage joint venture company established in 1996 between Hangzhou Wahaha Group ("Wahaha Group"), the largest beverage producer in China, and Groupe Danone ("Danone"), a

---

[6] "Harvard Business Review on Strategic Alliances", Harvard Business School Press, 2002, p. 3

[7] T.K. Das, "Strategic Alliances in a Globalizing World", Information Age Publishing, Inc. 2011, p. 94.

French food products multi-national corporation based in Paris. Zong Qinghou ("Zong"), one of China's wealthiest men, was the founder and controlling shareholder of Wahaha Group.[8]

Zong originally started Wahaha Group in a mini grocery located in a school in Hangzhou, China in 1986, targeting kids and their parents with his beverages. The name "Wahaha" sounds like an infant's laugh and means "laughing baby" in Chinese.[9]

In 1996, Danone contributed $45 million U.S. dollars and a trademark transfer fee of $7.33 million in exchange for 51% of the shares of the Joint Venture, with the other 49% of the shares taken by Wahaha Group.[10] The Joint Venture ended in 2009 after 30 law suits were filed in seven different countries between the Joint Venture partners, including a law suit launched in the U.S. against Zong's wife and daughters. Danone's interest in the Joint Venture was bought out by Zong and his entities in 2009 for a reported 300 million Euros (approximately $400 million).[11]

Initially, the Joint Venture was extremely successful and enjoyed very substantial profits. The partners set up 39 joint ventures in which Danone owned 51% while its Chinese partner owned the remaining 49%. These 39 joint ventures produced and marketed various Wahaha-branded drinks and snacks.[12] So what went wrong?

The first problem was that the Joint Venture was not properly structured to align the interest of both partners. Not all of Zong's beverage companies were transferred into the Joint Venture, thereby creating potential conflicts of interest. In fact, five of the

---

[8] Russell Flannery, "China Rich List, Beverage Billionaire", Forbes.com, 11/16/09, http://www.forbes.com/global/2009/1116/china-billionaires-09-wahaha-zong-qinghou-beverage-billionaire.html

[9] Malcolm Moore, "Zong Qinghou named as China's richest man", Telegraph Media Group Limited, September 29, 2010, http://www.telegraph.co.uk/finance/china-business/8033446/Zong-Qinghou-named-as-Chinas-richest-man.html

[10] "Danone Splits from Wahaha, Amicably", China Business Focus, December 2009, http://en.cbf.net.au/Item/418.aspx

[11] Id.

[12] Vivian Wai-yin Kwok, "Danone Gives UP China Fight", Forbes.com, 09/30/09, http://www.forbes.com/2009/09/30/danone-wahaha-dispute-markets-business-trademark.html

Wahaha Group companies remained outside of the Joint Venture and were operated by Zong and his family.[13]

Second, the joint venture contract was not as clear as it might have been concerning Zong's activities outside of the Joint Venture, including Zong's ability to use the Wahaha trademark.

In 2006, the then-president of the Joint Venture, Emmanuel Faber ("Faber") accused Zong of setting up some non-joint venture companies. These non-joint venture companies were controlled by some state-owned enterprises and their employees and used the same trademark as the Joint Venture. Faber approached Zong to buy 51% of the shares of the non-joint venture companies and his proposal was rejected by Zong. This rejection triggered the series of lawsuits, which culminated, after many millions of dollars in legal expense, in the buyout of Danone.[14]

However, long before 2006, cultural conflicts occurred which may have significantly contributed to the lawsuits and the ultimate breakup of the Joint Venture. According to one article, Danone never performed a "cultural integration risk analysis" when the parties originally formed the Joint Venture.[15] As a result, Danone was insensitive to a slight given unintentionally to Zong when the Joint Venture was formed, which Zong never forgot. When Danone invited Wahaha Group to come to France for a joint meeting with Danone, Danone charged 12,000 Euros for each delegate from Wahaha Group who participated. However, when Wahaha Group invited Danone to Indonesia for a discussion concerning a quality control problem, Danone never paid a comparable fee for its delegates. Zong remembered this insult for many years. When the lawsuits arose, Zong wrote a 10,000 word public letter characterizing Danone as "stingy misers".[16]

---

[13] Wahaha Communiqué: The truth behind the Wahaha dispute with Danone, Sina Finance, April 13, 2007, http://finance.sina.com.cn/chanjing/b/20070413/10043499496.shtml (Chinese)

[14] "Danone Splits from Wahaha, Amicably", China Business Focus, December 2009, http://en.cbf.net.au/Item/418.aspx

[15] Morgan Qu, Communications in the matter of Danone and Wahaha", Chinese Marketing 2007, Vol 97, http://www.glocalstrategy.com/english/service/Danone.htm

[16] Id.

Takeaways

Middle-market and smaller companies must develop cultural sensitivity to their Asian partners and learn what is and what is not an insult. Equally important is the necessity that the joint venture contract be crystal clear as to conflicts of interests and be properly structured to avoid such conflicts.

Our next example, the Corning-Samsung Joint Venture, which has been very successful for many years, reflects how important international growth can be to U.S. companies.

Corning-Samsung Joint Venture

Corning Incorporated ("Corning"), whose headquarters is in Corning, NY, is a leader in growing its business through both domestic and international joint ventures. Corning is ranked No. 328 on the Fortune 500 list. (All references to the Fortune 500 list in this book is as of May 21, 2012.) The company traces its origin to a glass business established in 1851. Today it is a global, technology-based corporation which manufactures and processes products at approximately 60 plants in 14 countries.[17]

In 2010, Corning had net income of approximately $3.6 billion. Of that amount, Corning's 50% equity in Samsung Corning Precision accounted for $1.5 billion, or approximately 41% of its net income.

The joint venture with Samsung was created in 1995. In 1996, less than 15% of Corning's net income was represented by this joint venture. The Corning-Samsung joint venture allowed Corning to enter the Korean market with a prestigious local manufacturer of consumer electronics. Corning invented an all glass television tube and was a major supplier worldwide, but did not have access to the Asian market. Samsung was interested in developing its television manufacturing business, so there was a mutuality of interests.[18]

---

[17] Corning Incorporated Form 10-K Report for 2000.
[18] Larraine Segil, "Intelligent Business Alliances", Three Rivers Press, 1996, p. 151.

When the Samsung Corning joint venture was originally created, it had three potential customers in Korea, namely Samsung,
Goldstar, and Daewoo. Officials at Corning visited these customers to learn how to win orders before the joint venture was
created. The venture was managed by Samsung and was an
important source of products and services to Samsung.[19]

Samsung Corning Precision is currently a producer of glass
panels and funnels for cathode ray tubes for televisions and
computer monitors, and has manufacturing facilities in Korea,
Germany, China and Malaysia.[20] Samsung Electronics Company,
Ltd., a Korean company, and its affiliates own the other 50%
interest in Samsung Corning Precision.

Corning has relied on joint ventures to create many of its successful businesses. More than 25% of its revenues came from
these strategic alliances in the mid-1990s. Corning typically uses
an informal governance structure. Strategic alliances were part
of the Corning business model for more than half a century and
have resulted in a substantial part of its business growth.[21]

The good marriage between Samsung and Corning continues
to produce new equity ventures. In February 2012, Corning and
Samsung announced an agreement to establish a new equity venture, located in Korea, To manufacture "lotus glass", which is used
in smartphones produced under the Galaxy umbrella, as well as
organic light emitting diodes ("OLED"), which are used in super
OLED televisions.[22]

[19] Id.

[20] Id.

[21] James D. Bamford, Benjamin Gomes-Casseres, Michael S. Robinson,
"Mastering Alliance Strategy" (Jossey-Bass, 2003)

[22] Joseph Volpe, "Corning and Samsung ink new joint venture, plot Lotus
Glass future for OLED devices", www.engadget.com, 2012; http://
www.engadget.com/2012/02/03/corning-and-samsung-ink-new-joint-
venture-plot-lotus-glass-futu/

Takeaways

- Corning's original management decision in 1995 to risk growing its business internationally has paid off handsomely for its shareholders.
- Had Corning decided to remain solely in the U.S. market, its income would have been approximately 40% less than its current income.

International Research and Development Joint Ventures

An international joint venture can spread the cost and limit the risk of commercializing new technologies. These R&D joint ventures are of growing significance as the cost of R&D increase and competition for funding sources becomes more intense.[23]

Typically middle-market and smaller companies will be less interested in R&D joint ventures than Fortune 500 companies. However, small university sponsored start-ups in the U.S. will often participate with large Asian companies in these R&D joint ventures. The so-called "born global phenomena", discussed in Chapter 2, typically consists of an R&D joint venture between an Asian company and a U.S. start-up company which grew out of a university research program.

In 2010, General Electric announced that it would use $500 million to set up customer innovation centers and enhance R&D activities in China. The centers were intended to focus on product development engineering and sourcing support and delivery in key development areas for China, such as world healthcare, renewable and clean energy, rail and aviation.[24]

---

[23] John Hagedoorn, Hans van Kranenburg and Richard N. Osborn, "Joint Patenting Amongst Companies – Expoloring the Effects of Inter-Firm R&D Partnering and Experience, Managerial and Decision Economics, John Wiley & Sons, Ltd. 2003, pgs. 71-84

[24] "GE to invest $2 bln in China on research, development, joint ventures", Xinhua News Agency, 2010, http://news.xinhuanet.com/english2010/business/2010-11/09/c_13598812.htm

Recent Growth of International Alliances

Every day one reads about a new alliance between an Asian company and a U.S. company.

BURGER KING

On June 15, 2012, Burger King Worldwide Holding Inc. stated that it would open 1,000 restaurants in China over the next five to seven years in a joint venture with the Kurdoglu family, which runs 450 Burger King restaurants in Turkey. The expansion in China is to be financed by Cartesian Capital Group. At the time of the announcement, Burger King had just 63 restaurants in China.

QVC, INC.

On March 20, 2012, online and television retailer QVC Inc., a division of Liberty Interactive Corp. (No. 230 on the Fortune 500), announced that it was entering China's growing consumer and media market through a joint venture with the country's national radio broadcaster.

QVC said it would acquire a 49% stake in China National Radio's home-shopping TV channel, which already reaches approximately 35 million Chinese households. China National Radio will hold the remaining 51%.

The American company hopes to reach more of the 195 million Chinese households with digital cable through its joint venture, called Home Shopping Co., QVC's Chief Executive Mike George said in an interview:

"We think this will potentially be one of the strongest markets we have for e-commerce in addition to traditional television," Mr. George said.

In the U.S., QVC reaches approximately 100 million households, or 75% of the country's population, and for years has looked to growth opportunities abroad. Around one-third of its revenue is generated from operations in Europe and Japan. QVC's German and Japanese divisions, which reach roughly the same amount of cable viewers as China National Radio's retail channel, generated more than $1 billion in revenue for 2011, Mr. George said.[25]

STARBUCKS

A typical cross-border joint venture involves a U.S. company and a strong foreign company which can provide the local know-how and distribution capabilities. For example, it was announced on January 31, 2012 that Starbucks Corp. (No. 227 on Fortune 500) planned to open 50 cafes in India by the end of 2012. Starbucks set up a joint venture with the Tata Group, an Indian flagship conglomerate, and its affiliate, Tata Global Beverage Ltd., which owns Eight O'Clock Coffee in the U.S. The two companies will start in India with an investment of $80 million and plan to add funds as the business expands. The first cafes would be open in either Delhi or Mumbai, India's two largest cities.[26]

HONEYWELL INTERNATIONAL, INC.

On October 10, 2011, Honeywell International, Inc. (No. 77 on Fortune 500) and Sinochem Group announced that they had

---

[25] William Launder, "QVC Forms Venture in China", The Wall Street Journal, March 20, 2012.

[26] Megha Bahree, "Starbucks Will Open Cafes in India", The Wall Street Journal, January 31, 2012, p. B10.

signed an agreement to form a 50/50 joint venture to produce and sell blowing agents for energy efficient foam insulation in China to meet growing demand in the Asian region for more energy efficient and environmentally-friendlier materials. The formation of the joint venture was subject to Chinese government approval.

The joint venture, located in Taicang, Jiangsu Province, will produce HFC-245fa, a non-ozone depleting foam blowing agent used in insulation for appliances, construction, transportation and other applications where maximum energy efficiency is required. The venture is expected to begin production in late 2013. Honeywell's newly-launched next generation HFO lower global warming potential blowing agent – Solstice ™ Liquid Blowing Agent – may also be produced by the joint venture.

"This joint venture with Sinochem, one of the strongest companies in China, will help meet growing demand for this material as Asian customers rapidly adopt more energy efficient and environmentally compliant materials," said Andreas Kramvis, president and CEO of Honeywell Specialty Materials. "Having Asian supply close to local customers is important to ensure global supply of this material in the future."

"Honeywell is a globally renowned multinational company with diversified leading technologies, products and services," said Yinping Want, vice president of Sinochem Group.

"The formation of the joint venture enhances our product portfolios and service capabilities in energy efficient and environmentally friendly materials, which aligns with both companies' business development strategies and reinforces the foundation for cooperation in depth. The joint venture depicts an exciting prospect."

Takeaway

All of these Fortune 500 companies believe that their future depends upon growing internationally through joint ventures and other strategic alliances. Middle-market and smaller companies would do well to consider a similar strategy consistent with their own resources. Although middle-market and smaller companies do not have the resources to enter into the global market place at the same level as Fortune 500 companies, there is no reason they should not consider strategic alliances with smaller companies in Asia who also may be looking for international partners.

What is a Strategic Alliance?

One way of describing a strategic alliance is a business relationship in which two or more independent firms:[27]

1. Work cooperatively on a specific project that is clearly bounded in terms of activity, geography, product, process and time.

2. Retain an agreed upon level of flexibility. While each firm makes specific commitments to each other within the scope of the alliance, each can work independently of the other on projects outside the alliance.

3. Share in rewards and risks of the project, which may go beyond measurable financial returns to include new intellectual property, skill sets, opportunity costs and market position.

4. Commit resources to the relationship to accomplish the objectives of the alliance.

The Merger Alternative

One alternative to the strategic alliance is the merger, at least in countries which permit foreign control of their enterprises. A study in 2004 reported a significant decline in the use of joint ventures over the previous 20 years, relying on data from the Bureau of Economic Analysis (BEA) annual survey of U.S. foreign direct investment from 1982 to 1997. Over this time frame, the prevalence of minority-owned affiliates (i.e., joint

---

[27] Gene Slowinski & Matthew W. Sagal, "The Strongest Link: Forging a Profitable & Enduring Corporate Alliance", AMACON (2003) p. 4

ventures) declined from 17.9% of affiliates to 10.6%; in contrast, the prevalence of wholly-owned affiliates increased from 72.3% of affiliates to 80.4%.[28]

Some mergers are actually joint ventures and some are not. The word "merger" is used in this book colloquially to include all forms of acquisition, whether or not the transaction is a technical merger.

Assume that an international company wishes to acquire 100% of the equity of a U.S. company but retains the management team of the U.S. company. The foreign company will typically provide incentives for outstanding performance to the management team, which may take the form of equity or cash, or both. To the extent that equity incentives, such as stock options or stock appreciation rights, etc., are awarded to the key management members, the relationship between the management and international company begins to look like a joint venture between the acquirer and the management. Arguably, therefore, there is no sharp distinction between a merger and other types of joint ventures, especially where the management team is provided with equity incentives.

Chinese Direct U.S. Investment

At one time, it was a joint venture initiated by a U.S. company based in an Asian country. Today it is the Chinese, Japanese and other Asian companies that are interested in establishing an operation in the U.S. Therefore, this book analyzes not only operations based in China or other Asian countries but also operations in the U.S.

For example, China's foreign direct investment in all countries grew from an annual average of below $3 billion before 2005 to over $60 billion in 2010. However, this investment was concentrated in developing countries and investments in the U.S. were very few. Since 2008 that story began to change. Direct investment expenditures by Chinese firms in the U.S. grew more than 130% per year during 2009 and 2010. According to one study,

---

[28] Desai et al., 2004, p. 329

"Chinese firms spent more than US$ 5 billion in the U.S. on 25 greenfield projects and 34 acquisitions. Today, Chinese firms have investments in at least 35 of the country's 50 states, across a wide range of industries."[29]

In the third quarter of 2011, Chinese investors expanded their foothold in the United States, spending $1.03 billion for nine greenfield projects and nine acquisitions.[30] In the fourth quarter, Chinese direct investment in the United States dipped to $69 million, dragging down the full year figure to $4.5 billion.[31]

For example, the White House announced in January 2011 that LP Amina, a multinational environmental engineer company headquartered in Novi, Michigan, signed a Memorandum of Understanding (MOU) with Yi Xing Union Congregation Co., Ltd., a Chinese energy and chemical company. The MOU will formalize plans in advance of an expected contract signing, which will establish a collaborative pilot project to demonstrate LP Amina's patent-pending Coal to Chemicals System. This innovative technology will couple chemical production with power generation and enable the use of thermal energy generated from the chemical production for additional efficiency power generation. This process would also reduce emissions by nearly 90% compared to the conventional production process in use today. Once commercialized, LP Amina estimates that this technology could be deployed in the United States creating up to 500 jobs.[32]

In January 2012, Sinopec, China's second-largest oil company by market capitalization, unveiled a $2.5 billion deal with Oklahoma-based Devon Energy to invest in five new development

---

[29] Thilo Hanemann and Daniel H. Rosen, "Chinese FDI in the United States is taking off: How to maximize its benefits?", Vale Columbia Center on Sustainable International Investors, http://www.vcc.columbia.edu/content/chinese-fdi-united-states-taking-how-maximize-its-benefits

[30] http://rhgroup.net/notes/chinese-fdi-in-the-united-states-q3-2011-update

[31] http://rhgroup.net/notes/chinese-fdi-in-the-united-states-q4-2011-update

[32] "LP Amina MOU with Yixing Union Congregation Co. Ltd.", Fact Sheet: U.S. China Commercial Relations, The White House, Office of the Press Secretary, January 19, 2011, http://www.whitehouse.gov/the-press-office/2011/01/19/fact-sheet-us-china-commercial-relations

areas for shale oil from Ohio to Alabama.[33] Sinopec is taking one-third of Devon's take in the five oil projects but will pay 80% of the development costs, or up to $1.6 billion, as well as paying $900 million in cash.[34]

Devon has a strong balance sheet with $6.8 billion in cash, but most of that is held offshore and liable for tax if repatriated to the U.S. That makes it more attractive for the company to seek other funding for its American projects.[35]

Takeaway

Larger Chinese companies are beginning to look for joint ventures in the U.S. This is evidence that Chinese businesses are beginning to follow the same pattern as Japanese businesses in the late 1980s. Although large Chinese businesses typically wish to deal only with large U.S. businesses at least initially, there may be opportunities with these large Chinese businesses in the future for middle-market and smaller companies. Moreover, there are plenty of middle-market and smaller companies in China that also want to grow internationally and may be interested in following the example of the larger Chinese companies.

Our next chapter deals with selecting the right partner for your international strategic alliance.

---

[33] Ed Crooks, James Boxell and Adam Jones, "China and France chase US shale assets", Financial Times, January 3, 2012, http://www.ft.com/cms/s/0/30c4c46e-35e2-11e1-9f98-00144feabdc0.html#axzz1tw4Lf9rd

[34] Id.

[35] Id.

Chapter 2

Selecting the Right Partner

Strategic alliances, particularly joint ventures, have a high failure rate.[36] The key to a successful arrangement for most companies is to gain significant experience with the proposed partner before formulating the joint venture. This experience can help the two parties establish trust in their relationship, create better understanding of each other's culture and business methods, and help clarify the objectives of the joint venture.

For example, an initial strategic alliance can be created with a simple distributorship or license contract for a few years before trying to create a complex joint venture. Likewise creating a simple non-equity joint venture can pave the way for an equity joint venture in which each party invests capital. Finally, a limited territorial joint venture can be used as a beta site before embarking on a country of world-wide joint venture.

Carrefour first started its operations in Taiwan for many years before expanding to mainland China. According to its manager, "We discovered Chinese culture and the way to work with the Chinese in Taiwan when the retail sector in mainland China was totally closed. International companies that decided to enter

---

[36] Kathryn Rudie Harrigan, *Beyond the Vision: Making Strategic Alliances Work*, keynote address at the Corporate Venturing Conference, Boston, June 1989; Bleeke, J., & Ernst, D. (1991), November – December). The way to win in cross-border alliances, *Harvard Business Review*, 127-135.

Taiwan – not Hong Kong – 15 or 20 years ago have a fantastic advantage in China, and that was the case for Carrefour."[37]

Another example of the benefits of the trial period was the introduction in 2009 of the Virtual Computing Environment Coalition consisting of Cisco, EMC, and VMware.[38] These companies worked closely during 2009 on a shared vision for the future of enterprise IT infrastructure, namely private cloud computing. A private cloud is a virtual IT infrastructure that is securely controlled and operated solely for one organization. The one-year collaboration enabled each of the parties to get to know each other better and to help ensure the success of the venture.

There are many large companies, such as Cisco, that have very sophisticated strategic alliance managers in large portfolio of alliances. For example, Steven Steinhilber, a vice president of Strategic Alliances at Cisco, manages a portfolio of alliances across multiple industry sectors, technologies, and geographies, with a cumulative annual value of more than $4.5 billion in business impact to Cisco and much more than that to our alliance partners.[39] These companies have sufficient background and experience in strategic alliances so they may elect to skip some of the initial steps described above and proceed directly to a formal joint venture.

However, many smaller companies that lack skilled management personnel with significant alliance experience would do well to proceed cautiously with any proposed international strategic alliance until they have gained sufficient knowledge and experience to justify a more complex arrangement.

---

[37] Child, P. (2006) Lessons from a global retailer: An interview with the president of Carrefour China. *McKinsey Quarterly*, special edition, 70-81.

[38] Press Release, Cisco, The Network, November 3, 2009, http://newsroom.cisco.com/dlls/2009/corp_110309.html

[39] Steve Steinhilber, "Strategic Alliances: Three Ways To Make Them Work", Harvard Business Review Press, 2008.

Yahoo! Inc. Alliances

According to the *Wall Street Journal* of May 14, 2012, the majority of Yahoo! Inc.'s ("Yahoo!") $18.5 billion market valuation is tied to two cross-border joint ventures, one in China and one in Japan. As of May 2012, Yahoo! owned 42% of a China-based Internet company called Alibaba Group Holding Ltd. ("Alibaba") and 35% of Yahoo Japan Corporation ("Yahoo Japan"). Yahoo! is No. 483 of the Fortune 500.

On October 23, 2005, Yahoo! Inc. acquired approximately 46% of the outstanding common stock of Alibaba, which represented approximately 40% on a fully-diluted basis, in exchange for $1.0 billion in cash, the contribution of Yahoo!'s China-based businesses, including 3721 Network Software Company Limited ("Yahoo! China"), and direct transaction costs of $8 million. Another investor in Alibaba is Softbank Corp., a Japanese corporation ("Softbank"). Alibaba is a privately-held company. Through its investment in Alibaba, Yahoo! combined its search capabilities with Alibaba's leading online marketplace and online payment system and Alibaba's strong local presence, expertise, and vision in the Chinese market. These factors contributed to a purchase price in excess of Yahoo!'s share of the fair value of Alibaba's net tangible and intangible assets acquired resulting in goodwill.[40]

During April 1996, Yahoo! signed a joint venture agreement with Softbank, which was amended in September 1997, whereby Yahoo Japan was formed. Yahoo Japan was formed to establish and manage a local version of Yahoo! in Japan.[41] According to the Form 10-K for 2011, the fair value of Yahoo!'s 35% ownership in the common stock of Yahoo Japan was approximately $6 billion as of December 31, 2011.

If we add the $6 billion valuation for Yahoo!'s stake in the Japanese joint venture to the $4 - $8 billion estimate of the value of Yahoo!'s stake in Alibaba, it is clear that at least a majority of Yahoo!'s total market valuation is tied to these two joint ventures. Indeed, the net income contributable to Yahoo!'s stake in Alibaba alone constituted approximately 25% of Yahoo!'s net income for

---

[40] Yahoo! Inc. Form 10-K for 2011
[41] Id.

2011. Yahoo! sold its Alibaba stake for $7.6 billion in September 2012.

Takeaway

The decision by Yahoo! in 2005 to create joint ventures in China and Japan with Internet companies has kept Yahoo!, despite its problems in the U.S., on the Fortune 500 list and has helped to maintain the value of its stock. The investment in Alibaba and Yahoo Japan has paid off handsomely because Yahoo! picked the right partners.

Alliances Outside of Your Industry

If your company is entering into a foreign country and needs knowledge of the local situation, it may not be necessary to enter into an alliance with someone in your same industry. Rather, what you need is a local company with the knowledge of the culture and country in which you want to expand, particularly companies that are potential suppliers to the joint venture.

For example, Kentucky Fried Chicken ("KFC"), a U.S. company, wanted to sell fried chicken in Japan and needed to know more about the culture, about the country and where to buy or lease real estate in Japan. Mitsubishi Corporation ("Mitsubishi") had this knowledge and capability, and wanted to develop domestic demand for its poultry operations.[42] Their alliance posed almost no threat of competition or conflict, since each was in an entirely different industry. Therefore, the alliance made a lot of sense.[43]

KFC and Mitsubishi first crossed paths back in the 1960s. At that time, the broiler chicken industry was flourishing in the U.S. and the largest buyer of chickens was none other than Colonel

---

[42] Angelina Jao, "The Fast Food Industry: Kentucky Fried Chicken", 1/29/2005, http://angelinajao.wordpress.com/2005/01/29/the-fast-food-industry-kentucky-fried-chicken/

[43] James D. Bamford et al, "Mastering Alliance Strategy", Jossey-Bass, 2003, P.25

Harlan Sanders' KFC. Colonel Sanders had been very successful in the U.S. in franchising his fried chicken restaurants and
Mitsubishi was interested in developing KFC stores in Japan
which would purchase poultry from Mitsubishi's poultry operations. A Mitsubishi employee who was in charge of food-related
business visited Colonel Sanders many times, and after four years
of negotiations, a joint venture was negotiated. [44]

A test store was opened at the Osaka World Expo in early
1970. The store offered a 350-yen combo meal, consisting of fried
chicken, French fries and a roll. It was an instant success, with the
store selling some 4,600 meals a day and posting average daily
sales of 1.6 million yen. After the successful test debut, Kentucky
Fried Chicken Japan Ltd. (KFCJ) was established in July 1970.[45]

A conflict of opinion on store locations soon developed
between KFC and Mitsubishi. Based on KFC's experience in
the U.S., KFC proposed opening stores near suburban shopping
centers. However, as the use of family cars had not yet become
widespread in Japan, Mitsubishi argued against that approach,
saying it would be best to begin by establishing stores in downtown locations. In the end, KFC was not convinced by these
arguments and the suburban strategy was adopted.[46]

The first store opened in Nagoya on November 12, 1970 to
great fanfare, including fireworks and balloons. Two other stores
were soon opened in Osaka. All the stores had been built in the
parking lots of shopping malls and were complete with play
areas for children. However, the stores struggled, just as people
at Mitsubishi had feared since shopping malls were not yet popular in Japan. Before a year had passed, KFCJ was running at a
significant loss, with a capital deficit reaching 100 million yen.[47]

According to Mitsubishi, investigations into possibly withdrawing from the venture were begun inside Mitsubishi. It was

---

[44] "KFC Japan: Endless Quest for Great Taste and Innovation", Mitsubishi
Corporation – MC Library – Our Endeavors – vol.2 KFC Japan, www.
mitsubishicorp.com/jp/en/mclibrary/projectstory/vol02/
[45] Id.
[46] Id.
[47] Id.

obvious from the initial failures that selecting the right location would be crucial to success.[48]

According to Mitsubishi, it developed the following strategy: "Let's enhance the visibility of our stores by developing smaller outlets inside buildings in downtown districts and upscale residential areas. We'll give it one more shot – this time with locations that we believe will work." Everything hinged on the success of this new strategy. The location chosen for this new strategy was Tor Road in Kobe, a district with many foreign residents, bordered by upscale residential developments.[49]

The Tor Road Store, which opened in 1972, carried the joint venture's hopes for survival. After 4 months, the store reached monthly sales of 3.6 million yen. The confidence of those involved with the new strategy grew. Thereafter, they opened their first store in Tokyo and the Aoyama Store opened later in 1972. The new locations became profitable and it wasn't long before KFC became a household name.[50]

In December 1973, KFCJ opened its 100th store. Around this time, stores were reflecting revenues of 3 million yen and the joint venture's performance stabilized. In December 1974, KFCJ began to extensively promote its Christmas campaign. In 1985, KFCJ introduced the Party Barrel, consisting of chicken, salad and ice cream. After this, the idea of having chicken on Christmas continued to spread and it is now an annual tradition for many Japanese.

Colonel Sanders became imbedded in Japanese culture in 1985 when an alleged curse was placed by Colonel Sanders on the Japanese Kansai-based Hanshin Tigers baseball team. Elated fans of the Hanshin team, excited over winning the 1985 championship series, tossed the statue of Colonel Sanders into the Dotonbori River. The team subsequently had a long losing streak. Despondent fans soon began to talk of "the curse of Colonel Sanders" which resulted from his anger over the treatment of the statue.

---

[48] Id.

[49] Id.

[50] Id.

KFCJ also introduced its own system for accrediting its suppliers. In 1988, Japan Farm's Tarumi Plant became the first cut chicken plant to win approval under this system. Although efforts to ensure safety have become common in the food industry, it was KFCJ that led the way in Japan.[51]

In 1990, 20 years after the joint venture was established, KFCJ stock was listed on the second section of the Tokyo Stock Exchange. In the following year, KFCJ expanded into the pizza delivery business with its Pizza Hut operations. In 2009, KFCJ launched a new buffet-style restaurant called "Pizza Hut Natural."[52]

KFCJ also pioneered various new menu items, such as "Red Hot Chicken" and "Paripari Umami Chicken" (Crispy Delicious Chicken), which suited the Japanese taste. [53]

In December 2007, Mitsubishi successfully completed a friendly takeover of KFCJ, which then owned more than 1,500 KFC and Pizza Hut restaurants around the country, for a purchase price exceeding $14 billion.[54]

Takeaway

Alliances outside of your industry can actually be more beneficial than alliances inside of your industry, since you are not creating an international competitor. Mitsubishi's desire to develop Japanese demand for its poultry operations meshed completely with KFC's need to expand its retail stores to Japan which sold fried chicken. Therefore, middle-market and smaller companies wishing to select the right international partner should think about creating joint ventures with international suppliers who can benefit from the growth of their business in the country in which the joint venture will be based. For U.S. companies that

---

[51] Id.

[52] Id.

[53] Id.

[54] "Mitsubishi takes over Kentucky Fried Chicken Japan for $14.83 billion", The Japan Times, Dec. 9, 2007, www.japantimes.co.jp/text/nb20071209a1. html.

wish to expand in Asia, look for suppliers in the Asian country in which you wish to expand. For Asian companies that wish to expand to the U.S., look for U.S. companies that are potential suppliers to your business in the U.S.

Aligning Strategic Objectives

Both venture partners must clearly identify their strategic objectives in the alliance to make certain that they mesh and are achievable. Achieving strategic objectives sometimes even requires each partner to make an investment in the other.

An example is the global alliance between The Goodyear Tire & Rubber Company ("Goodyear") and Sumitomo Rubber Industries, Ltd. ("Sumitomo"), which was announced on February 3, 1999, pursuant to a Memorandum of Understanding signed by the chairman, CEO and president of Goodyear and the president of Sumitomo. Goodyear's president stated "This combination supports both companies' strategic objectives for growth and cost leadership. As a result of these ventures, both will be able to compete more effectively, improve our performance through enhanced brand offerings, and generate benefits for our customers, shareholders, associates and suppliers....In addition, cost improvement and rationalization will add a combined estimated $300-$360 million to the operating profits of the joint ventures during the next three years."[55]

The operating joint ventures in North America and Europe would be owned 75% by Goodyear and 25% by Sumitomo. In Japan, Sumitomo would own 75% of two joint ventures and Goodyear would own 25%. Voting rights would be shared 70/30. The difference between the value of the respective businesses being consolidated and the agreed upon shareholding ratios would be settled through a balancing cash payment of $936 million to be paid by Goodyear to Sumitomo at the date the joint ventures go into effect.

---

[55] "Goodyear and Sumitomo Rubber Industries, Ltd., to Form Global Alliance", The AutoChanel, February 3, 1999, http://www.theautochannel.com/news/press/date/19990203/press003282.html

Separately, to demonstrate both parties' commitment to the overall relationship, establishment of a cross-shareholding was planned. Goodyear planned to acquire a 10% interest in Sumitomo and Sumitomo planned to acquire an equivalent dollar value of Goodyear shares.

In addition, the operating joint ventures would be supported by two service joint ventures. The first, involving technology-sharing, would be 51% owned by Goodyear and 49% by Sumitomo. The second, for global purchasing, would be 80% Goodyear-owned and 20% owned by Sumitomo.

Sumitomo traces its roots back to 1909 when the Sumitomo Group made an investment in Dunlop Tires, a newly formed Japanese subsidiary of the British company, Dunlop UK. The joint venture established Japan's first modern rubber factory and began production of bicycle tires and tubes and solid rickshaw tires.[56] In 1913, Sumitomo produced Japan's first automobile tires and was incorporated as a Japanese company in 1917. In 1985, Sumitomo acquired Dunlop Tire Corporation in the United States.[57]

There were four joint venture operating companies formed by Goodyear and Sumitomo – one in North America, one in Europe and two in Japan. In addition, two support ventures were formed by Goodyear and Sumitomo based in the U.S., one for global purchasing and one for sharing tire technology.[58]

The umbrella agreement between Goodyear and Sumitomo (also called SRI) contains the following interesting provision for top-level cooperation:

"13.01   TOP   LEVEL   MEETINGS   AND   GENERAL COOPERATION. Goodyear and SRI shall meet regularly to review the functioning of the Alliance and to discuss additional business opportunities including possible geographic

---

[56] www.srigroup.co/jp/english/corporate/history.html

[57] Id.

[58] "Goodyear and Sumitomo Rubber Industries, Ltd., to Form Global Alliance", The AutoChanel, February 3, 1999, http://www.theautochannel.com/news/press/date/19990203/press003282.html

or functional extensions of the Alliance. Notwithstanding any other meetings and discussions the Parties may have, Goodyear and SRI shall hold at least two Top Level Meetings per year. As used in this Agreement, a Top Level Meeting shall mean a meeting between, on the one hand, one or two persons who hold the title of chairman, chief executive officer, chief operating officer, and/or president of Goodyear and, on the other hand, one or two persons who hold the title of chairman or president of SRI. These meetings shall be at such times and places as the Parties may agree."[59]

Goodyear is currently No. 126 on the Fortune 500 list.

Takeaway

Selecting the right partner may, on occasion, require making mutual equity investments in each other. Although this is not a standard method of aligning strategic objectives, it worked for both Goodyear and Sumitomo.

Post-Joint Venture Alignments

Even after the strategic alliance has been formed it may be necessary to accommodate to the strategic objectives of the other party.

For example, it was announced on April 19, 2012 that General Motors Co. ("GM") (No. 5 on the Fortune 500 list) and its big Chinese partner, Shanghai Automotive Industry Corp. ("Shanghai Automotive") agreed to restructure their joint venture to give GM equal say in key decisions as their alliance expanded outside of China.[60] The joint venture between GM and Shanghai Automotive was originally formed in 1998.

Prior to April 19, 2012, Shanghai Automotive controlled 51% of the joint venture with GM, which had commenced as a 50-50

---

[59] Form 10Q Report of the Goodyear Tire and Rubber Company for the Quarterly Period Ended June 20, 1999.

[60] Sharon Terlep,"GM Seeks Sway in China", The Wall Street Journal, April 19, 2012.

joint venture. In 2009, on the eve of GM's bankruptcy filing, GM agreed to give Shanghai Automotive majority control by selling 1% to Shanghai Automotive of the joint venture in exchange for $84.5 million and help in obtaining a $400 million line of credit that GM used to rescue its Korean operation. When GM sold the 1% stake in the joint venture, called Shanghai General Motors, Shanghai Automotive committed to a call option that would permit GM to purchase back the 1%. That option was contingent on Shanghai Automotive's ability to book revenue from Shanghai General Motors. This condition was satisfied by virtue of changes in Chinese accounting rules. In 2011, the joint venture, Shanghai General Motors, sold 2.6 million vehicles, had revenue of $30.5 billion and profit of $1.5 billion.[61]

The adjustment in the relationship between GM and Shanghai Automotive satisfied the strategic objectives of each party, initially helping fund GM's bankruptcy and also protecting SIAC's accounting ability to reflect profits of Shanghai General Motors.[62]

Born Global Phenomena

There is at least anecdotal evidence in the academic literature that some companies have, from inception, adopted an international strategy. Start-up firms that internationalize early in their lifespan typically use foreign-based resources owned by other firms throughout their value chain as a means of overcoming the "liability of newness".[63] This phenomenon has been driven by small and medium size businesses, including high technology start-ups.

---

[61] Id.

[62] Id.

[63] Phiri, T.; Jones, M.V. & Wheeler, C. 2004; T.K. Das, Strategic Alliances in a Globalizing World, Information Age Publishing, Inc. (2011), p. 140

These born global firms have immediate access to international customers, markets, suppliers and collaborators.[64] In some cases research and development alliances are developed.[65]

One academic study sampled small and medium size exporting firms from Norway, Denmark and France. One-third of the firms sampled reported that the time period between establishment of the firm and the commencement of export was less than two years.[66]

Is there a Die Global Phenomenon?

The counterpart of the "born global" phenomenon is what we call the "die global" phenomenon. An example of "die global" is Groen Brothers Aviation, Inc. ("Groen"), a public company whose stock was traded on the so-called "Pink Sheets" under the symbol GNBA, and which was engaged in the development of an easy-to-fly and cost-efficient gyroplane called the SparrowHawk. In its fiscal year ended in 2011, Groen had revenues of only $4,000 and its auditors had substantial doubt about its ability to continue as a going concern. Nevertheless, it announced in January 2011 that it had entered into an agreement with Guangzhou Suntrans Aviation Science and Technology Co., Ltd. to form a Cooperative (contractual) Joint Venture ("CJV"). The CJV would be a Chinese limited liability company whose purpose was to produce in China for sales worldwide light gyroplanes based upon Groen's SparrowHawk design. The agreement generally provided for CJV to assemble, manufacture, sell and provide related services

---

[64] Andersson, S., & Wictor, I. (2003). Innovative internationalization in new firms: Born Global – The Swedish case. *Journal of International Entrepreneurship*, 1, 249-276

[65] Knight, G. & Cavusgil, S. (1996). The born global firm: A challenge to traditional internationalization theory. *Advances in International Marketing*, 11-26; Knight, G. & Cavusgil, S. (2004). Innovation, organizational, capabilities, and the born-global firm. *Journal of International Business Studies*, 35, 124-141.

[66] Oystein Moen and Per Servais, Born Global or Gradual Global? Examining the Export Behavior of Small and Medium-Sized Enterprises, *Journal of International Marketing*, Vol 10, No. 3 (2002), pp. 49-71, American Marketing Association.

for Groen's SparrowHawk. It was expected that CJV would reintroduce the SparrowHawk III Kit into the U.S. and world markets, followed over the next few years by a fully assembled light gyroplane using technology transferred by Groen to the CJV. In May, 2012, Groen announced a composition with its many creditors and thus may yet survive.

Joint Venture Saves Xerox

Choosing the right international partner can save even the larger and more prestigious partner. Take the example of the Fuji/Xerox joint venture. Appendix 1 of this book is a Harvard Business School case study entitled "Xerox and Fuji Xerox" which contains a fulsome description of this relationship.

Fuji Xerox Co. Ltd was originally established in 1962 as a 50:50 partnership between Rank Xerox (later absorbed into Xerox Corporation in 1997), an American document management and business process company, and Fuji Photo Film Company, a Japanese photo film company (also called "Fuji Photo Film"). Originally only a distributor of Rank Xerox products, Fuji Xerox was interested in the low-end copier market and launched the Fuji Xerox 914.[67] Compared to Xerox, Fuji was initially the weaker partner in the alliance.

Fuji Photo Film was a photographic film manufacturer, but in second place to Kodak. Its sales of photographic film in 1962 gave it revenues approximating that of Xerox, but it was not growing as quickly. Fuji Photo Film was attempting to diversify away from silver-base photography and had begun researching xerography and its plain-paper technology. Under the agreement with Rank Xerox, the joint venture received the exclusive rights to xerography patents in its territory.[68]

Jefferson Kennard was selected by Xerox to manage the Fuji Xerox alliance in the 1970s and remained in that role for three decades. Kennard was sent to Japan as Xerox resident director

---

[67] http://www.fujixerox.com/eng/company/profile/history/corporate.html
[68] http://www.alliancestrategy.com/PDFs/BGC%20Fuji%20Xerox%20%20 SnB97.pdf

when Fuji Xerox was just getting out of the start-up stage. He developed a long-term relationship with Tony Kobayashi, the Chief Executive Officer of Fuji Xerox. Kennard served as the executive assistant to Kobayashi as well as the Xerox resident director. This relationship of trust and confidence was a key to the ultimate success of Fuji Xerox.[69]

Professor Benjamin Gomes-Casseres has argued that Fuji Xerox may have saved Xerox from extinction. Although Xerox's revenues grew at a record pace in the 1960s, beginning in 1970 Xerox began suffering from increased competition. Many of the competitors came from Japan and produced high-quality, low-cost photocopiers. By 1975, Xerox's share of worldwide copier revenues had plummeted to 60% vs. 93% in 1971. Ricoh, a leader in the Japanese market, became the top U.S. seller in 1976. Other competitors such as Canon and Minolta also developed competitive products to Xerox. According to Xerox's CEO, "The Japanese were selling products in the United States for what it cost us to make them. We were losing market share rapidly, but didn't have the cost structure to do anything about it. I was not sure if Xerox would make it out of the 1980s."[70]

For a long time, Xerox executives had treated Fuji Xerox as an unimportant ally. This attitude changed dramatically in the 1980s as Fuji Xerox came to the rescue of Xerox with a series of product and manufacturing breakthroughs.[71]

Xerox's chief executive was quoted as saying: "The fact that we had this strong company in Japan was of extraordinary importance when other Japanese companies started coming after us. Fuji Xerox was able to see them coming earlier, and understood their development and manufacturing techniques. If Fuji Xerox were within our organization, it would be easier, but then we would lose certain benefits. They have always had a reasonable

---

[69] James D. Bamford, Benjamin Gomex-Casseres, Michael S. Robinson, "Mastering Alliance Strategy: A Comprehensive Guide to Design, Management, and Organization", Jossey-Bas 2003, pp. 188-189

[70]   http://www.alliancestrategy.com/PDFs/BGC%20Fuji%20Xerox%20%20 SnB97.pdf

[71] Id.

amount of autonomy. I can't take that away from them, and I wouldn't want to."[72]

In 2001, Fuji Photo Film Co. increased its equity percentage to 75%, with Xerox Corporation owning 25%. Many of the color printing devices sold by Xerox Corporation were originated by Fuji Xerox.[73]

This very successful joint venture accounted for over 10% of the net profits of Xerox Corporation for 2011.[74] Although Fuji Xerox is headquartered in Tokyo, its sales and service areas cover Japan, China and other Asia-Pacific countries and regions, including South Korea, the Philippines, Vietnam, Thailand, Malaysia, Singapore and New Zealand. Although Fuji Xerox has a base in the United States, sales and service in that region and Europe are covered by Xerox Corporation and Xerox Europe. Currently the company has over 40,000 employees and revenues exceeding 11 billion yen and profits of approximately 56 billion yen.[75]

This very important joint venture started with a modest investment of only two hundred million yen by the two joint venture partners.

Takeaway

By selecting the right foreign partner, Xerox saved its own business. The decision to partner with Fuji allowed Xerox to survive against formidable Japanese competitors. Xerox had developed a relationship with Fuji through its joint venture which permitted Fuji to help Xerox in its time of trouble. Middle-market and smaller companies could well learn from this example the importance of forging strong international ties.

An Asian joint venture may, in some cases, be an excellent defensive move for a middle-market or smaller company to maintain its market position. Just as Xerox was arguably saved by its Japanese partner, a middle-market and smaller company

---

[72] Id.

[73] http://www.fujixerox.com/eng/company/profile/history/corporate.html

[74] Form 10-K of Xerox Corporation for fiscal year ended December 31, 2011.

[75] http://www.fujixerox.com/eng/company/profile/history/corporate.html

may need the protection from aggressive Asian competitors who have low labor costs. For example, if the middle-market and smaller company produces high profit products which have significant labor content, they are potentially susceptible to having the selling price of their product undercut through Asian competitors. Having a strategic alliance in Asia will give them some protection from future Asian competitors, just as it protected Xerox.

Asian Partners With Political Connections

Throughout Asia, and particularly in China, many successful entrepreneurs have close relationships with politicians, especially local politicians. These political relationships can be very helpful to the joint venture, assuming that there is no violation of the Foreign Corrupt Practices Act (or comparable international laws). However, there is a downside. If the politician loses favor within the political party, the politician's associates, including the entrepreneur, also lose favor.

This happened to Xu Ming, whose business, called "Valian Shide Group", flourished because of his relationship with Bo Xilai, the Communist Party chief of Chongqing, China. In 2005, Xu Ming was rated by Forbes Magazine as the eighth-richest man in China. However, when Bo Xilai fell out of favor with the Chinese Communist Party, Xu Ming suffered along with him because of his close relationship.[76] Any joint venture affiliated with Xu Ming would likewise have also suffered due to its relationship to Bo Xilai.

Our next chapter explores why joint ventures fail and what lessons middle-market and smaller companies can learn from these failures.

---

[76] Alex Frangos, "A Tycoon Rises and Falls With a Chinese Political Boiss", The Wall Street Journal, June 22, 2012.

Chapter 3

Why Joint Ventures Fail

Middle-market and smaller companies must understand the major reasons why international joint ventures fail in order to avoid these pitfalls and have a greater chance for successful and profitable alliances. By being sensitive to these problem areas, negotiators of joint ventures can avoid these traps.

A 1991 Harvard Business Review study found that only 51 percent of the joint ventures studied were considered "successful". Success was defined as each partner achieving returns greater than their cost of capital.[77] In 2001, the same group did a follow-up study which looked at joint ventures again – a larger number this time – and found that success rates had "soared" to 53 percent. Clearly joint venture "success" remains elusive.[78] Another study in 2003 reported a failure rate between 30 – 61 percent, and that 60 percent of announced joint ventures failed to start, or faded away within five years.[79] One book reported that 70 percent of alliances failed.[80]

---

[77] Bamford, James, David Ernst and David G. Fubini. Launching a World-Class Joint Venture: Harvard Business Review. (Harvard Business School Publishing Corporation: February 2004)

[78] Tom MacMimllan, President and Chief Executive Officer, "CIBC Mellon: A Joint Venture Success Story", CIBC Mellon (Speech to the Financial Services Institute - November 2, 2006)

[79] Osborn, 2003. From http://www.blakenewport.co.uk/bna-news-and-media.asp?id=18

[80] Gene Slowinski & Matthew W. Sagal, "The Strongest Link: Forging a Profitable & Enduring Corporate Alliance, AMACOM (2003) p. ix

Many joint ventures in the automotive industry have failed to yield much of value. Although General Motors ("GM") has been a joint venture leader over the years, and has a successful joint venture in China with Shanghai Automotive Industry Corporation ("Shanghai Automotive"), it has also been a leader in producing failed joint ventures. In 2000, GM announced a joint venture with Fiat, which failed within a few years, with Fiat forcing GM to buy the entire company. Subsequently, there was the Isuzu/GM joint venture which also unraveled, although GM got its diesel engine from that joint venture. GM also had a joint venture with Suzuki from which nothing resulted. Likewise its joint venture with Subaru never produced any benefits to GM. However, GM has not been deterred by its dismal record on joint ventures. In February 2012, GM announced that it was taking a 7% equity stake in France's Peugeot Citroen.[81]Moreover, in 2011, GM had the number one market share in automobiles in China through its Chinese joint ventures.[82] GM sold more cars in China in both 2010 and 2011 than it sold in the U.S.[83]

Even prestigious foreign companies, such as Japan's Sony and South Korean rival Samsung, can have failed joint ventures. The joint venture was formed in 2004 when Sony, falling behind in flat panel televisions, invested in a Samsung panel factory to ensure a steady supply of panels for its LCD televisions. Sony's television operations lost money for seven straight years and, in December 2011, Sony announced that Samsung electronics would purchase all of Sony's shares in the joint venture. The price of televisions as well as panels had been dropping so it made greater business sense to purchase such panels on the open market rather than invest in production.[84]

---

[81]http://www.nytimes.com/2012/03/01/business/global/gm-to-take-stake-in-peugeot-in-new-al...

[82] General Motors Company Form 10-K, 2011, p34

[83] Alisa Priddle, "GM's big plans for China includes more Cadillac models", USA Today, 04/25/2012; http://content.usatoday.com/communities/driveon/post/2012/04/gm-general-motors-china-cadillac-big-plans/1

[84] "Sony, Samsung dissolve panel joint venture", 3News, December 28, 2011, http://www.3news.co.nz/Sony-Samsung-dissolve-panel-joint-venture/tabid/412/articleID/237812/Default.aspx

More important than the exact percentage of failed alliances are the reasons for the failure. These reasons provide the clues for the best practices in making the alliances work by avoiding these failure traps.

We can define the term "success" as each partner reaching a mutually-acceptable alliance arrangement that achieves each firm's strategic objectives. Therefore, a "failure" is an alliance which does not achieve each firm's strategic objectives. Since the goal of an alliance is not its survival but the achievement of the strategic objectives of the partners, there is nothing wrong with terminating an alliance which ultimately does not satisfy those strategic objectives.[85]

Takeaway

Given the high failure rate for joint ventures, middle-market and smaller companies must negotiate a joint venture agreement which contemplates the possibility of failure as well as the possibility of success. For example, will there be a non-competition provision between the partners once the joint venture terminates as well as during the joint venture? If the middle-market and smaller company is contributing equipment, licenses or other know-how to the joint venture, does the middle-market and smaller company have the right to receive these assets back upon termination of the joint venture? This subject is discussed more thoroughly in Chapter 7.

Primary Reasons for Failure

The following are 10 of the primary reasons why international strategic alliances, particularly joint ventures, fail:

---

[85] Ben Gomes-Casseres, "Alliance Strategy: Managing Beyond Alliance", CriticalEye, June-August 2004, www.criticaleye.net. See also "Strategy must lie at the heart of alliances", Financial Times, Mastering Management, pp. 14-15, October 16, 2000.

INADEQUATE DUE DILIGENCE

Many companies do not spend the time and effort to perform thorough due diligence on the market they wish to penetrate or the alliance partner they may have chosen for that purpose. Due diligence is expensive but it is usually much less expensive than engaging in a failed joint venture.

Middle-market and smaller companies typically do not have the internal staff to perform thorough due diligence. In addition, they may be naïve as to Asian business practices, particularly those in China. Accordingly, middle-market and smaller companies should consider hiring due diligence specialists in China to assist them.

A great introduction to due diligence specialists is the book entitled "Poorly Made in China" by Paul Midler (John Wiley & Sons, Inc., 2009). The author, Paul Midler, who lives in China, speaks Mandarin, and has a Wharton MBA, was requested to perform due diligence on a Chinese factory for Howard, a U.S. importer of ceramics from that factory. His book described what happened thereafter as follows:

"Importers that provided original designs were quoted low prices by Chinese manufacturers. They were offered a bargain in part because small importers [like Howard] paid more. Watching as some of ... factory workers packed up boxes for Howard, I noticed that some of the pieces were even defective, and I had an uneasy feeling about Howard's business prospects...Howard was disappointed, but resigned. He did not have the volume to justify hiring someone to design original pieces; and therefore, he felt at the mercy of the manufacturer. Howard also reiterated that he was in a hurry, and that he needed to take whatever he could get...We loaded Howard's product and shipped it overseas. Another few shipments later, Howard ran into trouble... As expected, his prices were too high. An importer of ceramics couldn't purchase product for only half of its retail price and survive. [The Chinese factory owner] knew it but pushed for the higher prices anyway."[86]

---

[86] Paul Midler, "Poorly Made in China, An Insider's Account of the Tactics Behind China's Production Game", John Wiley & Sons, Inc., 2009, p. 15.

Although the relationship between Howard and the Chinese factory owner was technically not an equity joint venture, the contract between Howard and the Chinese factory owner to provide the ceramics was a strategic alliance. Strategic alliances require the same due diligence as more complex joint ventures.

The following are some examples of poor due diligence in the context of an equity joint venture:

KFC/Mitsubishi

As noted in a prior chapter discussing the KFC/Mitsubishi joint venture, KFC proposed opening stores near suburban shopping centers. However, as the use of family cars had not yet become widespread in Japan, Mitsubishi argued against that approach, saying it would be best to begin by establishing stores in downtown locations. In the end, KFC was not convinced by these arguments, the suburban strategy was adopted and it almost ruined a very profitable joint venture. KFC's mistake was not only in failing to listen to the arguments of Mitsubishi, but also in not investing in the demographic and sociological due diligence necessary to find the proper location for its stores in Japan. KFC instead relied upon its knowledge of the U.S. market and the success of stores in shopping centers, which turned out to be inapplicable at that point to Japan.

Groupon/Tencent Holdings Ltd. Joint Venture

Groupon is a deal-of-the-day website that features discounted gift certificates usable at local and national companies. It was reported on September 13, 2011, that the Groupon joint venture with Tencent Holdings Ltd ("Tencent"), the Chinese social networking behemoth, was not doing well.[87] The Chinese joint venture is called Gaopeng and in September 2011 had to close 10 offices and fire as many as 400 employees. The Groupon joint venture focused its strategy on many smaller cities in China,

---

[87] Douglas Crets, "Groupon's Chinese Joint Venture Closes 10 Offices, Fires Hundreds, 'Changes Strategy'", Read Write Web, September 13, 2011, http://www.readwriteweb.com/archives/groupon_goes_too_fast_in_china_closes_offices_in_t.php

approximately 70 cities, in which its marketing strategy was not effective. Instead, the joint venture changed its focus to 20 larger cities such as Beijing, Guangzhou and Shanghai, etc., where people are more affluent, rather than the lower-tier smaller cities. This change in strategy is a result of poor due diligence initially in focusing on smaller Chinese cities where the Groupon business model was not effective. Moreover, the Groupon e-mail marketing strategy did not work well in China because China e-mail is much less popular than instant messaging services like Tencent's QQ, which Chinese consumers use almost every day. Again, this was a failure of marketing due diligence.[88] Fortunately, these initial due diligence failures are hopefully being corrected.

COMMERCIAL BRIBES AND REPUTATION

Many Asian companies are accustomed to marketing systems that involve bribes of government personnel. Although this information is difficult to obtain early in the relationship, U.S. companies cannot partner with such Asian companies because of the Foreign Corrupt Practices Act (or comparable international laws). This particular statute is vigorously enforced in the United States and will apply to joint ventures, as discussed below.

Checking out the operations of the proposed joint venture partner is vital to the success of the venture. The business reputation of the joint venture partner within the country is particularly important. The business reputation of the local joint venture partner can seriously influence the success or failure of the joint venture. If your joint venture partner has been involved in unethical business practices in the past or its products have a poor reputation, you should run – not walk – away from that potential partner.

---

[88] Ben Jiang, "Gaopeng, Groupon's Flagging Effort in China, May Be Headed For A merger with FTuan", Techcrunch.com. 04/18/2012, http://techcrunch.com/2012/04/18/gaopeng-groupons-flagging-effort-in-china-may-be-headed-for-a-merger-with-ftuan/

A joint venture strategy should only be considered in situations in which it is not feasible to start a business from scratch or to make an outright acquisition of a local company. The due diligence process helps to reveal whether these options, which may be superior to the joint venture, are feasible.

POOR COMMUNICATION OF STRATEGIC OBJECTIVES AND BUSINESS PLAN

Each of the firms must clearly understand their own strategic objectives and the business plan to achieve them. These strategic objectives and business plan must also be communicated to the other partner at some point during the negotiations.

There is a natural reluctance to reveal too much confidential information early in the negotiations for fear that it will be used by the other potential partner to become a competitor or in a manner detrimental to the disclosing party. However, the failure to fully communicate all strategic objectives and the business plan to the other alliance partner may doom the alliance from the beginning. A strong confidentiality agreement will help to protect each disclosing party.

At some point in the negotiations risks must be taken by each party to disclose all of their strategic objectives and business plan to the other. Without such mutual candor, the alliance is unlikely to succeed.

An example of good communication of strategic objectives was the 1983 negotiation by Fuji Photo ("Fuji") and Philip A. Hunt Chemical ("Hunt") for a joint venture aimed to penetrate the rapidly expanding market in Japan for electronic chemicals. Fuji, as well as Hunt, had each developed a photoresist technology and were potential competitors for the Japanese market. However, Fuji's priorities were elsewhere and it did not wish to expend its resources to further develop its photoresist technology. On the other hand, Hunt was a major player in the manufacturing of photoresist (i.e. sensitive coatings used in the electronic industry) in both the U.S. and Europe and had very little sales in Japan. Fuji's motivation was to obtain access to Hunt's technology, which was more developed than Fuji's, as well as to share resources and risks. Hunt's motivation was to quickly gain access to the Japanese market before competitors, such as Allied Corp. and DuPont, entered the business and was willing to provide Fuji access to its technology in the joint venture in exchange for this Japanese market share. The joint venture (called "Fuji-Hunt") was successful because each of the partners clearly revealed their motivations to the other in the negotiations.[89]

It has been suggested that once an agreement has been reached, the two joint venture partners should engage in a systematic "alliance relationship launch". This is a practice followed by Schering-Plough and 93 other companies who engage in strategic alliances.[90] This launch process, which may take several weeks, involves many meetings during which the partners explore the potential challenges of working together and establish detailed mechanisms for day-to-day operations. This alliance launch process is an important planning tool to ensure a successful initial operation of the joint venture.

BAD IDEA AND CONCEPT

The alliance partners must each benefit from the relationship. Each of the founding partners must bring something special to the relationship that the other lacks. Each of the joint venture partners must have carefully thought through and researched their respective strategic objectives and business plan.

Many times the business plan, even if thoroughly researched, turns out poorly. Unanticipated events can kill an idea that seems

[89] Kathryn Rudie Harrigan, "Joint Ventures, Alliances, and Corporate Strategy", Beard Books, 2003.
[90] Jonathan Hughes and Jeff Weiss, "Simple Rules for Making Alliances Work", Harvard Business Review, November 2007.

great on paper. Many times business plans that sound wonderful in concept do not produce sufficient tangible benefits to the alliance partners to be worth the effort.

One example is a major manufacturer of tires who created an alliance with a biotechnology company. The strategic objective of the tire manufacturer was to understand how biotechnology might impact its business and to obtain some useful insights which might be helpful in its planning. The articulation of the strategic objective and business plan sounded great on paper but failed to produce sufficient tangible benefits for the tire manufacturer to continue the alliance.[91] The alliance did not have sufficient relationship to the core business of either company to make the effort productive.

Any company participating in a joint venture should develop an alternative plan or an exit plan in case it turns out that the original business plan is not feasible.

Occasionally, joint ventures are formed by two companies who are too weak to survive alone. Putting two failing business together will not necessarily make a good business.

POOR PLANNING

The joint venture partners must agree up-front to a comprehensive plan outlining the business transaction. The plan must include detailed governance, dispute resolution, ownership of intellectual property, how each party will contribute to the joint venture (whether it's money, expertise, technology, etc.) and other matters that are necessary to the business operation.

Early in the negotiations difficult topics must be raised. For example, what happens if a competitor of either party produces a superior product? Will that event permit the other party to withdraw from the alliance? Who will determine if the competitor's product is superior?

---

[91] Id at p. 8

The leadership of the joint venture must be carefully identified. Leadership roles should be clearly designated in the strategic alliance contract. Placing a representative of each of the joint venture parties in a leadership position on each issue can produce a stalemate. Determinations must be made as to who will lead on specific issues if the parties cannot agree. In the case of a Chinese joint venture, it is important to determine who can appoint and remove the representative director and the general manager.

Poor planning can also lead to a lack of commitment by each of the joint venture parties. Some companies engage in joint ventures hoping for a quick profit. When a quick profit does not materialize, they lose interest and commitment. A comprehensive plan with well-defined goals as well as a timeline is critical to maintaining the commitment of each party.

WRONG PERSONNEL

Each organization must assign people to the joint venture company who can develop a close working relationship. International joint ventures suffer from serious cultural differences and these differences must be transcended. Even the best business plan for the joint venture will be unsuccessful if the assigned personnel do not develop the close personal relationship necessary to overcome both the working conflicts as well as the cultural differences.

Relationships must be at the top of each company. In discussing the Toshiba/General Electric joint venture, both companies emphasized the important role that senior management plays in the relationship. According to Tsuyoshi Kawanishi, a Toshiba director and senior executive vice president of partnerships and alliances, "During honeymoon time, everything is great. But, as you know, divorce is always a possibility, and that's when things can get bitter."[92] One big reason that an ugly falling out had not

---

[92] Brenton R. Schlender "How Toshiba Makes Alliances Work: The partners start out with the corporate equivalent of a prenuptial agreement just in case. But there hasn't been an ugly divorce yet." Fortune Magazine, 10/4/1993, http://

occurred in the Toshiba/GE alliance was the key role played by senior management in the relationship. According to Jack Welch, CEO of GE, "I've dealt with Toshiba for 15 years, and it's always been a very easy relationship. When things go awry, a call to Sato-san will take care of the problem in 24 hours."[93]

The example of Fuji Xerox in a prior chapter illustrates what is necessary to be successful. Jefferson Kennard was selected by Xerox to manage the Fuji Xerox alliance in the 1970s and remained in this role for three decades. Kennard was sent to Japan as Xerox resident director when Fuji Xerox was just getting out of the start-up stage. He developed a long-term relationship with Tony Kobayashi, the Chief Executive Officer of Fuji Xerox. Kennard served as the executive assistant to Kobayashi as well as the Xerox resident director. This relationship of trust and confidence was a key to the ultimate success of Fuji Xerox.[94]

Each of the parties must have or develop a counterpart to Jefferson Kennard and Toby Kobayashi. In the case of middle-market and smaller companies, leadership must be at the CEO level.

INADEQUATE CAPITALIZATION

A major reason for the failure of a joint venture is inadequate capitalization. Each of the parties must have realistic expectations of the amount of capital and the ability to provide that capital.

In contrast to Fortune 500 companies, middle-market and smaller companies do not have deep pockets and typically underestimate the amount of negative cash flow the joint venture will suffer. The time to ramp-up a joint venture until it is

money.cnn.com/magazines/fortune/fortune_archive/1993/10/04/78406/index.htm

[93] Id.

[94] James D. Bamford, Benjamin Gomex-Casseres, Michael S. Robinson, "Mastering Alliance Strategy: A Comprehensive Guide to Design, Management, and Organization", Jossey-Bas 2003, pp. 188-189

cash-positive is easily underestimated. Rosy budget projections of cash flow need to be carefully reviewed. These projections should be "shocked" by assuming that it takes three or four times as long to get to positive cash flow in order to determine how much capital will really be needed by the joint venture.

FAILURE TO DRAFT A COMPLETE JOINT VENTURE AGREEMENT

The joint venture agreement must cover all important business issues relating to the operations of the joint venture entity. The failure to cover certain business issues can breed conflicts which can adversely affect the joint venture. Negotiating key business points helps to identify areas in which the strategic objectives of the parties may conflict.

Omitting the resolution of major business issues in the joint venture agreement merely postpones the day when those issues must be decided by the parties. It is far better to take the time to negotiate a comprehensive agreement than to argue later as to the intention of the parties after they have committed their time and capital to the venture.

FAILURE TO MONITOR AND MAKE CONTRIBUTIONS TO JOINT VENTURE OPERATIONS

The U.S. partner must constantly monitor what is going on with the joint venture. Deferring to the Chinese joint venture partner because "it knows China" is not effective. The Chinese joint venture partner may know China, but it may not necessarily know marketing, production, management, finances, operations or any other business function as well as the U.S. partner.

If the U.S. partner is no longer making important contributions to the joint venture, or even if the Chinese joint venture partner wrongly believes the U.S. partner is no longer making important contributions to the joint venture, it may try to eliminate the U.S. partner. The Chinese joint venture partner may do this by withholding information and by deliberately lowering profits. Therefore, the U.S. partner must continue to impress the Chinese partner with their contributions to the joint venture.

CULTURAL DIFFERENCES, INCLUDING LANGUAGE BARRIERS

In Chapter One of this book we discussed the Wahaha joint venture in which a perceived slight contributed to bad feelings by the Chinese partner for many years.

It has long been known that it is difficult to mesh the cultures of two organizations, even when they are in the same country. The cultural problems are geometrically increased when the collaboration is between organizations in different countries.

Middle-market and smaller companies may need to adjust their own culture to accommodate the culture of their international joint venture partners. This is a difficult process for many companies and some fail miserably at it.

A special report prepared for the Association of Strategic Alliance Professionals came to the following three conclusions[95]:

- *Alliance culture matters and has a significant impact on alliance success.* "Our study shows that having alliance culture, especially in the area of norms and partner focus, is an important differentiator between companies with a

---

[95] "Alliance Culture: It's in the DNA!" ASAP White Paper on Alliance Culture – June 2010

high alliance success rate and those with a low alliance success rate."

- *Strong alliance cultures can be created in any sector, in any country; only company differences matter.* "There are no differences between sector or country regarding the extent of implementation of alliance cultures. Companies cannot claim that in their country or industry constraints exist which make it particularly hard to develop an alliance culture. It is completely up to the company to develop and manage its alliance culture."

- *Alliance culture needs to be internalized.* "Companies will only be successful when they have internalized their alliance culture as behaviors and company processes."

Language barriers are extremely serious problems in joint ventures. In Chinese joint ventures, there are more than 50 local dialects and approximately half of the country does not speak Mandarin. If the proposed Chinese joint venture partner cannot be understood except through interpreters, it may be best to look elsewhere for a partner. There are too many business issues which can be mistranslated by even the best interpreter. Moreover, having to use an interpreter can try the patience of most U.S. negotiators as well as lead to serious misunderstandings.

In Part II of this book we will discuss joint ventures based in China and start with the general description of the Chinese economy by Professor Larry D. Qiu.

PART II

Joint Ventures based in China

Chapter 4

The Chinese Economy

By Professor Larry D. Qiu
The University of Hong Kong

Doing business in another country or doing business with people from another country requires knowledge about that nation's economy. In this part, several important aspects of the Chinese economy are described with a focus on recent developments. Most of the data and figures presented in this part are directly drawn or calculated from various issues of the *Chinese Statistical Yearbook*. China began to reform its economy when it introduced the open-door policy in 1979. The objective of the reform is to change the economy from the centrally-planned system to a market system, and from a closed economy to an open one. Since that time, the Chinese economy has undergone tremendous changes and is now playing a very important role in the global economy in many dimensions.

The Macro Economy

Although China is still a developing country, the size of its economy – as commonly measured by gross domestic product (GDP) – has grown into one of the three largest in the world, with the United States remaining the biggest. China has doubled its GDP many times during the 30 years of reform, and its GDP increased from USD $1,198 billion in 2000 to USD $6,937 billion[96] in 2011, as shown in Figure 4.1, with the annual growth rate ranging from 8 percent to 14 percent over the last decade. China is among the few countries in the world with fast, stable and long-lasting growth. With the largest population in the world, China's corresponding large GDP does not necessarily translate to a high standard of living; its GDP per capita being one measure of such. In fact, when ranked according to national income per capita, China does not even rank in the top 100 globally. However, the improvement of income is very fast-paced in China, with its GDP per capita increasing from USD $949 in 2000 to USD $4,428 in 2010 as shown in Figure 4.2. The annual growth rate of GDP per capita is between 8 and 14 percent during that period, which is equally as impressive as the growth of overall GDP. With the current status, the large size of the economy means huge demand and large production capacity while the relatively low GDP per capita implies different consumption patterns from high-income countries. Nevertheless, with the rapid growth of both GDP and GDP per capita, the Chinese market will become increasingly important for all types of products and services.

Inflation rate, i.e., price change, in China fluctuates much more than GDP. The average inflation rate was about 4 percent during the period from 2000-2010, but in some years it reached 8 percent, which is quite high. Similar to other economic indicators such as unemployment and income distribution, inflation could become a big concern to Chinese society.

---

[96] All U.S. dollar figures are based on exchange rates of 1 Chinese yuan equals 0.1570 U.S. dollars. All charts contained in this chapter are derived from the China Statistical Yearbook 2011, as published by the National Bureau of Statistics of China.

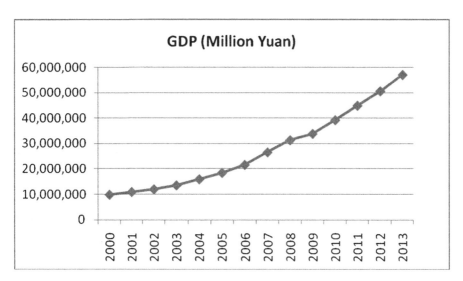

Figure 4.1: China's GDP (million yuan): the size of the economy

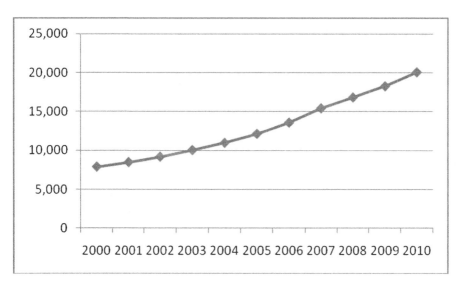

Figure 4.2: China's GDP per capita (yuan): the richness of the population

In recent years, the Chinese government relied more on using monetary tools – such as interest rate and bank's reserve requirement ratio – to control inflation. This makes the policy more transparent than in the early years of the reform. However, the main problem of Chinese inflation in recent years is not its level and volatility, but rather the structure. Some key driving factors behind the high inflation are the soaring prices of both food products and housing. They affect the daily life of low-income families more than middle- and high-income groups.

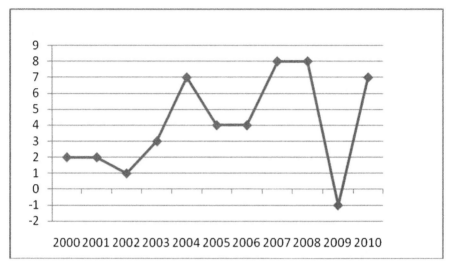

Figure 4.3: China's inflation rates (GDP deflator, %)

China has a very large pool of labor, especially low-skill labor. This provides comparative advantages for China in many labor-intensive industries and services. Unemployment has always been a big concern of the government. The government has been trying to keep the economic growth high and encourage export, largely done in an effort to sustain employment. With all the efforts, the urban registered unemployment rate remains reasonably low and quite stable. It ranged from a low of 3.1 percent in 2000 to 4.1 percent in 2010, with the highest coming in 2003 at 4.3 (the SARS period) and 2009 (the recent financial crisis year). Although keeping a low unemployment rate using various measures may result in low efficiency, it helps keep society more stable, which in turn helps the sustainability of economic growth.

Regional Imbalances

When one first looks at the key macroeconomic indicators of China, he/she will find that they all look healthy at the aggregate level: stable growth, low inflation, low unemployment, high investment, etc. However, China is a very large country and those macroeconomic performances vary tremendously across the nation's 31 administrative regions (province, autonomous regions, and direct municipalities), which can also be divided into three areas: east, middle and west. The eastern area is the most developed of the three, while the western area is the least economically developed.

Figure 4.4 indicates the dominance of the eastern area and its majority contribution to the country's total GDP. The eastern area is not only the largest in economic size, but the people who reside in it are also the richest.

Figure 4.5 shows that people in the western area have the lowest per capita income, which is about one-third of that in the east. This income inequality is even larger when looking at a comparison of income per capita across the 31 administrative regions. Shanghai has the highest income per capita, which was RMB76,074 yuan in 2010, while Guizhou – at RMB13,119 yuan in that same year – has the lowest.

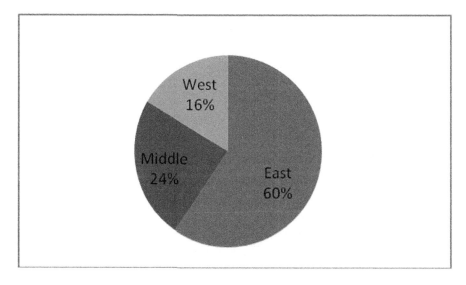

Figure 4.4: GDP distribution across regions in 2010

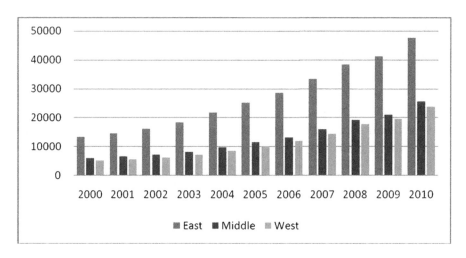

Figure 4.5: GDP per capita cross regions, 2000-2010

Although there are large imbalances across regions and areas in their respective economic developments, the growth rates are quite similar in recent years, as shown by Figure 4.6. This indicates that the less-developed regions are improving, which is partly the result of the government's assistance in both policies and transfers to those regions.

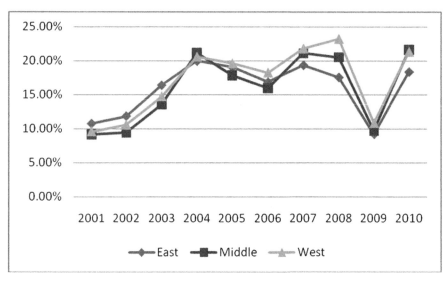

Figure 4.6: GDP growth rates cross regions, 2001-2010

The aggregate economic indicators imply the great potential of the Chinese market. However, the large imbalance of developments across regions indicates that one should view China as having many markets. Demand and business costs in the eastern area are very different from those in the middle and western areas. Different companies should enter different regions (markets) according to the nature of their businesses.

Sectoral Development

At the beginning of the economic reform, China was basically an agricultural economy with more than 80 percent of the labor force located in the rural area and a large share of primary sector in its GDP. The term "primary sector" refers to agriculture, fishing and extraction, such as mining. This contrasts with the secondary sector which is approximately the same as manufacturing and the tertiary sector, which is the service sector.

The reform has successfully changed the structure of the economy. By 2000, the primary sector's contribution to GDP had been reduced to 15.1 percent, which has since continued to drop, reaching to only 9.5 percent, as shown in Figure 4.7. Thus, the Chinese economy is no longer an agricultural one. In contrast, the tertiary or service sector grew very fast. Its GDP contribution was below 20 percent in the early period of the reform, reached 39 percent in 2000, and continued to grow to 45.9 percent in 2010. The secondary or manufacturing sector remained quite stable in terms of its share of GDP. In 2010, the tertiary or service sector surpassed the secondary sector (44.6 percent) to become the largest sector of the economy. This transformation has very strong implications on the markets.

The faster growth of the tertiary or service sector is a direct result of the economic development. When income reaches a certain level, the demand for services becomes greater. As services are mostly produced locally, this structure change also implies the importance of internal demand in the Chinese economy. That is, there is a shift from external demand to internal demand, which has a huge impact on the global economy given the sheer size of the Chinese economy. The implication for companies in the service industry is also clear: the rapid growth of demand in the Chinese market for your service products.

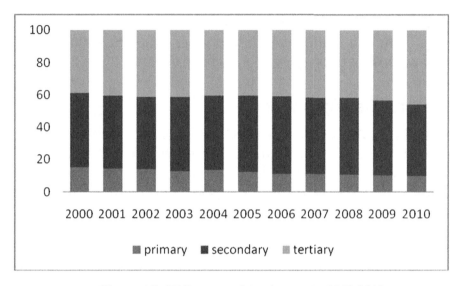

Figure 4.7: GDP composition by sector, 2000-2010

China's Globalization

Before 1979, the Chinese economy was immensely closed because the Government's objective was to develop its economy so that it would not need to rely heavily on foreign countries, especially those in the western part of the world. In 1979, the government launched its open-door policy which decentralized the trade decisions to production enterprises, lowered import protection, and provided incentives to exports. The results of China's globalization are as impressive as, or perhaps even more impressive than, those of the domestic economic reforms. In 1979, China's total trade ranked 32nd in the world. In 2006, China overtook the United States as the second-largest exporter, and in 2009, China surpassed Germany and became the world's largest exporter.

China contributes nearly 10 percent of the world's exports. By the end of 2009, China's imports ranked second in the world after the U.S., accounting for 8 percent of the world imports while the U.S. accounts for 13 percent.

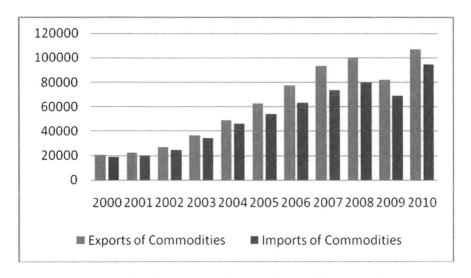

Figure 4.8: China's export and import (100 million yuan), 2000-2010

With the exception of 2009 – when the financial crises hit most of the world's economies – both import growth and export growth remain strong almost every year. Even in the recent decade, China was able to maintain an average of 20 percent annual growth in both export and import, as indicated by Figure 4.8, which gives the total values of commodities for imports and exports, respectively.

A substantial share of China's trade is in the form of process-ing trade in which China imports materials from abroad and uses them to produce the final goods exclusively for exports. This type of trade reflects China's labor cost advantage.

Foreign funded enterprises, including wholly-owned foreign firms and Sino-foreign joint ventures, contribute to roughly half of China's total trade. The substantial processing trade activity and foreign capital's involvement in China's trade implies that foreign acquisitions in China do not necessarily have to target the Chinese market. Export-platform investment/acquisitions – namely acquiring a Chinese firm for the purpose of using it as a platform for export – prove profitable.

Another important aspect of globalization is foreign direct investment (FDI). Figure 4.9 represents the values of both FDI inflows (foreign companies investing in China) and FDI outflows (Chinese companies investing abroad). Partly due to the asymmetric restrictions and incentives given to capital outflows and inflows, there are much larger FDI inflows than outflows.

When foreign multinationals invest in China, they either make a Greenfield investment (building the plants themselves) or acquire local Chinese firms. The investments can be also viewed from the ownership structure angle: investments wholly-owned by foreign enterprises or joint ventures with Chinese firms. Joint venture was a more popular mode of investment in the early period, but wholly-owned has become the dominant mode of investment in the recent decade, accounting for about 80 percent of the new investments.

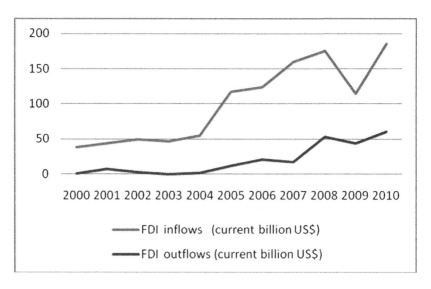

Figure 4.9: China's FDI inflows and outflows, 2000-2010

One of the drastic reforms in China in recent years is the exchange rate regime and policy. China maintained the fixed exchange rate system from 1996 to 2005, largely by restricting capital flows. RMB was fixed to the U.S. dollar at the rate of 8.28

yuan per dollar until July 2005. Ever since then, RMB has appreciated against the dollar by more than 20 percent. See Figure 4.10.

However, China has not switched completely to the flexible exchange system yet. The government still limits the daily fluctuation of the exchange rate to a small range and RMB is not fully convertible in the sense that people are not allowed to buy and sell in a large quantity without conditions. It is a common view that RMB is still undervalued and the general trend is that it will continue to appreciate slowly in the near future.

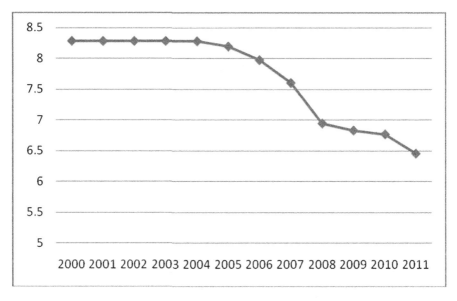

Figure 4.10: Exchange rates (yuan per dollar)

Government's Plans

It is impossible to review the government's policies in this section. The best way to have a sense of what direction future policies might take is to look at the government's plans. The Chinese government has produced five-year plans since the 1950s. The five-year plan lays down the foundations/themes for future developments while detailed policies and implementation are launched during the course of the corresponding sixty-month span. In March 2011, the government announced the 12ᵗʰ 5-year plan for 2011-2015. That current plan emphasizes "higher quality growth." With such an emphasis on quality, the GDP growth target is set at 7 percent per annum over the five-year period.

Surrounding the above-mentioned current central theme of "higher quality growth" are seven supporting ones: (1) sustainable growth, (2) moving up the value chain, (3) reducing disparities, (4) scientific development, (5) environmental protection, (6) energy efficiency and (7) domestic consumption. These themes have strong implications on the future policy introduction.

For example, to reduce disparities, the Chinese government will give resources and incentives in an effort to assist the development of the western regions. To switch to domestic consumption, the government will withdraw some incentives/subsidies given to the promotion of export in the past. With regard to industry developments, the government has identified seven priority industries in accordance with the other themes: (1) new energy (nuclear, wind and solar power); (2) energy conservation and environmental protection; (3) biotechnology (drugs and medical devices); (4) new materials (rare earths and high-end semiconductors); (5) new IT (broadband networks, internet security infrastructure, network convergence); (6) high-end equipment manufacturing (aerospace and telecom equipment); and (7) clean energy vehicles. Moreover, the government has announced its targets of increasing urbanization from 47.5% in 2011 to 51.5% by 2015, increasing services sector contribution to GDP from 43% to 47%, and increasing R&D spending to 2.2% of GDP.

Although the targets may eventually be achieved, it is clear that policies need to be designed to help reach them. This is important for businesses; knowing the direction of the country's economic future is critical for long-term investments.

Our next chapter deals with how to negotiate a joint venture based in China.

Chapter 5

Negotiating a Joint Venture Based in China

Negotiating a joint venture agreement internationally requires an intimate knowledge of the culture of the other party and the legal restrictions. The next chapter will deal with the legal restrictions in a Chinese-based joint venture, including investment restrictions. The purpose of this chapter is to discuss cultural issues involved in the negotiation of a China-based joint venture.

Ignorance of cultural differences can cause the failure of even the most promising of cross-border strategic alliances. One classic example of cultural ignorance is the story of a U.S. salesman who is trying to obtain a multi-million dollar contract from a potential Saudi-Arabian client. He presented the proposal to the Saudi-Arabian client in a pigskin binder. Muslims are prohibited from eating pork and the importation of pork products is illegal in Saudi Arabia.[97] The salesman and his company were then blacklisted from working with Saudi businesses.[98]

Before negotiating a cross-border alliance, it is important to study the peculiarities of the country. There are many books which cover cultural dos and don'ts, such as "Kiss, Bow, or Shake Hands: Asia".[99] In general, there are 12 major areas of personal

---

[97] Terri Morrison and Wayne A. Conaway, "Kiss, Bow, or Shake Hands", 2nd Edition, Adams Media, July 24, 2006, p. 430

[98] James K. Sebenius, "The Hidden Challenge of Cross-Border Negotiations", Harvard Review, March 2002

[99] Terri Morrison and Wayne A. Conaway, "Kiss, Bow or Shake Hands: Asia", Adams Media, 2007

and cultural differences that affect business relationships between people of different countries:

- **Business Cards** - What role do business cards play within the culture? How should your business card look to obtain maximum benefit?
- **Greetings** - How do people greet each other in the culture?[100] In group settings, whom should you greet first?
- **Degree of Formality** - How formally do you address or interact within the culture?
- **Gift Giving** - What role does gift giving have within the culture?
- **Touching** - Are there taboos about body contact?
- **Eye Contact** - What level of eye contact is expected?
- **General Deportment** - Are there taboos related to how a foreigner should carry themselves?
- **Emotions** - What displays of emotions are considered polite?
- **Silence** - Is silence during the negotiating process considered proper?
- **Eating** - What are the proper methods of dining?
- **Body Language** - Are certain forms of body language considered unacceptable? For example, showing the bottom of one's shoe by crossing your leg can be a sign of disrespect in certain cultures.
- **Punctuality** - Are you expected to be punctual or are schedules and agendas flexible?

Chinese Negotiating Strategies

China does not have the lowest labor cost of any Asian country. However, it has many other attributes that encourage business and joint ventures. Chinese factories can take any product and move it quickly into production. The Chinese show an incredible willingness and enthusiasm in getting a relationship started. A

---

[100] Terri Morrison and Wayne A. Conaway, "Kiss, Bow or Shake Hands", 2nd Edition, Adams Media, July 24, 2006.

foreign importer is typically treated "like a king."[101] China is on a mission to build its economy and typically provides the red carpet for those who will make investments.

Moreover, business travelers to China do not have to worry about being kidnapped or otherwise molested. Vietnam, which has a lower labor cost than China, is one of the countries in which petty theft is commonplace.[102]

It is extremely important to have your own interpreter available for negotiations. Do not rely on the interpreter hired by the Chinese company. Your own interpreter can make certain that your words and their correct meaning are faithfully conveyed to your Chinese counterparts.

Now let us review the Chinese style of negotiation and some of the 12 major areas of personal and cultural differences that affect business relationships, keeping in mind that Hong Kong, and to some degree Shanghai and Beijing, tend to be a bit less formal than the rest of China.

MEANING OF "YES"

Before applying these personal and cultural differences to a negotiation with a Chinese business owner, it is important to understand the meaning of the word "yes" in China and in all of Asia. In western culture, we tend to assume that the word "yes" means "I agree". Unfortunately, this is not necessarily true in the Asian culture. "Yes" may mean that "I am listening." Sometimes it means "maybe" and at other times "yes" may mean only that "you have been heard."[103]

When there is a risk of losing face (yours or theirs), the Chinese and other Asians may pretend to understand your

---

[101] Paul Midler, "Poorly Made in China: An Insider's Account of the Tactics Behind China's Production Game", John Wiley & Sons, Inc., 2009, p.22.

[102] Id.

[103] Mia Doucet, "What part of yes don't you understand?", Mechanical Engineering, November 2008

need by replying "yes". This could be particularly true if the Chinese responder did not understand your English and may feel ashamed at not understanding your language. The response "yes" should be considered a neutral response and not a meaningful response.[104]

NEGOTIATING STYLE

U.S. business owners tend to value assertiveness and individualism and prefer to start their negotiations fairly quickly. In China, business is a long courting process. You must build your "guanxi", which is loosely translated as your "social capital". The core of Chinese business is mixing business and friendship. This takes time and patience. Socialization with your potential business partners is absolutely essential. You may even have to sing Karaoke. This gives the Chinese the opportunity to observe how their potential partners behave in a social setting.

BUSINESS CARDS

Business cards are very important in Asian culture. Your full name should appear on the business card and your title. It should indicate a high position within your company. Business cards should be presented by holding it in both hands. Before going to China, you might consider inserting some Mandarin language on your business card. Finally, you should avoid placing the other person's card in your wallet or back pocket, which may be a sign of disrespect. Use your jacket or shirt pocket to store the other person's business card.

While it is important to be polite and follow local customs, do not be overly concerned if you take a business card with one hand

---

[104] Id.

instead of two and put it in your back pocket. At the end of the day, your success in China and other Asian countries depends more upon the fundamental soundness of your business plan rather than how many hands you use to take a business card or where you put it.

GREETINGS

Greetings tend to be formal. It is typical for the Chinese to nod or bow slightly upon greeting another person. However, handshakes are becoming more common. You should wait for your Chinese counterpart to extend their hand first.[105]

It is not unusual when you are visiting a Chinese factory to have the employees greet you with applause. The polite response is to applaud back.

GIFT-GIVING

Gift-giving is widespread in China even though it may occasionally violate Chinese law. A whole book can be written about the customs related to gift-giving in China.

In general, you should avoid giving anything of value in the presence of other persons, since it could cause the recipient both embarrassment and trouble. Always present a gift with both hands. Older Chinese will traditionally decline a gift two or three times before accepting it, which prevents them from appearing greedy. You should continue to insist that they accept the gift and indicate that you are pleased that they have done so.

It is best to not wrap a gift before arriving in China, since it may be unwrapped by PRC Customs. If possible, wrap gifts in

---

[105] Terri Morrison and Wayne A. Conaway, "Kiss, Bow or Shanke Hands: Asia", Adams Media, 2007

red, which is a lucky color, and preferably not white, which is a color used in funerals. Avoid gifts in sets of four (the Chinese word for "four" suggests death) or 13 (which connotes bad luck).[106] Chinese do not generally open gifts upon receipt.

The Chinese expect to exchange gifts at initial meetings, therefore you should be prepared to give a small gift to your Chinese colleagues and to each member of any Chinese delegation that meets you, in the order of introduction. A gift to a delegation as a group is an acceptable alternative to individual gifts provided the gift is given to the delegation leader.

It is likely that you will be treated to a banquet in China by a Chinese host. An appropriate gift might be a banquet in return.[107] Other acceptable gifts include cognac or other French brandy, whiskey, small items like cigarettes lighters, pens, or other desk items, books or framed paintings or gifts from your home region.

EATING

It is typical in China to have banquets. It is best to eat lightly at the beginning since many courses are usually served. It has been suggested that finishing all of your food at a banquet may be an insult to your host since it can mean that not sufficient food was provided. Likewise, leaving a bowl completely full may also be considered rude.[108]

---

[106] Mary Murray Bosrock, "Asian Business Customs & Manners", Meadowbrook Press, 2007.

[107] Kenneth A. Cutshaw, Michael E. Burke and Christopher A. Wagner, "Corporate Counsel's Guide to Doing Business in China, 3D", Thomson Reuters / West, 2010, p. 30; See also Terri Morrison and Wayne A. Conaway, "Kiss, Bow or Shanke Hands: Asia", Adams Media, 2007

[108] "Business-culture Briefing - China", Culturewise Ltd., 2004.

PUNCTUALITY

Punctuality is very important in China for both business as well as social occasions. Lateness is a serious affront.[109]

MEETINGS

Large meetings with Chinese tend to follow certain rituals. Chinese prefer to negotiate with a group of two to seven people. It is important in certain situations that your negotiating team includes middle-managers and technical experts. The level of management the Chinese send will match that of your team.

These large meetings follow a certain ritual. The highest ranking person from each party enters the room first. The rest of the foreign team enters the room together and then shakes hands with the Chinese team before formal introductions. The Chinese leader then welcomes everyone. The foreign leader introduces his or her team and then the members distribute their business cards to the Chinese team members. The leader of the foreign team then invites the Chinese leader to introduce the Chinese team, and the Chinese members distribute their business cards to the foreign team members.

For small groups, a member of the foreign team may distribute his or her business card before the foreign leader introduces the next person. This procedure permits the Chinese leader to see the importance of each team member of the foreign team.[110]

---

[109] Terri Morrison and Wayne A. Conaway, "Kiss, Bow or Shanke Hands: Asia", Adams Media, 2007

[110] Mary Murray Bosrock, "Asian Business Customs & Manners", Meadowbrook Press, 2007.

THE IMPORTANCE OF GUANXI

The Chinese place great importance in relationships. The key to successful negotiation is to develop guanxi, a term roughly meaning "connections."[111]   Guanxi emphasizes personal relationships in contrast to legal or contractual relationships or business practices.

The following are examples of how the leaders of three large U.S. companies developed guanxi in China. These examples serve as illustrations for middle-market and smaller companies that do not have the resources of these larger companies but that nevertheless can develop their own guanxi on a smaller scale.

GREENBERG/AIG GUANXI

Maurice R. Greenberg, the former CEO of U.S. insurance giant AIG, was a master at developing guanxi. The predecessor of AIG, a small Shanghai insurance company called American Asiatic Underwriters (later to become AIG), was founded in China by Cornelius Vander Starr in 1919. Maurice R. Greenberg was Starr's successor and developed relations with China's leadership, starting in 1975, prior to the time that China was opened to western business. Greenberg became the chairman of the Starr Foundation, which initially had over $3 billion in assets, and funded numerous fellowships with the Asian Cultural Council. Greenberg's lobbying efforts helped to support China's admission to the World Trade Organization in November 2001. He also guided the formation in 1980 of a 50/50 joint venture between AIG affiliates and the Peoples Insurance Company of China ("PICC"), which was the first joint venture in China with a foreign insurance organization and PICC. Greenberg also forged personal ties with China's future leadership and assisted Chinese government officials in introducing the international financial community to investment opportunities

---

[111] Robert Buderi and Gregory T. Huang, "Guanxi", Arrow Books Limited, New Ed edition (February 22,2007

in Shanghai. In 1992, American International Insurance, an AIG affiliate, established a Shanghai branch office and became the first foreign-owned insurance business to receive a license from the Peoples Bank of China. In 2005, AIG Private Bank became the first foreign private bank to be approved to open a Shanghai office.[112]

GALVIN/MOTOROLA GUANXI

Robert Galvin, Motorola's then CEO, entered China in 1987 with a $100 million investment, one of the first multi-national corporations to commence operations in China.[113] Motorola initially had an office in Beijing and in 1992 formed Motorola (China) Electronics Co., Ltd. The main products were mobile phones and other wireless communication equipment. By 2008, Motorola had invested $3.5 billion U.S. dollars in China and was one of the largest foreign-invested companies in China. In 1993, Motorola established Motorola University in Beijing to provide training both for its own staff and for its Chinese joint venture partners, suppliers, distributors, customers and, most importantly, PRC government officials. The curriculum was designed by professionals to ensure that it was adapted to the Chinese culture.[114]

Starting in 1998, Motorola cooperated with the Chinese Planning Committee and employed famous professors from universities in Beijing and Tianjin to teach. Through 2006, a total of 1,516 directors of state-owned enterprises, middle-management and technical personnel had taken part in the Motorola training.

---

[112] Richard Komaiko and Chris Stewart, "China's Imploding US ally", Asia Times, Sept. 18, 2008, http://www.atimes.com/atimes/China_Business/JI18Cb02.html

[113] Peter Svensson, "Robert Galvin, Longtime Motorola CEO and Cellphone Pioneer Dies at 89, Huff Post TECH, 10/12/11, http://www.huffingtonpost.com/2011/10/12/robert-galvin-dies_n_1007897.html

[114] Wang, Wen-Cheng, et al, "A Case Study on the Motorola China's Localization Strategy", The Journal of International Management Studies, Vol 5, Number 1, April 2010, p. 54.

At the urging of the Chinese Planning Committee, Motorola extended its training to the Chinese western provinces.[115]

This type of cooperation with the Chinese government earned Motorola much goodwill and Guanxi. In May 2012, Motorola Mobility Holdings Inc (a Motorola spin-off) was sold to Google for a cool $12.5 billion.[116]

GATES/ MICROSOFT GUANXI

Bill Gates first set foot in China in the late 1990s. He was scheduled to meet with the President of China, Jianj Xemin. He apparently did not study Chinese customs for attire, which, according to one book, required a dark suit and tie with dress shoes.[117]

Instead, Gates, being accustomed to the Silicon Valley informal attire, was dressed in his best blue jeans and a polo shirt to meet with the Chinese president. The purpose of his meeting was to try to establish a Chinese research laboratory.

Despite this inauspicious beginning, Gates, being a fast learner, started to attend countless dinners and banquets all over China to try to establish Quanxi. By 2006 the Microsoft Chinese Research Lab employed more than 400 of China's best and brightest and many of Microsoft's great products have come from this Beijing lab.[118]

[115] Id.

[116] John Letzing and Paul Mozur, "China Clears Google to Buy Motorola Mobility", The Wall Street Journal, May 20, 2012, http://online.wsj.com/article/SB10001424052702303360504577414280414923956.html

[117] Mary Murray Bosrock, "Asian Busines Customs & Manners", Meadowbrook Press, 2007.

[118] Robert Buderi and Gregory T. Huang, "Guanxi, The Art of Relationships: Microsoft, China, and Bill Gates's Plan to Win the Road Ahead", Simon & Schuster, May 9, 2006

GUIDELINES

Some of the guidelines for winning favor and establishing Quanxi are as follows:

- Trust
- Humility
- Mutual Respect
- Contribute to China First, Benefit Later
- Long Term Commitment in China
- Nurture Local Talent and Local Businesses[119]

THE ANATOMY OF NEGOTIATION

The best analysis of a Chinese joint venture negotiation is contained in a paper relating to the negotiations by Ericsson, a Swedish multi-national corporation, of different Chinese government projects in the telecommunication industry. Ericsson's negotiations for large mobile telecommunications projects occurred during the 1990s.[120]

The first co-author of the paper followed a China area manager at Ericsson Radio Systems AB, Stockholm, for three years in the early '90s and conducted in-depth interviews with him. The second co-author also conducted in-depth interviews, not only with a large number of Ericsson managers, but also with their Chinese negotiating partners. The authors divided the Chinese business negotiation process into three stages:

---

[119] Robert Buduri, "Guanxi: The Art of Relationships" Tiger.com, 10/29/10, http://21tiger.com/2010/10/29/guanxi-the-art-of-relationships-robert-buderi-and-gregory-t-huang/

[120] Pervez N. Ghauri and Tony Fang, "Negotiating with the Chinese: A Socio-Cultural Analysis", Journal of World Business, Autumn 2001, http://www-e.uni-magdeburg.de/evans/Journal%20Library/Intercultural%20Management/Negotiating%20with%20the%20Chinese.pdf

- Pre-negotiation – This includes lobbying presentations, informal discussions and trust building.
- Formal negotiation – This is the task-related exchange of information, persuasion, concessions and finally, agreement.
- Post-negotiation – Implementation of the project and new rounds of negotiation.

The authors noted that when dealing with the Chinese government bureaucracy, one should expect red-tape and observance of the cardinal principle: "He who does nothing makes no mistakes". Although Ericsson's negotiations occurred in the 1990s and was primarily with government officials, the negotiation process remains relevant today.

PRE-NEGOTIATION

The first step in Ericsson's negotiating process was to make presentations to let potential Chinese partners know more about the company, its products and the members of the negotiating team.   Ericsson provided all of the presentation material in Mandarin as well as in English. The presentations were followed by informal discussions between Ericsson and its Chinese counterparts. Ericsson attempted to convince the Chinese that although its price was much higher than that of the Japanese, its telecommunication system capacity was more powerful, its technology was better, and consequently this would facilitate future growth.

The next process involved trust building, to which the Chinese attach tremendous importance. An Ericsson manager noted that it was difficult to develop close social relations with the Chinese. For example, the Chinese seldom invited foreigners to their homes; this may be explained because of their embarrassment about their living condition. During this pre-negotiation phase, the Chinese sent delegations to Sweden for fact-finding tours and these tours provided an excellent opportunity for Ericsson to strengthen friendships with the Chinese. In Chinese culture, trust is high within the family but low outside the family.

Therefore, it was important for Ericsson to make the Chinese feel that they were dealing with a first-class firm.

FORMAL NEGOTIATION

The Chinese showed a strong interest in proceeding to a letter of intent, which was signed by both parties, and this started the formal negotiation stage. On the Chinese side were managers of companies under the Ministry of Post and Telecommunications, who were users of the Ericsson technology to be transferred, officials from the Bank of China (which controlled foreign exchange), designated staff from Chinese research institutes and occasionally from local government. On the Ericsson side were negotiators from Ericsson's Chinese area manager, a manager of product/technology, a lawyer and technical support, and an interpreter. Chinese lawyers seldom participate in the negotiations in contrast to foreign companies that may more often include an attorney.

There are five areas on which the negotiations concentrated:

- Equity Share – The Chinese insisted on having at least a 50% equity share, arguing that the equity share reflected "state sovereignty" and therefore had political significance.
- Respective Contributions – Ericsson's contribution consisted primarily of intangible resources, which were difficult to value, such as technology, managerial training, and know-how. The Chinese contribution included real estate, existing machinery and equipment and labor, which was much easier to value.
- Managerial Control – The Chinese wanted to share equal management positions with Ericsson, whereas Ericsson wanted its managers in a majority of the senior positions.
- Technology – Ericsson was concerned about how to protect its technology from being stolen. The Chinese, on the other hand, believed that once they had paid their share

of the joint venture, they should be entitled to whatever technologies Ericsson contributed for whatever purpose they wished.

- Price – As expected, there were significant conflicts on the technology transfer prices, royalty fees and other related fees, with the Chinese demanding very low prices. The Chinese argued about the tremendous value of the Chinese market which they were offering to Ericsson.

The Chinese used various tactics in their negotiations with Ericsson. These included flattery, identifying problems that Ericsson had, shaming, deception, and pitting competing foreign companies against Ericsson. For example, the Chinese entered into parallel negotiations with Nokia, a competitor, as well as Ericsson, thereby creating competitive pressure on Ericsson. At one point, the Chinese insisted that Ericsson's technology in Thailand had problems and did not work well. These tactics had to be countered by Ericsson.

CONCESSION AND FINAL AGREEMENT

The Chinese exhibited a desire to settle all outstanding issues with Ericsson on a "package basis." Although the Chinese made concessions, their concessions were not very substantial and were designed to attract Ericsson into making much more substantial concessions.

The Chinese were very careful in reviewing the words of the contract that would affect the Chinese. The agreement was executed in the presence of high-ranking Chinese government officials and was followed by lavish banquets and ceremonies.

One Ericsson negotiator described the following Chinese negotiating tactic:

"A tactic which I believe that the Chinese employ is that ... they set the deadline on a certain week and arrange a banquet long before the

contract is actually ready. They told us that things must be ready on Saturday when the mayor would come to the banquet. In this way the Chinese applied pressure on us to reach an agreement. This was common. ... You became a little disappointed the first time you came across such a situation. But, after a while, when you recognized the same thing happening again in other places, you knew that it was a tactic."

The Chinese negotiating team tended to be large. The Chinese reference to the Thailand project was directed at demonstrating Ericsson's weakness in quality in order to gain more bargaining power on the price issue. This is a typical Chinese negotiating tactic.

An excellent source for Chinese negotiating tactics is "The Thirty-Six Strategies of Ancient China"[121], which is based upon a biography of Wáng Jingé, a general who served in Southern Qi in the first Emperor Gao dynasty[122] Stratagem 2 entitled "Besiege Wei to rescue Zhao" suggests concentrating on the weaknesses of your opponent (i.e., the Thailand venture of Ericsson) to obtain concessions. This stratagem has been translated as follows:

"When the enemy is too strong to be attacked directly, then attack something he holds dear. Know that he cannot be superior in all things. Somewhere there is a gap in the armour, a weakness that can be attacked instead."

Stratagem 17 is entitled "Toss out a brick to attract a piece of jade." This tactic was used by the Chinese by making a small concession to obtain a big concession from Ericsson.

---

[121] Stefan H. Verstappen "The Thirty-six Strategies of Ancient China", China Books & Periodicals, January 30, 1999.

[122] "Original Text of the Biography of Wáng Jingé, Book of Qi (Traditional Chinese)".

POST-NEGOTIATION

A number of post-negotiation problems occurred, which required further rounds of negotiation. The joint venture agreement provided that the Swedish managing director would have a Western style residence in China. However, when he arrived in China, the Swedish managing director was afforded a Chinese residence similar to those of other Chinese senior executives. The Chinese argued that, despite the language in the contract, providing a Western type residence for the Swedish managing director was unfair to the Chinese senior executives who were part of the same joint venture. Ultimately a compromise was reached. Although the Chinese generally honored the contract, there was substantial negotiation after the execution of the formal agreement. The Chinese used the excuse of changing conditions to negotiate further concessions in the post-closing period and relied upon those changing conditions rather than being willing to adhere to the exact wording of the contract.

THE THIRTY-SIX STRATAGEMS -三十六𝑖† (SĀN SHÍ LIÙ JÌ)

The Chinese equate business with war. Therefore, the thirty-six stratagems of General Wáng Jingé are relevant to any business negotiation with the Chinese.

   The following thirty-six Chinese Strategies or Stratagems are a collection of tactics that can be applied to very different situations and are like proverbs or folklore. They have been described as "gems that speak to the cores of Chinese society." They are taught in school, found in literature, popular folk opera, and sometimes even in television programs. It is said that these strategies have become part of the "collective unconscious" of most Chinese people. The strategies are derived from military tactics applied during the Warring States Period (403-221 B.C.)

or during the Three Kingdom Period (265-220 B.C.). Just about anyone who has "grown up Chinese" (meaning that they have grown up in a Chinese home that respects and teaches Chinese traditions) knows these Thirty-six Strategies.[123]

1. **Cross the sea without Heaven's knowledge** –瞒 天 过海 **(mán tiān guò hǎi)**
   Prepare too much and you lose sight of the big picture; what you see often you do not doubt. Yin (the art of deception) is in Yang (acting in open). Too much Yang (transparency) hides Yin (true ruses).

2. **Besiege Wei to Rescue Zhao** – 围魏救赵**(wéi wèi jiù zhào)**
   When the enemy is too strong to be attacked directly, then attack something he holds dear. Know that he cannot be superior in all things. Somewhere there is a gap in the armour, a weakness that can be attacked instead.

3. **Kill with a borrowed knife** – 借刀杀人**(jiè dāo shā rén)**
   Attack using the strength of another (in a situation where using one's own strength is not favorable). Trick an ally into attacking him, bribe an official to turn traitor, or use the enemy's own strength against him.

4. **Await leisurely the exhausted enemy** –以逸待劳**(yǐ yì dài láo)**
   It is an advantage to choose the time and place for battle. In this way you know when and where the battle will take place, while your enemy does not. Encourage your enemy to expend his energy in futile quests while you conserve your strength. When he is

---

[123] "The 36 Chinese Strategies Applied to Negotiation" from John Barkai, Cultural Dimension Interests, the Dance of Negotiation, and Weather Forecasting: A Perspective on Cross-Cultural Negotiation and Dispute Resolution, 8 Pepperdine Dispute Resolution Law Journal 403 (2008).

exhausted and confused, you attack with energy and purpose.

5. **Loot a burning house** –趁火打劫(**chèn huǒ dǎ jié**)
    When a country is beset by internal conflicts, when disease and famine ravage the population, when corruption and crime are rampant, then it will be unable to deal with an outside threat. This is the time to attack.

6. **Clamor in the east but attack in the west** –声东击西 (**shēng dōng jī xī**)
    In any battle the element of surprise can provide an overwhelming advantage. Even when face to face with an enemy, surprise can still be employed by attacking where he least expects it. To do this you must create an expectation in the enemy's mind through the use of a feint.

7. **Create something out of nothing** –无中生有(**wú zhōng shēng yǒu**)
    A plain lie. Make somebody believe there was something when there is in fact nothing.

8. **Openly repair the walkway but secretly march to ChenCang** –明修栈道, 暗渡陈仓, (**Míng xiū zhàn dào, àn dù chén cāng**)
    Deceive the enemy with an obvious approach that will take a very long time, while surprising him by taking a shortcut and sneak up to him. As the enemy concentrates on the decoy, he will miss you sneaking up to him.

9. **Watch the fire burning from across the river** – .隔岸 观火(**gé àn guān huǒ**)
    Delay entering the field of battle until all the other players have become exhausted fighting amongst themselves. Then go in at full strength and pick up the pieces.

10. **Hide a knife in a smile** –笑里藏刀(**xiào lǐ cáng dāo**)
    Charm and ingratiate yourself to your enemy. When you have gained his trust, move against him in secret.

11. **Let the plum tree wither in place of the peach tree** –李代桃僵**(lǐ dài táo jiāng)**
There are circumstances in which you must sacrifice short-term objectives in order to gain the long-term goal. This is the scrapegoat stratagem whereby someone else suffers the consequences so that the rest do not.

12. **Lead away a goat in passing** –顺手牵羊**(shùn shǒu qiān yáng)**
While carrying out your plans be flexible enough to take advantage of any opportunity that presents itself, however small, and avail yourself of any profit, however slight.

13. **Beat the grass to startle the snake** –打草惊蛇**(dǎ cǎo jīng shé)**
Do something unaimed, but spectacular ("hitting the grass") to provoke a response of the enemy ("startle the snake"), thereby giving away his plans or position, or just taunt him. Do something unusual, strange, and unexpected as this will arouse the enemy's suspicion and disrupt his thinking. More widely used is "[Do not] startle the snake by hitting the grass". An imprudent act will give your position or intentions away to the enemy.

14. **Borrow a corpse to return the soul** –借尸还魂**(jiè shī hái hún)**
Take an institution, a technology, a method, or even an ideology that has been forgotten or discarded and appropriate it for your own purpose. Revive something from the past by giving it a new purpose or bring to life old ideas, customs, or traditions and reinterpret them to fit your purposes.

15. **Lure the tiger to leave the mountains** –调虎离山**(diào hǔ lí shān)**
Never directly attack an opponent whose advantage is derived from its position. Instead lure him away

from his position thus separating him from his source
of strength.

16. **In order to capture, first let it go** –欲擒故纵**(yù qín
    gù zòng)**
    Cornered prey will often mount a final desperate at-
    tack. To prevent this you let the enemy believe he
    still has a chance for freedom. His will to fight is thus
    dampened by his desire to escape. When in the end
    the freedom is proven a falsehood the enemy's mo-
    rale will be defeated and he will surrender without a
    fight.

17. **Toss out a brick to attract a piece of jade** –抛砖引玉
    (pāo zhuān yǐn yù)
    Bait someone by making him believe he gains some-
    thing or just make him react to it ("toss out a brick")
    and obtain something valuable from him in return
    ("get a jade gem").

18. **To capture bandits, first capture the ringleader** –擒
    贼擒王**(qín zéi qín wáng)**
    If the enemy's army is strong but is allied to the com-
    mander only by money, superstition or threats, then
    take aim at the leader. If the commander falls the rest
    of the army will disperse or come over to your side.
    If, however, they are allied to the leader through loy-
    alty then beware, the army can continue to fight on
    after his death out of vengeance.

19. **Remove the firewood from under the cooking pot**
    –釜底抽薪**(fǔ dǐ chōu xīn)**
    If something must be destroyed, destroy the source.

20. **Muddle the water to catch the fish** –混水摸鱼**(hún
    shuǐ mō yú)**
    Create confusion and use this confusion to further
    your own goals.

21. **The golden cicada sheds its shell** –金蝉脱壳**(jīn chán
    tuō ké)**
    It's a stratagem mainly used to escape from an en-
    emy of superior force. Mask yourself. Either leave

flamboyant traits behind, thus going incognito, or just masquerade yourself and create an illusion to fit your goals and distract others.

22. **Shut the door to catch the thief** –关门捉贼**(guān mén zhuō zéi)**

    To deliver/capture the enemy, you must plan prudently if you want to succeed. Do not rush into action. Before you "move in for the kill", first cut off your enemy's escape routes, and cut off any routes through which outside help can reach them.

23. **Befriend the distant states while attacking the nearby ones** –远交近攻**(yuǎn jiāo jìn gōng)**

    It is known that nations that border each other become enemies while nations separated by distance and obstacles make better allies. When you are the strongest in one field, your greatest threat is from the second strongest in your field, not the strongest from another field.

24. **Borrow the road to conquer Guo** –假途伐虢**(jiǎ tú fá guó)**

    Borrow the resources of an ally to attack a common enemy. Once the enemy is defeated, use those resources to turn on the ally that lent you them in the first place.

25. **Steam the beams and change the pillars** –偷梁换柱 **(tōu liáng huàn zhù)**

    Disrupt the enemy's formations, interfere with their methods of operations, change the rules that they are used to following, go contrary to their standard training. In this way you remove the supporting pillar, the common link that makes a group of men an effective fighting force.

26. **Point at the mulberry tree but curse the locust tree** –指桑骂槐**(zhǐ sāng mà huái)**

    To discipline, control, or warn others whose status or position excludes them from direct confrontation, use analogy and innuendo. When names are not used directly, those accused cannot retaliate without revealing their complicity.

27. **Play a sober-minded fool** –假痴不癫(jiǎ chī bú diān)
Hide behind the mask of a fool, a drunk, or a madman to create confusion about your intentions and motivations. Lure your opponent into underestimating your ability until, overconfident, he drops his guard. Then you may attack.

28. **Lure the enemy onto the roof, then take away the ladder** – 上屋抽梯(shàng wū chōu tī)
With baits and deceptions, lure your enemy into treacherous terrain. Then cut off his lines of communication and avenue of escape. To save himself, he must fight both your own forces and the elements of nature.

29. **Flowers bloom in the tree** –树上开花(shù shàng kāi huā)
Tying silk blossoms on a dead tree gives the illusion that the tree is healthy. Through the use of artifice and disguise, make something of no value appear valuable; of no threat appear dangerous; of no use appear useful.

30. **The guest becomes the host** –反客为主(Fǎn kè wéi zhǔ)
Usurp leadership in a situation where you are normally subordinate. Infiltrate your target. Initially, pretend to be a guest to be accepted, but develop from inside and become the owner later.

31. **The beautiful woman stratagem** –美人计 (Měi rén jì)
Send your enemy beautiful women to cause discord within his camp. This stratagem can work on three levels. First, the ruler becomes so enamored with the beauty that he neglects his duties and allows his vigilance to wane. Second, other males at court will begin to display aggressive behavior that inflames minor differences hindering co-operation and destroying

morale. Third, other females at court, motivated by jealousy and envy, begin to plot intrigues further exacerbating the situation.

32. **The empty city stratagem** –空城计 **(Kōng chéng jì)**
When the enemy is superior in numbers and your situation is such that you expect to be overrun at any moment, then drop all pretense of military preparedness and act calmly so that the enemy will think you are setting an ambush. This stratagem has to be used sparingly and only after one has first developed a reputation for military prowess. This also depends on having a clever opponent who, in perceiving a trap, may over-think his reaction.

33. **The counter-espionage stratagem** –反间计 **(Fǎn jiàn jì)**
Undermine your enemy's ability to fight by secretly causing discord between him and his friends, allies, advisors, family, commanders, soldiers, and population. While he is preoccupied settling internal disputes, his ability to attack or defend, is compromised.

34. **The self-torture stratagem** –苦肉计 **(Kǔ ròu jì)**
Pretending to be injured has two possible applications. In the first, the enemy is lulled into relaxing his guard since he no longer considers you to be an immediate threat. The second is a way of ingratiating yourself to your enemy by pretending the injury was caused by a mutual enemy.

35. **The stratagem of interrelated stratagems** –连环计 **(Lián huán jì)**
In important matters, one should use several stratagems applied simultaneously after another as in a chain of stratagems. Keep different plans operating in an overall scheme; however, in this manner if any one stratagem fails, then the chain breaks and the whole scheme fails.

36. **Running away is the best stratagem** –走为上 **(Zǒu wéi shàng)**

If it becomes obvious that your current course of action will lead to defeat, then retreat and regroup. When your side is losing, there are only three choices remaining: surrender, compromise, or escape. Surrender is complete defeat, compromise is half defeat, but escape is not defeat. As long as you are not defeated, you still have a chance.

In our next chapter we will discuss business and legal issues in creating a Chinese-based joint venture.

Chapter 6

Business and Legal Issues of Chinese-Based Joint Ventures

The purpose of this chapter is to discuss business and legal restrictions on joint ventures in China and business and legal issues that may arise when forming a Chinese-based joint venture. This chapter should be read in conjunction with Chapter 9, which discusses business and legal issues in forming a U.S.-based joint venture, since many of the business and legal issues are similar.

We begin with an analysis of Chinese laws which prescribe in detail the structure of Chinese-based joint ventures and the chapter ends with a discussion of two important U.S. laws which affect Chinese-based joint ventures, namely the U.S. Foreign Corrupt Practices Act and U.S. antitrust laws.

Chinese Investment Restrictions

Although restrictions on joint ventures in China were liberalized in 2011, opportunities for foreign investment are uneven across China's commercial landscape. According to the U.S. – China Business Council[124], though companies in many sectors can establish wholly foreign-owned enterprises (WFOEs), others are limited to joint ventures and minority equity investments. Some foreign investors face licensing requirements that effectively exclude them from the market altogether. These investment restrictions affect key segments of Chinese industry such as

---

[124]   http://www.uschina.org/info/members-survey/foreign-investment-restrictions.html

agriculture, automobiles, chemicals, energy, express delivery, insurance, securities, and telecommunications. In 2011, the Peoples Republic of China (PRC) issued a revised draft of the Catalogue Guiding Foreign Investment in Industry, which came into effect on January 30, 2012 ("2012 Catalogue"). The 2012 Catalogue is reproduced in Appendix 2.

The 2012 Catalogue categorizes foreign investment in products or sectors as either "encouraged", "restricted", or "prohibited". Even in the "encouraged" list, ownership restrictions may still be imposed.

The 2012 Catalogue recognizes the high-end manufacturing industry as a key "encouraged" sector. As a result, new products and technologies in textile, chemical and machine manufacturing industries have been added to the "encouraged" category in the 2012 Catalogue.[125]

The 2012 Catalogue also creates incentives for foreign investors to invest in the modern service industry, and nine new items have been added to the "encouraged" category, including motor vehicle charging stations, venture capital enterprises, intellectual property service and marine oil pollution clean-up service, as well as vocational training. In addition, foreign invested medical institutions and financial leasing companies, which used to belong to the restricted category in the superseded 2007 Catalogue, are now liberalized by the 2012 Catalogue as permitted sectors for foreign investments.[126]

Therefore, it is important to carefully review in which category the proposed joint venture will operate. It is clear that the PRC has a strategy to access foreign technology. The technology is typically licensed to a China-based entity in which the foreign company owns equity. In some cases the foreign investor can own 100% of the entity, so-called "WFOEs", which constitute 77% of foreign direct investment in China in 2011. In other cases, the foreign investor must form a joint venture with a Chinese partner

---

[125] David J. D. Dai and Mandy Yang, "China Issues New Foreign Investment Industrial Guidance Catalogue", MWE China Law Offices, http://www.mwechinalaw.com/news/2012/chinalawalert0112a.htm.htm
[126] Id.

and license that entity with the technology. In exchange for the license, the foreign investor negotiates a value for the technology to be transferred and receives a payment. The U.S. – China Business Council notes that the pressure to transfer technology is not required in all businesses in China but it does take place in key industries such as energy and transportation.

If the strategic objectives of the U.S. company can be accomplished using a WFOE, it is generally preferable to use a WFOE rather than create a joint venture. WFOEs permit the U.S. company sole, unilateral control of operations and eliminates any risk associated with a Chinese partner. However, if a WFOE is not currently legally permitted by the 2012 Catalogue for the industry or does not currently accomplish the strategic objectives of the U.S. partner, provisions may possibly be negotiated in the joint venture agreement to permit the creation of a WFOE if it is legally permitted in the future or otherwise can in the future better satisfy the strategic objectives of the U.S. partner.

Middle-market and smaller companies must carefully think through the problems of going it alone in China and many will conclude that a joint venture is at least initially preferable.

Representative Offices

Some U.S. companies are capable of accomplishing their objectives in China by establishing a "representative office", rather than creating a full subsidiary or joint venture. A representative office is not a legal entity and therefore does not have limited liability or separate legal person status.

Representative offices cannot engage in direct business activities and are limited to acting as a liaison for the foreign head office. They can be utilized to locate suppliers, find customers, and perform market research in China. The representative offices cannot engage in profit-making activities for their own account. Representative offices can be easily established by registering the foreign company with the State Administration of Industry and Commerce ("SAIC"). However, certain service providers, such as law firms, financial and insurance companies, and several other industries may require special approval.

Office space for a representative office may only be leased in certain designated buildings and the representative office may not directly employ Chinese nationals. Typically, representative offices must contract with Chinese service firms for staff services at the representative office.

Although representative offices are useful in attempting to select the right Chinese partner and perform market research, they cannot be effectively used as a vehicle for a joint venture because of the limitation on their profit-making activity as well as other restrictions.

Off-Shore Entities

A typical joint venture in China begins with a U.S. investor establishing an entity in a tax-free off-shore jurisdiction through which it holds its interest in the joint venture entity. These off-shore entities have traditionally been formed in the British Virgin Islands or the Cayman Islands, but there are many other tax-free off-shore jurisdictions.

The entity formed in the tax-free jurisdiction may then establish an intermediate Hong Kong company, which in turn makes the investments into the joint venture entity. This structure is not legally required but has the advantage of making it easier to avoid Chinese government restrictions on the transfer of equity in the joint venture and minimizing Chinese withholding tax. Within China, every equity transfer requires government approval. When the equity is received by the off-shore entity, no approval is required from the Chinese government. The foreign investor is therefore able to sell shares in the off-shore holding company in the British Virgin Islands, the Cayman Islands, etc. without Chinese government review or approval, assuming there is no monopoly concern and without the imposition of Chinese capital gains tax.

The motivation for establishing the intermediate Hong Kong company is because Chinese law provides a lower rate of tax on dividends paid to Hong Kong companies. Chinese tax authorities may challenge this lower rate of tax if the Hong Kong holding company does not have a reasonable business purpose. Another reason for using the Hong Kong intermediary company, apart from any tax advantage, is that Chinese government officials usually prefer investments by Hong Kong companies to those made by companies in other jurisdictions, and Hong Kong companies may have certain preferential access under the Closer Economic Partnership Arrangement ("CEPA") with Hong Kong.

It is not necessary to establish this complex structure for every joint venture entity. Many foreign investors have created much simpler structures for their investments.

Chinese Joint Venture Entities

Chinese companies established with at least 25% foreign investment are called FIEs, i.e., Foreign Invested Enterprises. There are two main sub-categories of FIEs:

- Entities wholly-owned by foreign companies, called WFOEs, which are not considered joint ventures since they have no Chinese ownership; and
- Joint ventures which consist of entities with some Chinese ownership and at least 25% foreign ownership.

In addition to these two main sub-categories of FIEs, there are two special forms of FIEs, namely foreign invested companies limited by shares (typically used for initial public offerings) and foreign invested holding companies (typically used to invest in other companies).

There are two basic forms of Chinese joint ventures:

- Equity joint ventures ("EJVs"); and
- Cooperative (or contractual) joint ventures ("CJVs").

In an EJV, board representation, profit distribution and rights upon liquidation strictly follow each party's relative equity contribution, whereas in a CJV there is greater flexibility to distribute profit in proportions that differ from the equity investments. Most investors use the EJV structure because authorities are generally more receptive to the EJV form.

A CJV may be established with or without a new legal entity separate from the partners. The primary advantages of a CJV, apart from not requiring profit distributions proportionate to equity investments, is the greater freedom to negotiate the CJV contract under PRC law. For example, CJVs have become attractive to foreign investors who prefer their Chinese partners to receive fixed payments only and to Chinese partners who do not have the necessary capital for an EJV. CJVs are also attractive to foreign investors who desire a quick return on their investment, but whose Chinese partners are reluctant to hand over long-term control. In this situation the foreign investor would have a controlling interest in the CJV at its inception and then gradually transfer control to the Chinese partner as the CJV became profitable. CJVs can also become attractive to foreign investors where a separate legal entity is not created since certain taxes and asset transfer fees can be avoided.[127] This is rare. As noted, it is more difficult, and sometimes impossible, to obtain government approval for a CJV rather than an EJV and the negotiations are typically more complex and detailed.[128]

Registered Capital and Total Investment

The registered capital is the amount of equity contributed to the entity and the investor's ownership interest in the company is determined by the proportion of the registered capital it contributes. For example, if the registered capital of an EJV is $5 million and the investor contributes $2.5 million of that

---

[127] Paul h. Folta, "Corporate Joint Ventures: Savvy foreign investors may wish to consider the benefits of this flexible investment structure", China Business Review, Jan-Feb. 2005, https://www.chinabusinessreview.com/public/0501/folta.html

[128] "Establishment of a Joint Venture (JV) in China", InterChina Consulting, July 2009, www.interchinaconsulting.com

registered capital, that investor would own 50% of the equity of the company.

The registered capital differs from the total investment and Chinese law requires a certain minimum percentage of the total investment to be registered capital. The excess of the total investment over the required registered capital would normally be debt. The following are the minimum ratios of registered capital to the total investment:

Total Investment	Minimum Registered Capital
Up to and including US$3 million	At least 70% of the total investment
Over US$3 million and up to and including US$10 million	Minimum of US$2.1 million, and at least 50% of the total investment
Over US$10 million and up to and including US$30 million	Minimum of US$5 million, and at least 40% of the total investment
Over US$30 million	Minimum of US$12 million, and at least one-third of the total investment

Thus, according to this chart, if the total investment is $1 million, $700,000 would have to be registered capital and $300,000 could be debt.

A minimum registered capital of RMB 30,000 is required for the most basic domestic enterprises.

The registered capital of a Chinese entity must be paid as follows: 15% of the total registered capital must be paid within 6 months of the issuance of the FIEs business license; the balance must be paid within 2 years after that license has been issued.

Foreign investors may contribute the registered capital in foreign currencies only except that RMB denominated contributions may be made to the extent that they derive from prior investments in China. Chinese law permits in-kind contributions such as machinery, equipment and intellectual property but usually limited to no more than 70% of the total registered capital.[129]

Almost all FIEs are limited liability entities with an investor's liability generally limited to its registered capital contribution.

Limitations on Existence of Business and Entity

Chinese entities are limited to the type of business set forth in both their business license and articles of association. Therefore, it is important to negotiate with the government authorities the broadest possible business scope of the joint venture.

Moreover, Chinese entities cannot be established for indefinite terms. FIEs have a limited term which is contained in their articles of association. It is wise to negotiate the term of existence of the entity with the government authorities who, in some cases, will agree to terms of existence as long as 50 years or more. The government authorities may be at the provincial, local level, or central level, depending upon the amount invested and whether the industry sector is encouraged or permitted or restricted. The term of existence of an FIE can be extended by filing an application 180 days prior to the expiration of its term.

Chinese government approval is generally required for all aspects of the joint venture, including the proposed Chinese partner as well as the foreign partner. Therefore, at an early stage of the negotiations, inquiry should be made of the proposed Chinese partner as to its qualifications to establish a joint venture.[130]

---

[129] Article 27 of the Law of the People's Republic of China on Joint Ventures Using Chinese and Foreign Investment provides that the machinery, equipment or other materials, industrial property or knowhow contributed by foreign participants as investment shall be submitted to the examination and approval authority for approval.

[130] "Establishment of a Joint Venture – China", HG Legal Directories, November 3, 2009, http://www.hg.org/article.asp?id=7496

Corporate Control

The board of directors is the highest governing body of an EJV and each investor's board representation is strictly proportional to its registered capital contribution. Chinese law specifies that certain corporate actions - including amendment of the articles of association, dissolution of the company - increase or decrease of the registered capital, and merger or division of the company, require unanimous board approval.

The Chinese company law requires limited liability companies to have a separate "board of supervisors" in addition to a board of directors. The board of supervisors serves as a check on the directors and officers. However, the same law permits companies with relatively few shareholders to have only a single supervisor or a pair of supervisors, rather than a supervisory board, thereby diminishing the practical effect of this requirement.

Foreign Currency Accounts

FIEs must establish both RMB and foreign currency bank accounts in the locality where they have been established. Once established, the FIE must apply to the State Administration of Foreign Exchange for a "foreign exchange registration certificate" and permission to open a foreign currency account. FIEs are required to separate their capital accounts from their current accounts. The State Administration of Foreign Exchange must approve any release from the capital account and oversees capital account distributions. Foreign exchange payments from the current account do not technically require government approval but there are still administrative procedures that must be followed. There are also limitations on how much foreign exchange receipts can be maintained in current accounts.

Dividends

Dividend payments in foreign currency require the approval of State Administration of Foreign Exchange.

Other Payments to Foreign Investors

Foreign investors may enter into management services agreements, technology and intellectual property licenses and other similar arrangements with their FIEs. Under these agreements, when an FIE pays out fees to foreign parties, including foreign investors, it may have the obligation to withhold and remit taxes on behalf of the recipient.

Real Property

While land cannot generally be "owned" under Chinese law, the right to engage in transactions involving both real and personal property is protected by China's Constitution. Under the Constitution, the State may grant the right to use land, for a limited time, to private persons. The maximum term of years on the use associated with the land is currently as follows:

- 70 years for residential;
- 50 years for industrial;
- 50 years for educational, scientific, technological, cultural, public health or sports-related;
- 40 years for commercial, tourist or recreational purposes;
- 50 years for mixed use or other purposes.[131]

The Joint Venture Contract

The joint venture contract is intended to express the mutual understanding of the parties on major issues which will, in all likelihood, be faced by the joint venture. A good joint venture contract will not compensate for poor advance planning. However, a poor joint venture contract, or one which does not correctly reflect the understanding of the parties, can lead to conflicting relationships between the joint venture partners.

---

[131] Kenneth A. Cutshat, Michael E. Burke and Christopher A. Wagner, "Corporate Counsel's Guide to Doing Business in China A, 3D, 2010-2011 Edition, West, 2010.

Bob Meredith, a lawyer by training and Xerox's resident director in Tokyo, described the role of these joint venture contracts in Xerox's strategy as follows:

"The legal contracts are flexible. We don't follow an adversarial, arm's-length approach, where you might try to gain short-term advantage or act opportunistically. The equity commitment focuses our relationship on one main objective: What is the profit-maximizing thing to do?"[132]

Who Holds the Chop?

Every company in China has a chop. It is the corporate seal with which the company is required to sign contracts. If you possess a chop, you have the legal right to contract for the company.[133] The chop is a vestige of a business system dating back to imperial times and is vital to core functions such as signing legal documents.

Any joint venture agreement in China should specify who holds the chop. Chops tend to be ornate and intricately designed.

The importance of chops was illustrated in the battle for control of ChinaCast Education Corporation, a small publicly-held Chinese education company with a market capitalization of slightly over $200 million. In March 2012, the company fired its chief executive officer, Ron Chan, for preventing its auditors, Deloitte & Touche L.P., from completing its audit. The directors were concerned that their inability to file financial statements might cost the company its NASDAQ listing. ChinaCast then sued Mr. Chan in a Shanghai court seeking the return of several chops. The complaint accused Mr. Chan of aiding in the disappearance of these chops. Mr. Chan, in turn, issued a letter to shareholders, declaring himself to be the victim of intimidation

---

[132] Krista McQuade and Professor Benjamin Gomes-Casseres, "Xerox and Fuji Xerox", Harvard Business School Publishing, 1991.

[133] Michael J. De La Merced, "Battle Over a Chinese Company Turns Physical", The New York Times, April 19, 2012, http://dealbook.nytimes.com/2012/04/19/battle-over-a-chinese-company-turns-physical/

by western investors seeking to wrest control of the company away from him, and denied holding any chops.[134]

Appointment and Removal of Representative Director and General Manager of Chinese Joint Venture Company

The chairman, who is the legal representative director of a Chinese joint venture, oversees the business operations and the general manager conducts its business operations on a day-to-day basis. A key issue in negotiating a joint venture agreement is the identity of each of these persons and who has the ability to remove them and appoint replacements. For example, if the joint venture agreement provides that both parties must agree on the removal and replacement of the representative director or general manager, a stalemate is possible. Since these are key positions, vital to the success of a Chinese joint venture, the parties must mutually develop mechanisms and possibly objective standards of performance to determine whether these persons should be replaced.

Some argue that no U.S. companies should agree to permit the Chinese joint venture partner to make these appointments.[135] However, the Chinese joint venture partner may not agree. Therefore, a possible compromise is developing objective standards of performance which would lead to the automatic removal of the representative director and the general manager.

Key Provisions of Joint Venture Agreements

The joint venture agreement is typically a heavily negotiated document designed to reflect the mutual understanding of the parties. The topics to be covered in the agreement will vary

---

[134] Id.

[135] Richard E. Weiner, "Four Steps to a Successful Joint Venture in China", Fredrikson & Byron P.A., February 2011, http://www.fredlaw.com/articles/international/intl_1102_rew.html

depending upon the nature of the joint venture and the countries in which it will operate.

For purposes of this discussion, we will assume that the joint venture is between a U.S. company and a Chinese company for a joint venture in China. The issues to be negotiated will be similar, but not identical, regardless of the location of the joint venture company.

Many wealthy Chinese businessmen have a number of affiliated companies that they control. Care must be taken in the joint venture agreement to make certain that revenues and assets are not diverted from the joint venture company to these other affiliates. Thus, any transaction with an affiliate of one partner should require the other partner's approval or approval by the board members appointed by that other partner.[136]

The following are some of the key topics to be covered in the joint venture agreement[137]:

- The name of the company and location of its principal office.
- The identification of the joint venture investors, including their respective percentage interests in the joint venture.
- The structure of the joint venture company and the scope of its business.
- For Chinese joint ventures, the amount of registered capital and the amount to be contributed by each party. In the case of assets contributed to the joint venture, which are not in cash, the valuation of such assets.
- The uses to which the registered capital of the company will be put.
- The dates on which registered capital will be contributed.
- The distribution of the net profits of the joint venture.

---

[136] Susan Perkins, Randall Morck, Bernard Yeung, "Innocents Abroad: The Hazards of international Joint Venture with Pyramidal Group Firms", National Bureau of Economic Research, April 2008, http://www.nber.org/papers/w13914

[137] Article 11 of the Regulations implementing the Law of the People's Republic of China on Joint Ventures Using Chinese and Foreign Investments contains the minimum requirements for a joint venture contract.

- If there are licensing agreements, management services agreements, research and development agreements, or supply agreements, each should be negotiated and attached to the joint venture agreement.
- The composition of the board of directors and methods of removal of directors.
- The method of conducting board meetings, who will conduct the board meeting and the designation of the chairperson of the board.
- Any veto rights that board members will have over significant joint venture company actions.
- Any supermajority vote of the board requirements for certain major actions.
- Methods of dealing with deadlocks of the board, such as arbitration.
- Chinese joint ventures require a board of supervisors to oversee accounting and financial activities of the company and monitor the conduct of the board and senior executives. The composition of the board of supervisors and their appointment and removal should be covered. Methods of conducting meetings of the board of supervisors and of handling deadlocks should also be included.
- Methods of calling meetings of the joint venture investors, the conduct of such meetings, joint venture voting rights and special approval rights or supermajority rights.
- Methods of handling deadlocks of the joint venture investors.
- The appointment and removal of officers and their powers and duties.
- Methods of adopting business plans.
- The financial statements that will be produced by the joint venture company, including internal controls and management information systems as well as the appointment of an independent auditor.
- The rights of joint venture investors to inspect joint ventures books and records and to discuss with the

company executives the affairs, finances and accounts of the company.

- The rights of each director, supervisor, or officer to indemnification and to be immunized from personal liability, including any director and officer insurance policy.
- Prohibitions on sale and other transfers by joint venture investors, including rights of first refusal.
- Buy/Sell provisions which may include Puts and Calls.
- Confidentiality provisions.
- Warranties and representations by each investor.
- The term of the joint venture agreement, events which cause the premature termination of the agreement and what provisions survive the termination.
- Governing law, which must be Chinese law for an EJV or a CJV.
- Agreement by the joint venture investors to not compete with the joint venture company.
- Agreement by the joint venture investors to refer new business opportunities to the joint venture company.
- General provisions dealing with expenses related to the agreement.
- Method of amending the agreement and anti-assignment clauses.

A joint venture agreement, dated August 17, 2011, between a U.S. company and a Chinese company, attached as Appendix 3, discusses each of these subjects and several more that we have not mentioned. This agreement is not intended as a model of a joint venture contract since it omits many important clauses. Nevertheless, it is typical of bare bones joint venture contracts in China.

The joint venture contract is between an affiliate of ZBB Energy Corporation, a start-up Wisconsin corporation with 54 employees, and several joint venture partners. The joint venture partners include PowerSav Inc., AnHui Zinlong Electrical Co. and Wuhu Huarui Power Transmission & Transformation Engineering Co. PowerSav Inc. provides vital "new energy" solutions to the

China market, enabling the country to alter the energy mix to high-efficiency renewable sources and away from coal and oil. "With breakthrough products in LED lighting, advanced energy storage and energy management systems, and 'Smart Grid' infrastructure, PowerSav Inc. addresses many of the highest growth markets in China. The PowerSav Inc. products and services are critical to supporting the needs of China's rapidly growing population." XinLong Electrical manufactures a wide range of power transmission and transformer equipment, including high and low-voltage power electronics, automation and control systems and power quality and conditioning systems. It is publicly traded on the Shenzhen Stock Exchange, with registered capital of RMB165 million. From 22 locations throughout China, XinLong Electrical has more than 450 sales resources, aftermarket field support personnel, and project integration teams serving key market segments such as State Grid and South Grid electricity and power projects, transportation, telecommunications, industrial and commercial building and manufacturing. Wuhu Huarui is a "distinct leader" in the design, engineering and deployment of UHV transmission systems, with major businesses located in more than 20 provinces throughout China. With 2010 revenue of $100 Million, WuHu Huarui specializes in electric power transmission and substation project construction, and has strong and long established relationships with both State Grid and South Grid companies. Wuhu Huarui has municipal engineering projects, covering power electricity, roads, railways, metro transport, shipbuilding and other segments.[138]

The joint venture was intended to operate through a jointly-owned Chinese company located in Wuhu City, Anhui Province named Anhui MeiXim Store Energy Co., Ltd (the "JV Company"). The JV Company was intended to initially assemble and ultimately manufacture ZBB products for sale in the power

---

[138] "PowerSav Inc. Invests in Joint Venture Company to Enter China's Energy Storage Market", Greentechmedia, August 30, 2011, http://www.greentechmedia.com/industry/read/powersav-inc.-invests-in-joint-venture-company-to-enter-china-20909/

management industry on an exclusive basis in mainland China and on a non-exclusive basis in Hong Kong and Taiwan.

The 10-K for ZZB Energy Corporation filed with the SEC in September 2011 describes ZBB as being in the business of designing, developing, and manufacturing advanced energy storage, and power electronic systems to solve a wide range of electrical system challenges in global markets for utility, governmental, commercial, industrial and residential customers. Notes to its financial statements describe the company business as providing advanced electrical power management platforms targeted at the growing global need for distributed renewable energy, energy efficiency, power quality, and grid modernization. The company and its power electronics subsidiary, Tier Electronics, "have developed a portfolio of intelligent power management platforms that directly integrate multiple renewal and conventional onsite generation sources with rechargeable zinc bromide flow batteries and other storage technology." The company also offers advanced systems to directly connect wind and solar equipment to other grid and systems that can form various levels of microgrids. Tier Electronics participates in the energy efficiency markets through its hybrid vehicle control systems, and power quality markets with its line of regulation solutions. "Together, these platforms solve a wide range of electrical system challenges in global markets for utility, governmental, commercial, industrial and residential end customers."

Interestingly enough, this standard joint venture agreement does not reflect who holds the chop!

Dispute Settlement

It is inevitable that disputes will occur in the operation of a joint venture, particularly in an international joint venture where there are cultural differences. The key to a successful cross-border alliance is to have personal high-level relationships with each joint venture partner and a clear understanding of the strategic objectives of each partner.

All joint venture agreements contain a dispute resolution clause. If it is necessary to have a legal determination of a dispute, it is likely that the joint venture will ultimately fail. However, there may be situations where the dispute is not of strategic importance to each partner and they would prefer to have a third party resolve it.

The Umbrella Agreement dated June 14, 1999, between Goodyear and Sumitomo, discussed in a prior chapter, contained the following dispute resolution:

"16.02 ARBITRATION. (a) Any Dispute arising out of, relating to or in connection with the Alliance Agreements, including, without limitation, any dispute regarding the validity or termination thereof, of the performance or breach thereof, or regarding the entitlement of a Party to exercise a Global Exit Right or Regional Exit Right under the terms of Article XVII hereof (but not a Dispute solely involving valuation in the case of a Global Exit Right or a Regional Exit Right, which shall be resolved as set forth in such Article XVII or, as regards valuations in connection with new equity fundings of the JVCs under the relevant Shareholders Agreement) shall be finally settled by arbitration administered by the International Chamber of Commerce ("ICC"). The arbitration shall be conducted in accordance with the Rules of Arbitration of the ICC in effect at the time of the arbitration ("ICC Rules"), except as they may be modified herein or by agreement of Goodyear and SRI. The arbitration shall be conducted by three arbitrators appointed in accordance with the ICC Rules.

"(b) The place of arbitration shall be Paris, France and the proceedings shall be conducted in the English language.

"(c) The Award rendered by the arbitrators (the "Award") shall be final and binding on the Parties and their respective Affiliates. Judgment on the Award may be entered in the Supreme Court of the State of New York or the U.S. Federal Court for the Southern District of New York and for the purposes hereof the Parties agree to consent and cause their respective Affiliates to consent to the jurisdiction of such

Courts. The Award may be enforced in any court having jurisdiction thereof.

"(d) In addition to any discovery permitted under the ICC Rules but subject to the determination of the tribunal, each Party shall produce relevant, non-privileged documents or copies thereof requested by the other Party within the time limits set by the tribunal. Depositions of Party witnesses may be ordered by the tribunal upon a showing of need.

"(e) All hearings shall be transcribed and the costs of such transcription shall be treated as costs of the arbitration.

"(f) By agreeing to arbitration, the Parties do not intend to deprive any court with jurisdiction of its ability to issue a preliminary injunction, attachment or other form of provisional remedy in aid of the arbitration and a request for such provisional remedies by a Party to a court shall not be deemed a waiver of this agreement to arbitrate. In addition to the authority conferred upon the tribunal by the ICC Rules specified above, the tribunal shall also have the authority to grant provisional remedies, including injunctive relief, and shall have the authority to award specific performance.

"(g) Except as may be required by applicable law or court order, the Parties agree to maintain confidentiality as to all aspects of the arbitration, including the existence and results, except that nothing herein shall prevent any Party from disclosing information regarding the arbitration for purposes of enforcing the Award or in and court proceeding involving the Parties. The Parties further agree to obtain the arbitrators' agreement to preserve the confidentiality of the arbitration."

Approval and Registration Process

The joint venture establishment process commences with the reservation of the company name with the State Administration for Industry and Commerce ("SAIC"). After the company's name has been reserved, the applicant must obtain "examination and approval" of the investment by the Ministry of Commerce of the PRC ("MOFCOM"). This requires the submission of all definitive documents and may also require a "feasibility study" concerning the project. MOFCOM may request additional documentation.

After receiving MOFCOM approval and the payment of the initial installment of registered capital, the parties may apply to the SAIC for a business license. The joint venture is officially established when its business license is issued and it thereby becomes a recognized legal entity in China.

U.S. Foreign Corrupt Practices Act and Similar International Laws

In contrast to Fortune 500 companies, middle-market and smaller companies do not have the benefit of large staffs of in-house lawyers to guide them through the provisions of the U.S. Foreign Corrupt Practices Act of 1977 ("FCPA"). Some private middle-market and smaller companies are under the mistaken belief that the statute does not apply to them because they are privately owned. That is a fallacy. Indeed, the first criminal prosecution under this statute in 1982 was against a middle-market Texas corporation called Crawford Industries and its president and owner, Donald G. Crawford, for bribing two top officials of Pemex, the national oil company of Mexico, in order to obtain several multi-million dollar equipment contracts.[139] Mr. Crawford pled no contest to the criminal indictment and was fined $309,000.[140]

Every international joint venture needs to be concerned with complying with both the FCPA and similar international laws. Even though a violation may be committed by a foreign joint venture, the U.S. joint venture partner may still be liable on various

---

[139] United States Court of Appeals, Fifth Circuit. – 826 F.2d 392, Justia US Law, September 10, 1987, http://law.justia.com/cases/federal/appellate-courts/F2/826/392/321307/

[140] Sherman & Sterling LLP, FCPA Digest, January 2012, p. 208, http://www.shearman.com/files/Publication/bb1a7bff-ad52-4cf9-88b9-9d99e001dd5f/Presentation/PublicationAttachment/590a9fc7-2617-41fc-9aef-04727f927e07/FCPA-Digest-Jan2012.pdf

legal theories, including the argument that the foreign joint venture was acting as an agent for the U.S. company.

Even huge organizations with many lawyers have difficulty complying with the FCPA with respect to their foreign operations. For example, it was reported in *The New York Times* of April 21, 2012[141] that Wal-Mart's largest foreign subsidiary, Wal-Mart de Mexico, had made hundreds of suspect payments, totaling more than $24 million, to mayors, city council members, obscure urban planners and low-level bureaucrats in Mexico – anyone who issued permits needed to permit Wal-Mart's growth in Mexico. The alleged bribes purchased zoning approvals for Wal-Mart stores in Mexico, reductions in environmental impact fees and allegiance of neighborhood leaders. Wal-Mart de Mexico allegedly perfected the art of bribery with fraudulent accounting and the allegations implicated many of Wal-Mart de Mexico's leaders, including its board of directors, general counsel, chief auditor and top real estate executive.

If Wal-Mart cannot control its Mexican affiliate, think about how much more difficult it would be for a middle-market or smaller company to control its foreign affiliate in China.

Recently, there has been increased enforcement of the FCPA, which has extraterritorial application in the global marketplace. The civil and criminal penalties attached to violations of this law can create substantial liabilities. For example, in the Spring of 2007, Baker Hughes Incorporated paid a total of $45 million for violating the FCPA, which consisted of a criminal fine, a civil penalty, a disgorgement of profits and prejudgment interest resulting from a $5.2 million bribe of foreign officials in Kazakhstan.[142] Although the bribe was $5.2 million, the disgorgement of profits from the entire venture by Baker Hughes was $23 million, well in excess of the bribe.

In addition to the FCPA, the Organization for Economic Co-Operation and Development (OECD) Convention on Combating Bribery of Foreign Public Officials in International

---

[141] David Barstow, "Vast Mexico Bribery Case Hushed Up by Wal-Mart After Top-Level Struggle", The New York Times, April 21, 2012.

[142] SEC Release Number 2007-77 (April 26, 2007)

Business Transactions has resulted in the adoption of FCPA-type laws by a growing number of international jurisdictions. For example, India has its own version of the FCPA. Both the UN and the World Bank are also intensifying their anti-corruption efforts, in addition to the efforts of the OECD and local law enforcement authorities.

The FCPA was the result of SEC investigations in the mid-1970s when over 400 U.S. companies admitted making questionable or illegal payments in excess of $300 million to foreign government officials, politicians, and political parties. The abuses ran the gamut from bribery of high foreign officials to secure some type of favorable action by a foreign government to so-called facilitating payments that allegedly were made to ensure that government functionaries discharged certain ministerial or clerical duties. The U.S. Congress enacted the FCPA to bring a halt to the bribery of foreign officials and to restore public confidence in the integrity of the American business system.

Foreign Bribes

Corruption is a major problem in China, particularly on the local official level. Although Chinese leaders hold frequent political campaigns against government corruption, such corruption still persists.

The FCPA proscribes and criminalizes foreign corrupt payments by either a public company or a "domestic concern." The term "domestic concern" includes any individual who is a U.S. citizen, national, or resident. The term also includes any corporation, partnership, association, joint-stock company, business trust, unincorporated organization, or sole proprietorship which has its principal place of business in the U.S., or which is organized under the laws of a state of the U.S. or a territory, possession, or commonwealth of the U.S.

The FCPA applies generally to middle-market or smaller companies, whether privately owned or publicly held and their officers, directors, employees, agents and stockholders, if certain jurisdictional means are used. Generally speaking, the FCPA makes it illegal to offer, pay, promise to pay, or authorize the payment of any money or anything of value to:

- any official of a foreign government or instrumentality of a foreign government;
- any foreign political party;
- any candidate for foreign political office; or
- any person while knowing that that such person will offer or make a proscribed payment, or will promise to make a proscribed payment,

for the purpose of: (a) influencing any act or decision of such foreign official, political party, party official or candidate in his or its official capacity; (b) inducing any act or decision which violates a lawful duty; or (c) securing any improper advantage, in each case, for the purpose of obtaining or retaining business for or with, or directing business to any person.

In order to fall within the FCPA's proscriptions, the payment, or promise or authorization of payment, must be "corrupt"; that is, whether or not it is legal under the laws of the foreign jurisdiction, it must be intended to induce the recipient to use his official position for the benefit of the person offering the payment or his client. The FCPA prohibits not only the payment of, but also the promise or authorization of, a corrupt foreign payment. Therefore, the law can be violated even if the payment is never in fact made. Since a corrupt payment which is requested by the foreign official (rather than offered to him) involves a decision to accede to the request, it is not a defense that the payment was requested. However, payments which are extorted and are made to protect physical assets from capricious destruction are not within the ambit of the FCPA. In addition, so-called "grease payments" (e.g., payments to ministerial or clerical employees of foreign government or agencies to facilitate, expedite or secure performance of their routine duties) are not prohibited by the FCPA.

However, not all of the international counterparts to the FCPA contain this exception for "grease payments". For example, the

U.K. Bribery Act of 2010 has no exception for so-called "grease payments".[143] Moreover, the U.K. Bribery Act is broader in its reach than the FCPA. Thus, an Asian joint venture that did some business in the U.K., but did not have a U.K. office, may be criminally liable if an agent, employee or subsidiary offered or accepted a bribe anywhere in the world, regardless of whether the misconduct involved the U.K. business or occurred in the U.K., and even if the joint venture had only limited contacts with the U.K.[144]

It is clear that, if authorized, the making of a foreign corrupt payment by a foreign subsidiary of a United States company is prohibited by the FCPA. Also prohibited are payments to an agent (even one who is not himself subject to the FCPA) when it is known that they will be used to make corrupt payments.

If a middle-market or smaller company engages in foreign transactions through a joint venture, particularly those involving an agent, great care should be exercised to secure documentation to prove that the FCPA was not violated. It is prudent to secure an affidavit from any agents who are paid commissions attesting to their compliance with the FCPA. Obviously, such an affidavit is useless if company officials have reason to know that it is false.

Violations of the corrupt payment provisions of the FCPA are punishable by fines and civil penalties against corporations or business entities of up to $2,000,000, plus up to a $10,000 civil penalty. In addition, officers, directors, employees, agents and stockholders can be fined up to $100,000 (plus up to a $10,000 civil penalty) or imprisoned for not more than five years, or both, for violations of the corrupt payment provisions of the FCPA. The FCPA further provides that fines imposed on an individual violator cannot be paid, directly or indirectly, by the company for whose benefit the bribe was paid or promised.

---

[143] Michelle Duncan, Palmina Fava & Samantha Kakati, "A Comparison of the U.S. Foreign Corrupt Practices Act and the U.K. Bribery Act", Paul Hastings, October 2010.
[144] Id.

Recent Examples of Violations of Foreign Bribe Provisions

The FCPA applies to bribes of "any official of a foreign government or instrumentality of a foreign government." In a number of countries, the government is an owner or partial owner of all sorts of ventures. In China, the government is an owner or government officials are owners of what appears to be commercial ventures and that government ownership creates major issues from an FCPA perspective. For example, in May 2005, a wholly-owned Chinese subsidiary of Diagnostic Products Corp. (DPC), a U.S.-based medical equipment firm, pled guilty to criminal charges arising out of approximately $1.6 million in sales "commissions" made by DPC, through its subsidiary, to doctors and laboratory staff employed by state-owned hospitals in China in order to generate business. The doctors and laboratory staff were considered officials of a foreign government or its instrumentality.[145]

The FCPA anti-bribery provisions apply to payments to foreign officials. The problem in China is the large number of officials to which these prohibitions apply. The dominant corporate players in many Chinese industries are state-owned enterprises. Employees of these companies may be considered technically "foreign officials" for purposes of the FCPA.

The broad scope of the foreign bribe provisions of the FCPA are best illustrated by the following case dealing with travel and entertainment expenses for Chinese foreign officials:

In *SEC v. Lucent Technologies, Inc.*[146], the Commission's complaint alleged that over a three-year period Lucent, through a subsidiary, paid over $10 million for about 1,000 Chinese foreign officials to travel to the U.S. The SEC concluded that about 315 of the trips included a disproportionate amount of sightseeing, entertainment and leisure. Some of the trips were, in fact, vacations to places such as Hawaii, Las Vegas, the Grand Canyon,

---

[145] Securities Exchange Act of 1934 Release No. 51724 / May 20, 2005

[146] *SEC v. Lucent Technologies, Inc.*, Civil Action No. 07-092301 (D.D.C. Filed December 21, 2007)

Disney World and similar venues. These expenses, for officials Lucent was either doing business with or attempting to do business with, were booked to a factory inspection account. The company failed over the years to provide adequate FCPA training.

To resolve the SEC's case, Lucent consented to an injunction prohibiting future violations of the FCPA books and records provisions. In addition, the company agreed to pay a $1.5 million civil penalty.

The SEC action against The Dow Chemical Company in 2007[147] also involved the question of travel and entertainment expenses. In its complaint, the SEC alleged that a Dow subsidiary in India made improper payments to an Indian government official consisting of over $37,000 in gifts, travel, entertainment and other items. Payments were also made to an official of the Central Insecticides Board to expedite the registration of three products. To resolve the SEC action, Dow consented to the entry of a permanent injunction prohibiting future violations of the books and records provisions of the FCPA. The company also agreed to pay a civil penalty of $325,000.

ACCOUNTING STANDARDS

Public companies are subject to special accounting standards. These standards are not applicable until after a U.S. IPO or other event which causes the company's securities to be registered under the Securities Exchange Act of 1934 (the "1934 Act"). Once the accounting standards are applicable, the public company is required to:

A. make and keep books, records and accounts, which, in reasonable detail, accurately and fairly reflect the transactions and dispositions of the assets of the company; and

B. devise and maintain a system of internal accounting controls sufficient to provide reasonable assurance that:

---

[147] *SEC v. The Dow Chemical Company*, Civil Action No. 07-00336 (D.D.C. Filed February 13, 2007

(i)   transactions are executed in accordance with management's general or specific authorization;

(ii) transactions are recorded as necessary (a) to permit preparation of financial statements in conformity with generally accepted accounting principles or any other criteria applicable to such statements, and (b) to maintain accountability for assets;

(iii) access to assets is permitted only in accordance with management's general or specific authorization; and

(iv) the recorded accountability for assets is compared with the existing assets at reasonable intervals and appropriate action is taken with respect to any differences.

The 1934 Act's requirements with regard to the maintenance of books and records and a system of internal control were enacted largely in response to disclosures that many United States corporations had established so-called "off-the-book" accounts and "slush funds." However, they are applicable to all U.S. public companies, whether or not they engage in foreign business or employ slush funds.

It must be borne in mind that the accounting standards imposed by the 1934 Act are directed at the accuracy of the company's books, records and accounts, not its financial statements. Thus, even though the company has not paid foreign bribes and even though its published financial statements may be accurate in all respects, it could nonetheless be in violation of the 1934 Act if, for example, its books and records improperly characterize the nature of a perfectly legitimate item of expense.

Antitrust Issues

International strategic alliances between or among competitors or potential competitors can create issues under U.S. and foreign antitrust laws. For information on U.S. laws, see the Antitrust Guidelines for Collaborations among Competitors issued by the U.S. Federal Trade Commission and the U.S. Department of

Justice.[148] Strategic alliances may also trigger filing requirements under the U.S. Hart-Scott-Rodino Act.

Moreover, merely satisfying U.S. laws is not sufficient since China has its own Antimonopoly Law, which includes both horizontal and vertical monopoly agreements. This law generally regulates (a) monopoly agreements, (b) abuses of dominant positions, (c) mergers, acquisitions and other concentrations that restrict competition (including establishing pre-merger notification and review) and (d) abuses of government administrative powers that inhibit competition.

If a middle-market or smaller company is contemplating a joint venture with a Chinese competitor or potential competitor or which may have other anticompetitive effects, it will need the help of an antitrust lawyer in both the U.S. and China.

Our next chapter will discuss selected issues in operating a joint venture based in China and some of the problems with terminating a joint venture.

---

[148] www.usdoj.gov/atr

Chapter 7

Operating and Terminating the Joint Venture in China

The purpose of this chapter is to review a few major issues in operating a joint venture based in China and some of the difficult issues involved in terminating the joint venture.

The following are four major operational issues:

- Dealing with government officials;
- Protecting intellectual property;
- Employment law and relationships; and
- Chinese business taxes.

The chapter ends with the problems involved in terminating a joint venture.

Dealing With Chinese Government Officials

Middle-market and smaller companies wishing to expand their business to China must understand the degree of influence of Chinese government entities throughout the Chinese economy. For example to expand in Macau, which generates more than five times as much gambling revenue as the Las Vegas Strip, U.S. casino operators had to grapple with a "complicated and opaque" government approval process.[149]

---

[149] Kate O'Keefe, "In Wynn's Macau Deal, Web of Political Ties", The Wall Street Journal, July 2, 2012, p. B7.

A Wall Street Journal article in 2011[150] illustrates how the Chinese government officials push around even big companies, such as Wal-Mart. Clearly, smaller companies have even less protection. However, the main advantage of the medium size and smaller U.S. companies is that they tend to fly under the radar screen of the Chinese government regulators.

According to the article, in Wal-Mart stores in the city of Chongqing, nonorganic pork was labeled "organic", which was a mistake. The pork was otherwise fine. Seizing on this error at a time when inflation is a hot-button issue in China, officials accused Wal-Mart of cheating the public by charging premium prices for regular meat. They fined the company, shut down all 13 Wal-Mart stores in the city and jailed a number of Wal-Mart employees. The actions played well in the national media.

Since Wal-Mart had nearly 350 stores in China with revenue of $7.5 billion, Wal-Mart apologized. It issued a statement declaring "the rights of consumers were infringed," and said it accepted the fifteen-day forced closure of its stores as an opportunity "to focus on implementing corrective actions."

This obsequious response by Wal-Mart is a reflection of the pervasive power of government officials in China.

Another example of China's occasional discrimination against foreign companies can be found in its government procurement rules giving preferences to Chinese products. Nationalistic pride is endemic in Chinese society and occasionally manifests itself against foreigners. However, xenophobia is not limited to China but occasionally occurs in other Asian countries as well as non-Asian countries.

U.S. companies must be concerned not only with their relations with national government officials but also with provincial and local government officials as well. Provincial and local government officials may, in fact, be more important to middle-market and smaller companies than national government officials.

It is important that middle-market and smaller U.S. companies recognize the power of these provincial and local government

---

[150] John Bussey, "China: Bullying to Prosperity", The Wall Street Journal, October 14, 2011, B1

officials and occasionally socialize with them and attempt to maintain good relationships with them. Having dinner periodically with key provincial and local officials to update them on the activities of the joint venture is an important ingredient of good relations.

We discussed in the last chapter the U.S. Foreign Corrupt Practices Act ("FCPA") and similar international laws which criminalize corrupt payments to foreign officials. Care must be taken by any Asian joint venture to scrupulously comply with these laws.

Some Chinese government officials refuse to meet except over a very expensive and lavish meal, including shark's fin, abalone, bear's paw, etc. Although the FCPA permits "reasonable and bona fide" business entertainment, some of these very expensive meals can present problems under the FCPA. Likewise, gift-giving, particularly at the Chinese New Year and the Mid-Autumn Festival, if deemed to be excessively lavish, can create issues under the FCPA. One may argue that these lavish meals and entertainment are not for a "corrupt" purpose and therefore do not violate the FCPA.

Intellectual Property Protection

In May 2012, Steve Ballmer, CEO of Microsoft, complained about China's lack of intellectual property protection. Speaking at Peking University in Beijing, Ballmer stated that China's protection for intellectual property rights was "still weak", thereby making it difficult to sell legitimate software there.[151]

Even Baidu, the Chinese government-sponsored search-engine, provides links to third-party websites that offer online counterfeit products as well as access to counterfeit hardware and merchandise.[152]

---

[151] Lea Bell, "Ballmer moans about China intellectual property rights", The Inquirer, May 24, 2012, http://www.theinquirer.net/inquirer/news/2179501/ballmer-moans-china-intellectual-property-rights

[152] "U.S. says China's Baidu is notorious pirated goods market", BBC News, March 1, 2011, http://www.bbc.co.uk/news/business-12605067

China has broad legal protection for intellectual property through an extensive series of statutes. Although things are improving, it is still difficult to enforce these laws. Unfortunately, the court system is weak and the remedies for violations of patents, trademarks, copyrights and trade secrets tend to be inadequate.

Foreign firms have often complained of biased local courts. Some provincial courts may favor local firms over outsiders, whether these outsiders are Chinese or foreign. In addition, damage awards in China are so meager (less than $30,000 per victory, by one estimate[153]) that they do not justify the costs of litigation. Judges often do not publish detailed rulings, or do so after much delay.

Although intellectual property laws are promulgated by China's central authorities, they are implemented by local author-ities. In some areas, infringement and piracy plays a significant role in local commerce, stimulating jobs and income for the local population and resulting in higher tax collections for the local authorities. For example, local governments earn significant rental income from booths at state-owned markets where pirated and counterfeit products are typically sold.

However, things are improving. In 2012, Ashland, a chemi-cal firm, received a damage award of $3.5 million.[154] In addi-tion, Chinese leaders are recognizing the importance of intel-lectual property protection as they make investments in foreign countries.[155]

Middle-market and smaller companies would do well to take advantage of whatever intellectual property protection is avail-able under Chinese law. There is very little downside in doing so and at some point in the future this protection may prove

---

[153] "Still murky: Is the Middle Kingdom getting serious about protecting intellectual property?" The Economist, April 21, 2012. http://www.economist.com/node/21553040

[154] Id.

[155] Id.

valuable. In fact in 2011 China became the world's top patent filer, surpassing the U.S. and Japan.[156]

The following is a very abbreviated summary of Chinese laws relating to patents, trademarks, copyrights and trade secrets.

PATENTS

China is a first-to-file country, meaning that priority is given to date of the filing of the patent application rather than the date the invention was created. There are three types of patents available:

- Invention Patent:

  - Substantive examination required
  - Patent Term: 20 years from earliest priority date
  - Analogous to utility patent in U.S.

- Utility Model Patent:

  - Minor improvements in shape, structure of a product, or the combination thereof
  - No substantive examination

- Industrial Design Patent:

  - No substantive examination
  - Patent term: 10 years from earliest priority date

---

[156] Lee Chyen Yee, "China tops U.S., Japan to become top patent filer", Reuters. com, December 21, 2011; http://www.reuters.com/article/2011/12/21/us-china-patents-idUSTRE7BK0LQ20111221

TRADEMARKS

China is a first-to-file country also with respect to trademarks. Only registration of the mark confers exclusive rights. Intellectual property attorneys generally encourage applicants to file their trademark applications in the Chinese language in addition to the original filings. Registration of a mark does not offer protection from infringers using the Chinese translation or transliteration of the mark.

Registerable trademarks include any of the following:

- Any visual sign capable of distinguishing goods or services from others;
- Words, designs, letters, numerals, three-dimensional symbols, combinations of colors, or a combination of any of the aforementioned elements;
- Packaging may also be protected (as long as the shape is not necessary to obtain a technical result or give a substantial value to the goods).

Service marks, geographic indications and collective marks are also registerable.

COPYRIGHTS

Registration of a copyright is not required in order to receive copyright protection if the copyright holder is from a country that is a member of the Berne Convention (which includes the U.S.), but it can be difficult to enforce a copyright without registration. However, some countries counsel their citizens to not register software copyrights in China unless necessary, because of a risk that the publicly accessible part of the registered software code may be copied.

With registration, the owner establishes prima facie ownership of the copyright, and the owner can file a complaint with the Chinese Copyright Bureau anytime after discovering an act of infringement. A prima facie showing of ownership can be later rebutted. If an owner has not registered the copyright of his or her work, the owner must provide evidence, e.g. the original work, to prove ownership of the copyright. Failure on the part of the owner to provide sufficient evidence of his copyright ownership may preclude any action by the Copyright Bureau or other government agencies. Therefore, even though an owner can enjoy a copyright without registration, a copyright registration is often advisable for important works.

For individuals, the term of copyright protection is generally 50 years after the life of the individual author. For a work created in the course of employment, the term of copyright protection is generally 50 years after publication.

TRADE SECRETS

It is important to place confidentiality and non-compete provisions in employment contracts in order to protect trade secrets of the joint venture. This was illustrated in a famous case in which an employee of Nike (China) resigned his position as marketing manager and began working for the Beijing branch of Adidas (China), a competitor, and the Chinese court enforced the non-compete agreement.[157]

Article 10 of the Chinese Anti-Unfair Competition Law specifically protects "business secrets". The law prohibits "managers" from using any of the following methods to infringe upon "business secrecy":

- To steal, coerce, or use any other unfair method to obtain the other's business secrets;

---

[157] Kenneth A. Cutshaw, Michael E. Burke and Christopher A. Wagner, "Doing Business in China, 3D, 2010-2011 Edition, Thomson Reuters/West, pp. 587-588

- To disclose, use or permit others to use the business secrets mentioned in Section 1 of this Article; and
- To violate the contract or the requirement to publish, use or permit others to use the business secrets, which were maintained as secrets by the legal owner of the business secrecy.

"Business secrecy" is defined to mean "the utilized technical information and business information which is unknown by the public, which may create business interests or profit for its legal owners and also is maintained secrecy by its legal owners."

A third party who knows or should know of the illegal activities, and who gains, uses or publishes the business secrecy is also liable under the statute.

Chinese law also provides for criminal penalties for certain infringements of trade secrets.[158]

Employment Law and Relationships

Foreign investment enterprises in China may hire local employees either directly in the labor market or through a qualified labor service company. If employees are hired through a labor service company, these individuals remain employees of the labor service company even though all of their services are performed for the joint venture. Moreover, under the Labor Contract Law, the joint venture is required to treat such employees of the labor service company the same as direct employees in terms of salary and benefits.[159]

The Chinese Labor Contract Law requires all employers to enter into a written contract with their employees upon employment.[160] If the employer fails to do so within 1 month of employment, the employer is liable for a penalty of double salary beginning from the second month of employment until a written labor

---

[158] *Criminal Law of the People's Republic of China.*

[159] Labor Contract Law, arts. 62, 63.

[160] Labor Contract Law, art. 10; See, generally, Cutshaw et. al., Doing Business in China, 3D (West, 2010).

contract is established.[161] The penalty is payable directly to the employee.

A labor contract must contain the following clauses[162]:

- The employer's name, residence, legal representative or major principal;
- The worker's name, residence, number of identity card or number of any other valid identity certificate;
- The time limit for the labor contract;
- The work contents and place;
- The work time, rest and vocation;
- The remunerations;
- The social security;
- The labor protection, work conditions, and protection against and prevention of occupational harm; and
- Other matters that must be incorporated in the labor contract according to any law or regulation.

If there is still no written labor contract in place after 1 year of employment, a non-fixed term labor contract will be deemed to have been created.[163]

The Labor Contract Law permits provisions for the protection of confidential information and intellectual property of the employer without additional consideration. In addition, an employer may impose noncompetition restraints on certain key employees with a duration period not to exceed two years.[164] However, separate compensation must be paid for a noncompetition agreement after such employee's termination.[165]

An employer is permitted to terminate the employment of an employee by written notice if the employee refuses the employer's

---

[161] Labor Contract Law, art. 82; Labor Contract Law Implementing Regulations, art. 6

[162] Labor Contract Law, art. 16.

[163] Labor Contract Law, art 14; Labor Contract Law Implementing Regulations, art. 7

[164] Labor Contract Law, art 24

[165] Labor Contract Law, art 23

written request to enter into a written labor contract within the first month of employment.[166] In the event of such termination the employer must still pay the employee for the period actually worked.

Employers may terminate a labor contract with its employee under a variety of circumstances which are specified in the Labor Contract Law. The bases for terminating employment under the Labor Contract Law are not as liberal as the "at-will doctrine" under U.S. law, which permits employees to be terminated without cause.[167] Employers may only terminate employment at-will during the probation period, which is between 1 to 6 months after the beginning of the contract.[168]

PROBATIONARY PERIOD

The Labor Contract Law permits the following maximum employee probationary periods:[169]

Employment Term	Maximum Probationary Period
• Less than 3 months or not fixed but expires upon completion of a certain job	No probation period
• 3 months – less than 1 year	1 month
• 1 year – less than 3 years	Less than 2 months
• 3 years and non-fixed term	6 months

---

[166] Labor Contract Law Implementing Regulations, art. 5

[167] Labor Contract Law, arts. 37 through 41

[168] Labor Contract Law, art. 39; Labor Contract Law, art. 19

[169] Labor Contract Law, art. 19

No probation period may be contained in a labor contract with a period to complete the prescribed work or in a labor contract with a fixed period of less than 3 months.[170]

SEVERANCE

With the exception of employees who resign, reach retirement or are terminated for certain causes, all employees whose employment is terminated are entitled to receive severance payments under the Labor Contract Law, except for probationary employees. Employees entitled to severance include those who agree to mutual termination, or who are terminated for incompetence, or whose labor contract expires and is not renewed, but does not include probationary employees. [171] The amount of the severance payment is determined on the basis of 1 month's average wage (including guaranteed bonuses and allowances), multiplied by the number of years of service.[172] If the monthly wage is higher than three times the average monthly wage of employees in the location, the severance pay may be avoided.[173]

MINIMUM WAGE

The minimum wage standards apply on both a monthly and hourly basis and are set at the provincial and municipal level. Employers are prohibited from reaching an agreement with employees for wages that fall below the local minimum wage standard, regardless of whether or not the employee is still in a probationary period.

---

[170] Labor Contract Law, art. 19

[171] Labor Contract Law, art. 46

[172] Labor Contract Law, art. 47; See, generally, Cutshaw et. al., Doing Business in China, 3D (West, 2010).

[173] Labor Contact Law, art. 47

The minimum wage depends on the locality. In Shanghai the minimum for full time employees is RMB 1,120 per month. In the inland city of Chongqing, the minimum wage is RMB 870 per month.[174]

OVERTIME

Under Chinese law, an employer must pay overtime compensation to any employee who works more than 40 hours per week.[175] As a general rule, an employer cannot require overtime of more than 1 hour per day, or 3 hours per day under special circumstances, and no more than 36 hours per month.[176] White collar workers like managers and sales staff are often exempt from the overtime pay rules. The following payment schedule illustrates the overtime pay requirements:[177]

Extended Working Hours	Minimum Overtime Pay (percent of regular wages)
Typical working day	150 percent
Rest day (min. one per week) (i.e., weekend)	200 percent
National holiday	300 percent

---

[174] Nathan Jackson, "What are the major Aspects of Chinese Law?", The University of Iowa Center for International Finance and Development, April 2011, http://ebook.law.uiowa.edu/ebook/uicifd-ebook/what-are-relevant-issues-concerning-chinese-labor-and-employment-law

[175] Labor Contract Law, art 44; the State Council Regulations on Employee Working Time, art. 3.

[176] Labor Contract Law, art. 41.

[177] Labor Contract Law, art. 44

Despite these regulations, employers are able to avoid paying overtime by applying to the local labor authorities and asking for approval to use an alternative system of working hours.[178]

BENEFITS (EXCLUDING RETIREMENT)

Annual Leave

Employees with between 1 and 10 years of work experience are required to receive a minimum of 5 days annual leave per year.[179] Employees with between 10 and 20 years of work experience receive a minimum of 10 days per year.[180] For more than 20 years of work experience, the employee receives a minimum of 15 days per year.[181] These laws apply to all employees, including managers.

Holidays

In general, Chinese workers receive many more days of holiday than the U.S. Each year employees receive 11 days of national holiday, and women receive an extra half-day for Women's day.[182]

---

[178] Labor Contract Law, art. 39

[179] Labor Contract Law, art. 45; the Regulation on Paid Annual Leave for Employees, art.3

[180] Id.

[181] Id.

[182] Regulations on Public Holidays for National Annual Festivals and Memorial Days (2007 Revision), art. 2 and art. 3

Medical Insurance

Chinese law requires most employers to participate in the national basic medical insurance system.[183] Employers contribute approximately 6 percent of total staff payroll, and employees contribute 2 percent of their individual wages (capped at three times local average salary) to a pooled insurance fund and employee personal expense accounts.[184] The employee's contribution is placed in a personal medical expense account.[185] The employer's contribution is split into two portions: 30 percent of the employer's contribution is placed in the employee's personal medical expense account and the remaining 70 percent of the employer's contribution is transferred to the pooled fund.[186] Supplemental medical insurance is also common among white collar workers.

Maternity Leave

Female employees are entitled to a minimum of 90 days of maternity leave.[187] Employers are prohibited from discharging or discriminating against women because of pregnancy or status as mothers. Employers may not subject pregnant women to overtime or hazardous work.[188] China also has a maternity insurance fund that compensates a woman for any lost wages during maternity leave. The insurance fund is financed by employers

---

[183] Social Insurance law of the People's Republic of China, art. 23.

[184] Decision of the State Council on Establishing the Urban Employees' Basic Medical Insurance System, art. 2.

[185] Decision of the State Council on Establishing the Urban Employees' Basic Medical Insurance System, art. 3.

[186] Id.

[187] Labor Law, art. 62

[188] Labor Law, art. 61

that contribute roughly one percent of payroll expenses.[189] Men are not covered under the maternity leave provisions, although most employers allow men several days off following the birth of a child.

Unemployment Insurance

Urban residents with a proper household registration, working at a place of official registration, may be entitled to receive unemployment insurance.[190] The employees must fall within a working age range, be able to work, and register with the government. Approximately 15 percent of the total workforce is eligible. The unemployment insurance system is financed by employers who must pay two percent of payroll, with employees contributing one percent of their wages (capped at three times local average salary) to the fund.[191] To be entitled to receive unemployment benefits, the employee must be registered for benefits, have paid premiums for at least 1 year, have involuntarily lost employment, and be actively seeking work.[192]

Housing Funds

Local governments in urban areas typically operate housing funds.[193] Under these programs, the employer and employee contribute an amount each month to a fund dedicated to assisting employees in buying, refurbishing, or renting a home. If the

---

[189] Interim Provisions on Maternity Insurance for Enterprises Employees, art. 4

[190] Regulations of Unemployment Insurance, art. 2

[191] Regulations of Unemployment Insurance, art. 6

[192] Regulations of Unemployment Insurance, art. 14.

[193] Regulation on the Administration of Housing Accumulation Funds (2002 Revision), art. 8.

employee does not use the funds in their account for housing, they can only remove the funds for retirement, a permanent move overseas, or several other scenarios.[194]

RETIREMENT

Employers and employees must contribute to a basic pension insurance fund that is administered at the provincial or municipal level. Some cities have also set up supplementary pension insurance funds that employees have the option to join. Typically, employers contribute roughly 20 percent of total wages and employees contribute roughly 8 percent of wages (capped at three times local average salary).[195] It should be noted that most pension amounts are insufficient to support retirees. For this reason, the government offers and encourages workers to enroll in supplemental retirement plans.

The general retirement age for men is 60 and for women it is 55.[196] Employees are not allowed to make early withdrawals from their pension accounts, but the accounts are transferrable when the employee changes employers or moves to a new city.[197] Employer contributions are subject to strong enforcement and employer defaults can be subject to very large fines. When an employer defaults on pension payments, the local government is permitted

---

[194] Regulation on the Administration of Housing Accumulation Funds (2002 Revision), art 24.

[195] The contribution rates to pension insurance between employer and employee are slightly different, such as the current employer's contribution rate is 22%, and employees contribution rate is 8% in Shanghai, while the current employer's contribution rate is 20%, and employees contribution rate is 8% in Beijing.

[196] Interim Regulations of State Council on Settlement of the Old, Weak, Sic and Disabled Officers, art. 4.

[197] Notice of the General Office of the State Council on Forwarding the Interim Measures of the Ministry of Human Resources and Social Security and the Ministry of Finance for the Transfer and Continuation of the Basic Pension Insurance Relations of Urban Employee, art. 3

to garnish the payments from the employer's property. This is typically done through the largely state-run banking system.

WORKMAN'S COMPENSATION

Each province in China has its own regulations that require employers to pay the medical expenses of injuries, disability, and occupational diseases. The regulations cover all companies, including unregistered companies and those that illegally avoid paying the premiums. The insurance fund is financed through employer-paid premiums that the government establishes by determining the dangers inherent in the workplace.[198] For example, an employer with low risk work, like accounting, pays 0.5 percent of total payroll expenses into the insurance fund, while an employer with high risk work, like shipbuilding, pays 2 percent of total payroll into the fund.[199]

The law prohibits employers and employees from contractually opting out of the system. However, many employees are unfamiliar with this worker's compensation program, or attempt to avoid it and the system is generally underfunded.

UNIONS

Although it is easy to form a union in China, the primary function of a union is to avoid labor unrest, rather than promoting the interest of workers. Unions typically discourage employee members from airing grievances or striking.[200] Only 25 workers

---

[198] Regulation on Work-Related Injury Insurance (2010 Revision), art. 7

[199] Regulation on Work-Related Injury Insurance (2010 Revision), art. 8

[200] Trade Union Law of the People's Republic of China (2001 Amendment), art. 27.

are necessary to join a union and the employer will usually be required to accept the union.[201]

Although labor unions may only be established by employees voluntarily, employers often encourage unions in order to pre-empt the organization by workers. These are called company unions. Company union officials are often members of management paid directly by the company.

Occasionally, workers do strike. For example, in June 2011, it was reported that workers at the Tandy Electronics Co. Ltd., located in Huizhou, China, had been on strike protesting the terms of a proposed compensation agreement as part of preparations for the plant's closure. Tandy Electronics Co. Ltd. is a joint venture company which is the largest wireless equipment manufacturer and supplier for RadioShack.[202]

CHILD LABOR

Under Chinese Child Labor Regulations, employers may not recruit, employ, or facilitate the employment of children under the age of sixteen.[203] Exceptions exist for child entertainers, athletes, or vocational training, but in these cases employers must ensure the health of the children.[204]

Employees between the ages of sixteen and eighteen are classified as underage employees and may not engage in mining, unhealthy or hazardous work, or highly labor-intensive work.[205] Employers of underage workers must arrange to have these workers receive regular physical examinations.[206]

[201] Trade Union Law of the People's Republic of China (2001 Amendment), art. 10

[202] "The Unfair Dismissal of Tandy Electronics Co. Ltd Workers", China Labor Watch, June 8, 2011, http://www.chinalaborwatch.org/pro/proshow-147.html

[203] Provisions on the Prohibition of Using Child Labor, art. 2.

[204] Provisions on the Prohibition of Using Child labor, art. 13.

[205] Labor Law, art. 58; Labor Law, art. 64

[206] Labor Law. art 65.

Despite the regulations that prohibit employment of children under the age of sixteen, exploitation of child employees is widespread in China.

Chinese Business Taxes

CORPORATE INCOME TAX

Under China's Enterprise Income Tax Law, effective January 1, 2008, both FIEs and domestic companies are subject to a corporate income tax on profits at the rate of 25%. FIEs must pay tax on their worldwide income, but tax credits may be available under dual tax treaties for income tax paid to other countries. Small companies can, in certain cases, pay a 20% corporate tax.

WITHHOLDING TAX

A 10% withholding tax is due on dividends from investments, royalties and rents paid to foreign entities from their China activities.

INDIVIDUAL INCOME TAX

During 2012, an individual's income is taxed progressively at rates ranging from 3% to 45%. FIEs must generally serve as a withholding agent for its employees. Capital gains for individuals are taxed at the rate of 20%.

VALUE ADDED TAX

China imposes a value added tax ("VAT") generally at the rate of 17% for certain necessities tax of 13%. The VAT applies to the sale of goods, except real estate properties, and the provision of labor services in relation to the processing of goods and repair and replacement services within China.

There are a variety of other taxes imposed by China such as sales taxes, real estate taxes, customs duties, resources tax, etc. which are beyond the scope of this book.

Terminating the Joint Venture[207]

There are many reasons why partners in a joint venture, even a modestly successful one, may wish to terminate it. These reasons range from changes in the marketplace or the strategic objectives of the parties to disagreements over management, the need for additional capital or the disposition of joint venture earnings.

Sometimes the motivation for withdraw is to disassociate from a partner who is in trouble. For example, it was announced in November 2011 that ThyssenKrupp AG was withdrawing from its joint venture, called Marine Force International ("MFI"), with Ferrostaal because of a corruption scandal involving Ferrostaal. Ferrostaal had been accused of paying millions of Euros in bribes to Greece related to the purchase of submarines and MFI was suspected of making illegal payments to South Korean officials in connection with its purchase of submarines.[208]

Sometimes the motivation for withdrawing from a joint venture is unhappiness with the original legal terms, including the inability to obtain control. For example, in 2008, Morgan Stanley sold its interest in a Chinese joint venture investment bank called China International Capital Corp ("CICC"), China's first investment bank, allegedly because Morgan Stanley did not control the business management of CICC. It had also been reported that Morgan Stanley had signed an agreement with Shanghai-based

---

[207] For a thoughtful discussion of this topic see Vol. 1, Chapter 2, "Transnational Joint Ventures", (2011) (Thomson Reuters/West).

[208] "Thyssen Plans Withdrawal from Submarine Joint Venture", Spiegel Online International, 11/8/2011, http://www.spiegel.de/international/business/u-turn-on-u-boats-thyssen-plans-withdrawal-from-submarine-joint-venture-a-796474.html

China Fortune Securities for a joint venture investment bank and might be interested in a controlling stake.[209]

Any person thinking about entering into an international joint venture must carefully consider the process for terminating it. The absence of mutually agreed provisions relating to the termination of the joint venture may make the process both protracted and more expensive.

The first question to consider is which of the partners will receive the assets of the joint venture. In general, if assets, such as machinery, equipment, technology, trademarks, etc. have been contributed by Partner A, Partner A should receive those assets. The problem is that some of these assets are not easily returnable, especially technology, once revealed.

Partner B may object to all of these assets going back to Partner A because it undervalues the contributions of Partner B. The return of contributed assets to Partner A may give more value to Partner A than the respective equity percentage of Partner A.

One neat method of resolving this problem on the breakup of a joint venture is to allow the partner who wants out to set a price at which they will buy or sell and allow the partner who does not want the breakup to make the choice of buying or selling. While this methodology works well in countries which do not restrict foreign ownership, it does not work well in countries, such as China, where there is a restriction on foreign ownership. In China it may be impossible for the U.S. partner to become 100% owner of the business because of investment restrictions.

A second problem in drafting a breakup clause is whether there is any restrictions on post-termination competition by either of the partners. The joint venture may have inadvertently created a worldwide competitor for the U.S. partner.

A third problem is the ownership after the breakup of trademarks, patents and other intellectual property which were owned by the joint venture entity. These may be the most valuable assets

---

[209] "Morgan Stanley to withdraw from China joint venture: Report", The Economic Times, January 8, 2008, http://articles.economictimes.indiatimes.com/2008-01-08/news/28494652_1_morgan-stanley-joint-venture-china-investment-corporation

of the joint venture and each partner may wish to have rights to use the trademarks, patents and other intellectual property.

A fourth problem is what to do with the joint venture personnel and who bears the responsibility for any severance payments or other termination payments required by law. For example, in June 2011, Desay Group, a main supplier for RadioShack, decided to withdraw from a joint venture agreement with RadioShack which created a factory in Huizhou, China, operated by a joint venture company called Tandy Electronics Co. Ltd. Unfortunately, the joint venture partners did not agree in advance on the termination compensation arrangements for the approximately 1,000 workers at the factory in Huizhou, China and this resulted in a strike by these workers.[210]

Finally, a question may arise if the assets of the joint venture are not sufficient to pay its creditors. Which of the partners, if any, should be responsible? In most cases, the joint venture partners will rely upon the limited liability of the joint venture and not legally obligate themselves to pay creditors.

The foregoing are only a few of the problems involved in negotiating and drafting a breakup provision. Since the determination of these issues creates many difficult problems, many middle-market and smaller companies may choose to avoid raising them in the negotiations of the joint venture. As a result, these breakup issues get resolved on an ad hoc basis at such time as the joint venture terminates.

Part III of this book is intended as a guide for Chinese and other Asian companies and individuals in establishing a joint venture based in the United States.

---

[210] "The Unfair Dismissal of Tandy Electronics Co. Ltd Workers", China Labor Watch, June 8, 2011, http://www.chinalaborwatch.org/pro/proshow-147.html

PART III

Joint Ventures Based In The United States

Chapter 8

Establishing A U.S.-Based Cross-Border Alliance

The purpose of the next two chapters is to educate Chinese and other international companies who wish to form strategic alliances based in the United States with U.S. companies or to acquire U.S. companies. Although this process is in the very early stages of development, it may be expected that in the next several decades, more and more Asian companies will wish to establish joint ventures in the United States.

At the end of this chapter is a discussion of restrictions on foreign investment in certain strategic U.S. industries.

The motivation for middle-market and smaller Chinese and other Asian companies to establish alliances with U.S. companies or to acquire them will vary. However, the following are some of the major motivating factors:

- To save on transportation costs to the U.S. for products that have low labor content
- To create research and development alliances to take advantage of areas in which U.S. technology is superior
- To establish better distribution in the U.S. of Asian-made products
- To better market products to Asian-American citizens
- To obtain Green Cards which will permit the owner of the business, and his or her family, access to the U.S. and possibly U.S. citizenship. This topic is covered in Chapter 10.

During the 1980s, large Japanese companies started slowly moving capital into the U.S. to effectuate strategic alliances and acquisitions, including real estate investments. Japanese direct investment in the U.S. reached a record of $20 billion in 1990, with acquisitions during the period of 1988 through 1990 valued at $750 million, accounting for a quarter to half of the annual investment inflow from Japan.[211] This trend culminated in the Japanese ultimately establishing manufacturing plants in the U.S. (such as Toyota and Honda) to take better advantage of the U.S. markets.

The primary reason behind the late 1990s' surge in Japanese direct investment in the U.S. was the availability of inexpensive capital in Japan, as stock markets roughly tripled in value between 1985 and 1990. That factor, combined with an appreciating yen over much of the 1980s and the relatively weak prices of assets in the U.S. gave corporate Japan sufficient purchasing power to establish or acquire thousands of U.S. businesses.[212]

Similarly, large Chinese companies are beginning to make investments in the U.S.

For example, on May 21, 2012, it was announced that AMC Entertainment Holdings would be acquired for $2.6 billion by Chinese conglomerate Dalian Wanda Group.[213] This proposed acquisition was the largest takeover of an American company by a Chinese company to date.[214]

On May 9, 2012, the Industrial and Commercial Bank of China, Ltd., one of the world's largest banking companies, received approval from the U.S. Federal Reserve, along with two other institutions – the China Investment Corporation and Central Huijin Investment – to purchase an 80 percent share in

[211] Arthur J. Alexander "Japanese Direct Investment in the United States: Revising and Updating Perceptions" Japanese Economic Institute, Report No. 42A, November 7, 1997

[212] Id.

[213] Richard Verrier and David Pierson, "Chinese firm's deal to buy AMC may spur others", Los Angeles Times, May 22, 2012

[214] "Chinese Firm Buying AMC Movie Theater Chain", The Associated Press, May 21, 2012

the Bank of East Asia's American arm.[215] The Bank of East Asia is a Hong Kong company which has 13 branches in New York and California, but these branches are small with only $780 million in assets. This is a relatively conservative investment by China's largest bank with $2.5 trillion in assets, compared with $2.3 trillion in assets for the largest U.S. bank, J. P. Morgan Chase & Co. According to a spokesman for the Chinese bank, their philosophy is to "go slow and learn the market."[216]

The approval of these acquisitions marks the first occasion on which the Federal Reserve Board approved the acquisition of a U.S. bank by a Chinese bank since the Foreign Bank Supervision Enhancement Act of 1991. This Act increased federal supervision of foreign banks operating in the U.S. and requires the Federal Reserve Board to make a finding that the foreign bank is subject to comprehensive supervision on a consolidated basis by its home country supervisor. This Federal Reserve Board approval should create the opportunity for other leading Chinese banks to acquire small U.S. banks since it creates a precedent for other similarly situated Chinese banks.

The Rhodium Group reported that China invested $264 million in renewable energy deals in the U.S. in 2011.[217]

According to a report by the Boston Consulting Group, sometime around 2015 it will be as economical to manufacture many goods for U.S. consumption in the United States as in China. The report pointed to seven industries that are nearing that breakpoint, namely electronics, appliances, machinery, transportation goods, fabricated metals, furniture and plastics and rubber. These are all products with relatively low labor content and high transportation costs.[218]

---

[215] Debbie Baratz, "Fed Gives Chinese Bank Clearance to Takeover Bank of East Asia", ValueWalk, May 10, 2012, http://www.valuewalk.com/2012/05/fed-gives-chinese-bank-clearance-to-takeover-bank-of-east-asia/

[216] Jon Hilsenrath, Robin Sidel and Lingling Wei, "Chinese Banks Get Nod in U.S., The Wall Street Journal, May 10, 2012, p. A2.

[217] Jeffrey Ball, "Beneath a War of Words, Money Paints a Different China-U.S. Picture", the Wall Street Journal, June 18, 2012, p. R5

[218] David Conrads, "As Chinese wages rise, US manufacturers heard back home", The Christian Science Monitor, May 10, 2012,

On March 5, 2012, Premier Wen Jiabao stated that China intended to relax its restrictions on individual investing overseas and will implement a "go global" strategy in 2012.[219]

The Professional Team

Chinese and other international investors need the assistance of skilled professionals in approaching investments in the U.S. market. The professional team should include experts on marketing products or services in the U.S., including actual and potential competition as well as important pricing issues. Chinese and other international investors should not rely solely upon their U.S. joint venture partner for this marketing study.

It is also important to retain a U.S. attorney who is familiar with joint ventures and other international alliances. The attorney can explain the pitfalls that you may face. It is extremely important that you obtain tax advice and have a full understanding as to the applicable federal, state, and local taxes to which your investment will be subject. Import and export regulations are also vital to the success of the joint venture and this information should be obtained from an attorney specializing in the area.

The type of expertise you are looking for in your attorney will be typically found in large U.S. law firms. These firms will also advise potential investors as to the proper legal entity to form to minimize taxes and protect them from potential liability.

As noted later in this chapter, there are many laws that protect employees. Potential investors must have a full understanding of the extent to which these laws differ from the protections available in their home country.

The professional team should also include a financial advisor to assist the investor in hedging against currency fluctuations. If the goal of the joint venture involves U.S. manufacturing,

---

http://www.csmonitor.com/Business/new-economy/2012/0510/ As-Chinese-wages-rise-US-manufacturers-head-back-home

[219] "China to relax overseas investment restrictions", chinadaily.com. cn, March 5, 2012; http://www.chinadaily.com.cn/china/2012-03/05/ content_14757284.htm

investors should consider adding to their professional team experts on manufacturing in the U.S.

Negotiating With a U.S. Partner

There is no single negotiating style for U.S. joint venture partners. Just as negotiating strategy and tactics can vary by region in China and in all of Asia, so are there significant variations in different regions of the United States. Negotiating a joint venture with a New York private equity fund which controls a portfolio company in the U.S. would be quite different from negotiating with a small to mid-size manufacturer in Iowa.

In general, the U.S. negotiating style is much more direct than the Chinese style. U.S. negotiators are willing to spend time getting to know the Chinese company, but have nowhere near the patience of Chinese negotiators for an extensive get-to-know-you period.

Compared to Chinese culture, business is done at lightning speed in the United States. It is not unusual for a U.S. salesperson to bring final contracts to their first meeting with prospective customers. Middle-managers may have the authority to enter into small contracts even without approval of higher-ups in the organization.

Role of Attorneys

In contrast to China, the United States is very litigious. It has over one million lawyers and any business conducted in the United States will be subject to significant litigation costs.

Attorneys play a much more important role in the U.S. negotiating process than occurs in China or other Asian countries. Tax attorneys will help to structure the transaction to minimize the impact of both U.S. federal, state and local taxes on the joint venture. The letter of intent and the definitive contract will be drafted by an attorney and the U.S. partner would expect the Chinese company to be represented by a sophisticated U.S. attorney.

It is important to obtain an attorney who specializes in mergers, acquisitions and joint ventures. As noted, most of these attorneys are with large law firms. Attorneys in the U.S. can be very expensive. Hourly rates in excess of $500 per hour or even $1,000 per hour are not unheard of. Indeed, if a law firm, which is ranked among the top 100, is used in the negotiations, an hourly rate in excess of $500 should be expected.

The Chinese company should attempt to obtain at least a budget for the work and, if possible, negotiate a fixed fee with its attorney.

Cultural Considerations

Many executives in the United States will tell acquaintances to use their first name almost immediately upon first being introduced. Even people with great authority like to cultivate down-to-earth images by promoting the use of their first name, or potentially their nickname.

Smoking is generally prohibited in most public and private buildings and is considered by many to be an annoying and unhealthful activity. Before smoking, ask if anyone minds, or wait to see if others smoke.

There are many women executives in the United States. In many parts of the United States, sexual innuendoes are considered bad behavior. Anti-sexual harassment laws are common throughout the United States.

In the United States, gift-giving is not as common as in China. Indeed, certain laws actually make business gifts illegal unless the gift is of a very modest amount. Therefore, be careful in providing gifts to U.S. executives. A modest gift after a transaction closes is not necessary but can be helpful for future relationships.

Many companies have adopted a "business casual" policy. In small towns and rural areas, clothing is less formal and more relaxed. There is nothing wrong with dressing in a suit and tie, even if the U.S. executives are more casually dressed.[220]

---

[220] Terri Morrison and Wayne A. Conaway, "Kiss, Bow, or Shake Hands", 2nd Edition, Adams Media, 2006

The U.S. Laws Restricting Foreign Ownership

In comparison to the detailed Chinese government restrictions on investment in the Peoples Republic of China, there are relatively few restrictions on investments in the U.S. industries by foreign nationals.

However, U.S. statutes contain major restrictions on foreign investment in the following industries, among others:[221]

- Shipping
- Aircraft
- Mining
- Energy
- Lands
- Communications
- Banking
- Government contracting
- Investment company regulation

In addition, there are four major federal statutes that impact U.S. foreign investment and are designed for information-gathering and disclosure. These four statutes are as follows: International Investment and Trade in Services Survey Act of 1976; Foreign Direct Investment and International Financial Data Improvements Act of 1990; Agricultural Foreign Investment Disclosure Act of 1978; and Domestic and Foreign Investment Improved Disclosure Act of 1977.[222]

International investors should bear in mind that there are specific restrictions in many states which can also impede foreign investment.[223]

---

[221] Michael V. Seitzinger, Esq., "CRS Report to Congress – Foreign Investment in the United States: Major Federal Statutory Restrictions", Congressional Research Service, March 27, 2008

[222] Id.

[223] *See* Jose E. Alverez, *Political Protectionism and United States Investment Obligations in Conflict: The Hazards of Exon-Florio*, 30 Va. J. Int'l L. 1, 159 (1989) (stating that U.S. reactions to foreign investment "appear schizophrenic" by restricting the foreign investments t hat other policies expressly attempt to

Committee on Foreign Investment in the United States

The Committee on Foreign Investment in the United States (CFIUS) is a multi-member board headed by the Secretary of the Treasury.[224] CFIUS may review any "covered transaction," defined as any merger, acquisition, or takeover by or with a foreign person which could result in foreign control of any person engaged in interstate commerce in the U.S.,[225] for its potential effect upon national security. This review includes domestic production needed for projected national defense requirements, the capability and capacity of domestic industries to meet national defense requirements, the control of domestic industries and commercial activity by foreign citizens as it affects the capability and capacity of the U.S. to meet the requirement of national security, and the potential impact of the proposed or pending transaction on U.S. international technological leadership in areas affecting U.S. national security.[226] A mandatory investigation is required in any situation in which an entity controlled by or acting on behalf of a foreign government seeks to engage in any merger, acquisition, or takeover which could result in control of a person engaged in interstate commerce in the U.S. that could affect the national security of the U.S. Among indicia of control is a purchase of voting securities or comparable interests in a U.S. person greater than 10% of the outstanding voting securities of a U.S. person.[227]

U.S. Currency Controls

There are very few currency controls in the U.S., in contrast to many other countries.

---

expand); *See also* Cheryl Tate, Note, *The Constitutionality of State Attempts to Regulate Foreign Investment*, 99 Yale L.J. 2023 (1990).

[224] 50 U.S.C. App §§ 2170 *et seq.*

[225] 50 U.S.C. App § 2170(a)

[226] 50 U.S.C. App. § 2170(f)

[227] *See* 31 C.F.R. § 800.302(d)(1)

It is legal to transport any amount of currency or other monetary instruments into or out of the U.S. However, if you transport, attempt to transport, or cause to be transported (including by mail or other means) currency or other monetary instruments in an aggregate amount exceeding $10,000 (or its foreign equivalent) at one time from the U.S. to any foreign place, or into the U.S. from any foreign place, you must file a report with U.S. Customs.[228] This report is called the Report of International Transportation of Currency or Monetary Instruments, Customs Form 4790. Furthermore, if you receive in the U.S., currency or other monetary instruments in an aggregate amount exceeding $10,000 (or its foreign equivalent) at one time which has been transported, mailed, or shipped to you from any foreign place, you must file a CF-4790. These forms can be obtained at all U.S. ports of entry and departure.

Monetary instruments include:

- U.S. or foreign coins and currency;
- Travelers checks in any form;
- Negotiable instruments (including checks, promissory notes, and money orders) that are either in bearer form, endorsed without restriction, made out to a fictitious payee, or otherwise in such form that title thereto passes upon delivery;
- Incomplete instruments (including checks, promissory notes, and money orders) signed, but with the payee's name omitted; and
- Securities or stock in bearer form or otherwise in such form that title thereto passes upon delivery. However, the term "monetary instruments" does not include:
  - Checks or money orders made payable to the order of a named person which have not been endorsed or which bear restrictive endorsements;
  - Warehouse receipts; or
  - Bills of lading.

---

[228] Currency Reporting For Travelers, Transportation Security Administration, http://www.tsa.gov/travelers/airtravel/assistant/editorial_1848.shtm

Reporting is required under the Currency and Foreign Transaction Reporting Act[229], as amended. Failure to comply can result in civil and criminal penalties and may lead to forfeiture of your monetary instrument(s).

Federal law requires financial institutions to report currency (cash or coin) transactions over $10,000 conducted by, or on behalf of, one person, as well as multiple currency transactions that aggregate to be over $10,000 in a single day. These transactions are reported on Currency Transaction Reports (CTRs). The federal law requiring these reports was passed to safeguard the financial industry from threats posed by money laundering and other financial crime. To comply with this law, financial institutions must obtain personal identification information about the individual conducting the transaction such as a Social Security number as well as a driver's license or other government-issued document. This requirement applies whether the individual conducting the transaction has an account relationship with the institution or not.

Locating Facilities in the U.S.

Many joint ventures will involve creating a new office or plant in the U.S. The following are some of the major factors that will influence the location of the office or plant:

- Available state and local subsidies. Many states and local governments would provide generous financing for facilities that will create employment. These subsidies are greater in states that have high unemployment rates.
- Availability of skilled workforce. A skilled workforce is a key to a successful joint venture in the United States. Many parts of the United States, particularly those with high unemployment, possess such a skilled workforce available for hiring.
- State and local taxes. In general, avoid locations in states with high state and local income taxes. However, many

---

[229] PL 97-258, 31 U.S.C. 5311, et seq

states, such as Pennsylvania, with high corporate income taxes may provide very generous subsidies to new plants that will generate significant employment.

- Transportation. The location of the plant should be reasonably convenient to the terminus of flights to the U.S. from China or other international locations to the U.S. Thus, even though a state in the Midwest of the U.S. may have lower taxes, travel to and from the facility may be very time-consuming if the facility is not located near an airport.
- Right to Work states. States named below have so-called "Right to Work" laws which make it more difficult for workers to be unionized. The following are the states with Right to Work laws as of July 1, 2012: Alabama, Arizona, Arkansas, Florida, Georgia, Guam, Idaho, Indiana, Iowa, Kansas, Louisiana, Mississippi, Nebraska, Nevada, North Carolina, North Dakota, Oklahoma, South Carolina, South Dakota, Tennessee, Texas, Utah, Virginia and Wyoming. Below is a map of the states that have a Right to Work law:

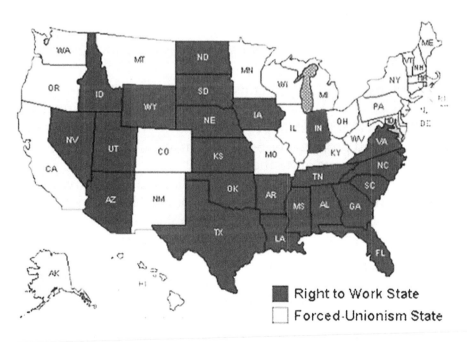

The location of your joint venture plant will, in part, depend upon the location of your joint venture U.S. partner. Your alliance partner may well wish to have a joint venture plant located near its own facilities in order to keep a better eye on the operations.

Forbes, Inc. annually publishes an article entitled "Best Places for Businesses and Careers." It is important to treat this article with skepticism since the ranking of the best places does not consider the availability of government subsidies or the availability of a skilled workforce. In general, the article will typically recommend places in the Midwest or with a strong university presence. Many of these places, such as Raleigh, North Carolina or Austin, Texas, may not have a government subsidy to the new business or the availability of a skilled workforce.[230]

State Subsidies

Pennsylvania is generally a high-tax state and in some of the major cities of Pennsylvania unions are extremely strong. Therefore, one might conclude that this was not a great state to locate a joint venture plant. However, Pennsylvania, like other northeastern states in the U.S., knows the disincentives to establishing businesses there and tries to offset these disincentives with very generous incentives.

For example, in 1997, Pennsylvania was so anxious to have Kvaerner ASA, a Norwegian corporation, build a shipyard in Philadelphia that the state provided $429 million in public funds to the shipyard project. The $429 million included 92.3% in grants and the rest in loans and other funds.[231]

In 1976, Volkswagen was provided with $70 million in Pennsylvania public funds when it announced its decision to construct its plant in an abandoned Chrysler Factory in Westmorland

---

[230] Kurt Badenhausen, "The Best Places For Business", Forbes.com, June 29, 2011, http://www.forbes.com/sites/kurtbadenhausen/2011/06/29/the-best-places-for-business-and-careers/

[231] "A Performance Audit of Commonwealth Spending For the Kvaerner-Philadelphia naval Shipyard Project Through January 14, 2000", http://www.auditorgen.state.pa.us/archives/performance/kvaernerrpt.html

County, PA, which is in the central part of Pennsylvania.[232] By 1980, the plant was turning out approximately 200,000 automobiles and employing close to 6,000 employees.[233] Despite initial success, in 1987 the plant was shut down and Pennsylvania was left holding the bag for many millions of dollars.[234]

In addition to Pennsylvania, other states that are suffering from high unemployment, such as Michigan and Rhode Island, will provide very generous financing packages for major employers. For example, in 2010 the State of Rhode Island "morally" guaranteed a $75 million loan to a retired famous U.S. baseball player. [235]

It is clear that joint ventures that benefit employment within a state can still obtain major subsidies of public funds.

Federal Legal Protections for U.S. Employees

There are numerous federal, state and local statutes that protect U.S. employees. Federal, state and local governments are generally active in enforcing these laws. In addition, there is no shortage of attorneys who are willing to represent employees on a so-called contingent fee basis (no fee unless there is a recovery) in lawsuits against employers.

Although China has laws that provide some protection for employees, a U.S. employee has much greater and substantial legal rights and privileges.

---

[232] David E. Buchholz, Ph.D., "Volkswagen: pining for the gentleman caller", CFED, http://development.cfed.org/focus.m?edit=0&parentid=1629&siteid=1629&id=1658

[233] Id.

[234] Id.

[235] Abby Goodnough, "Trouble in Rhode Island for Boston Baseball Hero Trying Out a new Game", The New York Times, May 20, 2012, http://www.nytimes.com/2012/05/21/us/curtschillings- business-trouble-in-rhode-island.html?_r=1; See also, Josh Barro, "Curt Schilling's Moral Obligations, and Rhode Island's", Bloomberg. com, July 27, 2012, http://www.bloomberg.com/news/2012-06-27/curt-schilling-s-moral-obligations-and-rhodeisland- s.html

Although the U.S. has many statutory worker protection laws, employees generally have relatively limited rights in the context of employment terminations, unless they are in a protected class of employees, have employment contracts, or are subject to collective bargaining agreements. The primary reason for this is a legal concept unique to the United States known as the "at will" employment doctrine. This doctrine permits an employer in the United States to freely terminate the employment of an employee at any time, without notice and without cause, so long as it is not for an unlawful reason.

Unfortunately, the doctrine of "at will" employment is not interpreted uniformly in all 50 states and is being eroded by court decisions. Moreover, there are many employees in protective classes such as older employees and minorities. For example, the Age Discrimination in Employment Act of 1967 and the Americans with Disabilities Act of 1990 prohibits discrimination based on age (40 and over) and disability, respectively. In addition, the Civil Rights Act of 1964 prohibits employment discrimination on the basis of race, color, religion, sex, national origin, pregnancy, childbirth or related medical conditions. Finally the Civil Rights Act of 1991 provides a federal remedy to employees or applicants alleging racial discrimination or harassment in employment. Some states expand upon the protective categories by prohibiting discrimination or harassment on the basis of marital status or sexual orientation.

In major metropolitan areas in the United States it is not uncommon for three sets of laws – federal, state and local – to apply to employees.

The following is a partial list of the statutes that have been passed by the U.S. Congress to protect employees (employers should also be aware that state laws may impose additional obligations):

- Wages and Hours Worked
  - Minimum Wage and Overtime Pay – Fair Labor Standards Act
  - Wage Garnishment – Fair Labor Standards Act

- Protection for Workers in Agriculture – Migrant and Seasonal Agricultural Worker Protection Act
- Child Labor Protections – Fair Labor Standard Act – Child Labor Provisions

- Safety and Health Standards
  - Occupational Safety and Health – Occupational Safety and Health Act
  - Mine Safety and Health – Mine Safety and Health Act
  - Worker Protections in Agriculture – Migrant and Seasonal Agricultural Worker Protection Act

- Health Benefits, Retirement Standards and Workers' Compensation
  - Employee Benefit Plans – Employee Retirement Income Security Act
  - Black Lung Compensation – Black Lung Benefits Act
  - Family and Medical leave – Family and Medical Leave Act

- Non-Discrimination
  - Discrimination – Title VII of the Civil Rights Act of 1964, as amended
  - Disability discrimination – The Americans with Disabilities Act ("ADA") and the Americans with Disabilities Act Amendments Act ("ADAAA")
  - Pregnancy discrimination – The Pregnancy Discrimination Act
  - Age Discrimination – The Age Discrimination in Employment Act
  - Affirmative Action – Executive Order 11246
  - Reemployment and Nondiscrimination Rights for Uniformed Services Members – Uniformed Services Employment and Reemployment Rights Act
  - Equal Pay for employees – Equal Pay Act and the Lilly Ledbetter Fair Pay Act

- Employment Nondiscrimination and Equal Opportunity for Qualified Individuals with Disabilities for recipients of federal funding – The Rehabilitation Act of 1973

- Other Workplace Standards
  - Labor Issues – The National Labor Relations Act
  - Lie Detector Tests – Employee Polygraph Protection Act
  - Whistleblower and Retaliation Protections – Occupational Safety and Health Act and The Dodd Frank False Claims Act
  - Notices for Plant Closings and Mass Layoffs – Worker Adjustment and Retraining Notification Act

- Work Authorization for Non-U.S. Citizens
  - Immigrant Visas – Immigration and Nationality Act and related federal regulations
  - Non-Immigrant Visas – Immigration and Nationality Act and related federal regulations

- Federal Contracts: Working Conditions
  - Wages in Supply & Equipment Contracts – Walsh-Healy Public Contracts Act
  - Prevailing Wages in Service Contracts – McNamara-O'Hara Service Contract Act
  - Prevailing Wages in Construction Contracts – Davis-Bacon and Related Acts
  - Hours and Safety Standards in Construction Contracts – Contract Work Hours and Safety Standards Act
  - Prohibition Against "Kickbacks" in Federally Funded – Copeland "Anti-Kickback" Act

Our next chapter discusses the business and legal issues involved in establishing a U.S.-based joint venture.

Chapter 9

Business and Legal Issues of U.S.-Based Joint Ventures

The purpose of this chapter is to explain to international companies some of the business and related legal issues involved in forming a U.S.-based joint venture.

One way of looking at a joint venture is to divide it up into four different periods and to establish terms and conditions for each of those four periods. The four periods would be as follows:

- Planning Phase: Starting with the time of locating a potential joint venture partner and ending with the closing of the definitive joint venture agreement. This may be viewed as the planning phase.
- Start-up Period: Joint venture start-up period during which the parties prepare to conduct business and test the validity of the assumptions made during the planning phase.
- Active Option: The active operation of the joint venture.
- Termination: The termination or other dissolution of the joint venture.

This chapter will primarily discuss the planning phase.

Confidentiality Agreements

The process of forming the joint venture can last from several months to several years. It is important to maintain confidentiality of the company's proprietary information throughout the process. The joint venture partner selected will want to perform due diligence on the company with whom they are negotiating just as your company will perform due diligence on the proposed joint venture partner. Proprietary information includes customer lists, trade secrets, methods of marketing, and so on.

There are three methods of maintaining the confidentiality of proprietary information:

- Give potential joint venture partners only enough information to permit them to make the joint venture decision, but no more.
- Require potential joint venture partners to sign a confidentiality agreement.
- Require potential joint venture partners to refrain from hiring the company's key employees.

It is recommended that all three methods be used to preserve confidentiality of proprietary information. Obviously any agreement by your potential joint venture partner will likely be reciprocal. One may argue that if your potential joint venture partner is not in a competitive business (example: Mitsubishi and Kentucky Fried Chicken discussed in a prior chapter), there is less need for confidentiality than if you are dealing with a potential competitor. However, even if your potential partner is not currently a potential competitor, they may, in the future, become a competitor. In addition, each joint venture partner will want to prevent the other from disclosing proprietary information to others who may in fact become competitors.

Accordingly, the joint venture attorney should draft a confidentiality agreement, preferably one that is reciprocal in its obligations, and have it signed before beginning joint venture negotiations. The agreement should typically restrict not only the use or disclosure of proprietary information, but should also obligate each party to not hire the key employees of the other during the period of the negotiations and for one or two years thereafter. Exceptions to this mutual obligation can be crafted if, for example, the key employee answers an unsolicited advertisement.

As mentioned previously, it is important to be frank with the proposed joint venture partner concerning your strategic objectives. This may involve revealing some confidential or proprietary information. At the right time during the negotiations, it may be necessary to reveal sensitive information in order to establish a level of trust with your proposed joint venture partner.

Letters of Intent

A letter of intent (also called an "agreement in principle") is a document signed by both potential joint venture partners that expresses their mutual intention of the parties to form a joint venture. The letter of intent is generally not legally binding except for any confidentiality and non-solicitation of employee provisions. The purpose of the letter of intent is to set forth the major business terms of the transaction and to confirm these terms in writing to prevent any misunderstanding. Typically, the letter of intent will state that it is not legally binding (except for the confidentiality and non-solicitation of employee provisions) and that the only legally binding document is the definitive joint venture agreement.

The problem with letters of intent is that sometimes they are legally binding even though the parties say that they are not. For example, an $11 billion judgment was rendered against Texaco, Inc. in the Getty merger in connection with a letter of intent signed by Getty with Pennzoil that was not supposed to be legally binding.

As a result of the Pennzoil case, some attorneys are reluctant to have their clients sign letters of intent and prefer instead to proceed to the final joint venture agreement. In addition, some attorneys believe that the letter of intent creates a moral obligation to proceed with the joint venture and therefore would prefer to proceed directly to the definitive joint venture agreement.

Another problem with letters of intent is the tendency of some attorneys to use the letter of intent to negotiate almost all of the joint venture transaction terms. This may result in expensive and protracted negotiations over the words of a document that is not intended to be legally binding.

In general, if there is a letter of intent, it should be confined to a few major business terms, leaving to the final joint venture agreement the detailed negotiations.

Equity vs. Non-Equity

Once the international business has selected the right U.S. partner, it will have to evaluate the possible forms that the cross-border alliance may take. This issue will be seriously affected by the degree of the involvement that each of the parties wish to have in the management of the strategic alliance and how long the alliance should last. As discussed in a previous chapter, an alliance may take the form of a contractual relationship which does not require the creation of a new legal entity separate from the two or more contracting parties. Such a contractual arrangement could include a license, a distributorship agreement, a research and development agreement, a joint bidding contract, etc. These types of strategic alliances are sometimes used for a short-term or one-time project. These types of contractual relationships typically do not require capital investment by either party and serve as a method to enter the U.S. market.

On the other hand, many strategic alliances do require the formation of a new legal entity separate from each of the contracting parties and do require equity investment by each of the contracting parties. Because of this equity investment, these alliances involve not only greater potential risk than non-equity alliances but also have greater potential reward. Moreover, negotiating an equity joint venture is much more complicated than a simple license, distributorship agreement, research development contract, joint bidding agreement, etc.

Thus, the first issue to be discussed in the negotiation is what form will the strategic alliance take and will it involve equity investment. For some kinds of investments in which foreign ownership is restricted, the maximum amount of equity which can be obtained by an international company will be limited by law.

Amount and Form of Contributions

If the joint venture requires a capital infusion, the parties must specify how much each will contribute. In addition, there may be some contribution in kind, such as equipment, furniture, fixtures, technology, etc. The parties must agree on the value of the equity contributions in kind.

The parties must also agree as to what amount of the required capital should be debt or equity. Unlike Chinese-based joint ventures, the U.S. government does not have a specific rule as to the ratio of debt to equity. However, the amount of equity should be sufficient to avoid piercing of the corporate veil and should be adequate for the needs of the business. Moreover, the amount of interest which may be deducted by the joint venture in computing its federal income tax liability may be limited if there is an excessive ratio of debt to equity.

Types of Entities

In the United States, there are various business forms that the law recognizes. There are sole proprietorships, general and limited partnerships, limited liability companies, corporations and joint ventures. The forms of business that are most often utilized by foreign investors are so-called C corporations and limited liability companies.

The final choice of entity will depend primarily upon tax considerations. In this regard, the limited liability company is usually the most tax efficient entity, since it avoids the higher tax applicable to so-called C corporations upon a sale of assets or other dissolution of the joint venture.

Chops Are Not Important; Apparent Authority

As previously discussed, the holder of the chop in a Chinese entity has legal authority to enter into binding contracts. This is not true of U.S. entities.

The closest analogy to the chop in a U.S. entity is a corporate seal. The corporate seal does not confer legal authority upon the holder to enter into contracts on behalf of the joint venture entity. The only effect of the corporate seal in a U.S. entity is, if the contract contains the seal, there may be in certain states a longer period to bring legal claims under the contract which are not barred by the statute of limitations and the legal defense of lack of consideration does not apply. The corporate seal in a U.S. entity has no other binding effect upon the entity except to the extent that it may create apparent authority in its holder to bind the joint venture with respect to third parties.

Under the laws of almost all states in the U.S., officers of the joint venture entity will generally be considered to have apparent authority to legally bind the joint venture entity to contracts that they execute even though they did not have actual authority to do so. Therefore, great care must be taken in selecting the officers of the joint venture entity.

Governance

A critical issue is how the U.S.-based joint venture will be governed. There are no specific rules dictated by the U.S. government except for certain protected industries as discussed in the prior chapter.

The governing documents as well as the joint venture agreement should spell out the governance structure in detail.

Among the issues to be addressed are the following:

- The composition of the board of directors;
- What decisions, if any, of the board of directors require a super majority vote;
- The methods of appointing directors and officers;

- Procedure for meetings of the board of directors and any committees of the board of directors; and
- On what issues must shareholders vote and is the vote required by either a simple majority or a super majority.

Termination Provisions

These provisions were discussed in Chapter 7.

Dispute Resolutions

There are three major arbitration institutions for handling international commercial disputes, namely:

- The American Arbitration Association (AAA), headquartered in New York, New York;
- The International Chamber of Commerce (ICC), headquartered in Paris, France; and

- The London Court of International Arbitration (LCIA), headquartered in London, England.

An Asian joint venture partner may be unwilling to use something called the American Arbitration Association to resolve disputes relating to the joint venture with a U.S. company. However, they may be willing to permit AAA to facilitate the arbitration process if a more neutral set of arbitration rules were used. The United Nations Commission on International Trade (UNCITRAL) has adopted arbitration rules that may be more acceptable to an international joint venture partner.

UNCITRAL was established by the United Nations to help harmonize and unify laws around the world related to international business and trade. It does this in part by promoting uniform practices and procedures and by creating model laws and rules, such as the UNCITRAL Arbitration Rules (as revised in 2010). UNCITRAL does not itself administer or become involved in individual arbitrations. Thus, the UNCITRAL rules can be administered by AAA and make the arbitration clause more acceptable to the foreign national. AAA has specific clauses which permit that result.

In general, it is best to have a very simple arbitration clause, since overemphasizing dispute potential is not conducive to friendly negotiations of an international joint venture.

A simple arbitration clause using the UNCITRAL model arbitration clause might read as follows:

"Any dispute, controversy or claim arising out of or relating to this contract, or the breach, termination or invalidity thereof, shall be settled by arbitration in accordance with the UNCITRAL Arbitration Rules. The appointing authority shall be the American Arbitration Association, New York, New York. The number of arbitrators shall be one and such person shall be a retired judge. The place of the arbitration shall be New York City, New York. The language to be used in the arbitration proceedings shall be English."

Since the arbitrators get paid by the number of hearings they hold, it might be useful to speed things along by adding the following provision: "The arbitrator shall not be paid for hearings held more than 1 year after the appointment of the arbitrator."

Another prominent international arbitral institution is the International Chamber of Commerce (ICC). The critical distinction between the ICC rules and UNCITRAL rules is that, while the UNCITRAL rules are not administered by any particular arbitration institution, the ICC Court of Arbitration administers and supports arbitrations under the ICC rules. The ICC Court of Arbitration formally appoints arbitrators, determines issues not agreed upon between the parties (e.g. number of arbitrators, seat of the arbitration, etc.) and challenges to the appointment of arbitrators, approves terms of reference, and scrutinizes awards before delivery to the parties.

Some Chinese and other Asian investors are motivated to form a U.S. joint venture in order to obtain the benefits of an EB-5 visa, which is discussed in the next chapter.

Chapter 10

Permanent U.S. Residency for Asian Investors

One of the major incentives for making an investment in a U.S. joint venture is to permit the investor and his or her family the ability to immigrate to the U.S.

The U.S. makes available 10,000 EB-5[236] visas each year to individuals who meet certain criteria. The individuals must invest at least $1 million in a new commercial enterprise in the U.S. as well as create a minimum of 10 full-time jobs for qualified U.S. workers (within two years after their admission to the U.S. as Conditional Permanent Residents). If the business is a "troubled business" (as defined below), maintenance of preexisting employment levels will be sufficient. In areas that are rural or dealing with high rates of unemployment (so-called "targeted employment area"), the amount of the investment is only $500,000. There are more than 200 regional centers in the U.S. to assist foreign investors under the pilot EB-5 program and many of these regional centers allow foreign investors to invest in prearranged programs for only $500,000, plus administrative fees.

Investments in joint ventures located in the United States count towards satisfying these requirements since multiple investor entrepreneurs qualify, even though some of the investors are U.S. citizens.[237] Investors meeting the EB-5 visa requirements, who must pass strict background checks for verifying wealth resources, may first gain conditional Green Cards and then see

---

[236] Section 203(b)(5) of the Immigration and Nationality Act.

[237] 8 CFR §204.6(g)

the conditions removed in two years and may choose to become U.S. citizens in five years. Spouses and children, accompanying the Green Card holders, are allowed to apply for authorization to work[238] or attend schools in the United States.

During fiscal year 2011, a total of 3,463 EB-5 visas were issued with the following Asian countries making the top 10[239]:

- People's Republic of China (2,408 or 69.5%)
- Republic of South Korea (254 or 7.3%)
- Taiwan (122 or 3.5%)
- India (37 or 1.1%)

The purpose of this chapter is to initially describe the EB-5 visa program. This chapter ends with the potential of the investor and his or her family to become U.S. citizens.

The EB-5 visa rules are extremely technical and you will need an immigration attorney to help you qualify. The following is a summary of the major requirements.

GENERALLY

To obtain immigrant visa status thorough investment, an alien entrepreneur must establish that he or she "has invested or is in the process of investing the required amount of capital" in a new U.S. commercial enterprise.[240] The investment must be "at risk", must come from a legitimate, lawful source, and cannot be debt. Additionally, the new enterprise must generate at least 10 employment opportunities for "qualifying employees",[241]

---

[238] 8 CFR §274a. 12(c)(9)

[239] "Final Visa Usage Statistics for FY2010" published by U.S. Department of State; see also http://blog.lucidtext.com/2011/02/10/eb-5-visa-usage-by-country-2010/

[240] 8 CFR §204.6(h).

[241] 8 CFR §204.6(e).

unless the enterprise is a "troubled business."[242] Although the alien entrepreneur must be engaged in the management of the enterprise, the activity may be limited to "policymaking" such as serving as a member of the Board of Directors.[243]

Initially, the alien entrepreneur is granted conditional resident status for a two-year period. Approximately 90 days prior to the two-year anniversary, the alien entrepreneur is required to file a petition removing the conditional status and submit evidence that the enterprise is ongoing and continues to meet the requirements of the EB-5 category. The entrepreneur is eligible to file for naturalization after having been a permanent resident for five years. If the entrepreneur dies during the prescribed two-year period of conditional permanent residence, the spouse and children of the entrepreneur will be eligible for removal of conditions if the conditions would have been satisfied by the entrepreneur under the regulations.

NEW COMMERCIAL ENTERPRISE

The commercial enterprise can be any type of business organization as long as the entity (and all subsidiaries for a holding company) are engaged in "for profit" activity.[244] To establish a "new" enterprise, the alien investor must either: (1) create an original business; (2) purchase an existing business and simultaneously or subsequently restructure or reorganize it so that a new enterprise results; or (3) expand an existing business resulting in a 40% increase in either the net worth or number of employees of the enterprise, so that the new net worth, or number of employees, amounts to at least 140% of the pre-expansion net worth or number of employees.[245] Even if the 140% test is met, the

---

[242] Id.

[243] 8 CFR §204.6(j)(5).

[244] 8 CFR §204.6(e).

[245] 8 CFR §204.6(h).

required investment amount and the 10 employee requirement must also be satisfied.

REQUIRED AMOUNT OF INVESTMENT

Generally, the amount of capital the petitioner must invest is $1 million. However, the amount can be reduced to $500,000.00 if the enterprise is principally doing business in a "targeted employment area"[246], defined as (a) a "rural area" namely any area not within (i) a metropolitan statistical area (as designated by the Office of Management and Budget) or (ii) the outer boundary of a city or town of more than 20,000 people, or (b) an area that has experienced high unemployment of at least 150% of the national average rate.[247]

Qualifying capital is defined as ". . . cash, equipment, inventory, other tangible property, cash equivalents, and indebtedness secured by assets owned by the alien entrepreneur, provided that the alien entrepreneur...is personally and primarily liable and that the assets of the new commercial enterprise upon which the petition is based are not used to secure any of the indebtedness"[248] of the entrepreneur. The capital may come from the alien's existing businesses in the U.S.

INVESTMENT "AT RISK"

The investment must be placed "at risk" for the purpose of generating a return on that capital. A mere intent to invest, or prospective investment arrangement entailing no present commitment from the alien entrepreneur, will not suffice

---

[246] 8 CFR §204.6(f)(2).

[247] INA §203(b)(5)(B) .

[248] 8 CFR §204.6(e).

to establish that the petitioner is actively in the process of investing.[249] To evidence that the investment is placed at risk, monies must be deposited in the enterprise's business accounts, assets must be purchased for use in the U.S. business, a transfer of monies to the commercial enterprise in exchange for shares of stock must have occurred, a transfer of assets from abroad for use of the commercial enterprise must have occurred, or a loan, mortgage agreement, promissory note, security agreement, or other evidence of the investor's borrowing (in which he/she is personally liable) must have been executed.[250]

With regards to promissory notes and escrow accounts, there are issues that warrant special consideration. Generally, both the U.S. Citizenship & Immigration Services (USCIS) and the Administrative Appeals Unit (AAO) have issued decisions and rulings, respectively, challenging the use of these schemes as not truly putting the investment "at risk". Use of promissory notes and escrow accounts are permissible however, provided that certain additional standards are met.

"LAWFUL MEANS"

The capital invested must have been obtained through lawful means in order to qualify for investment purposes.[251] The petitioner will have the burden to show source of funds and the legitimacy of the capital. Capital acquired by gift, inheritance, and loans can be considered as qualifying capital.

---

[249] 8 CFR §204.6(j)(2).

[250] Id.

[251] 8 CFR §204.6(j)(3).

TEN FULL-TIME POSITIONS FOR "QUALIFYING EMPLOYEES"

The enterprise must benefit the U.S. economy and must create ten full-time positions for at least 10 U.S. workers.[252] In the case of a joint venture with a U.S. citizen or others, all of the employees will be allocated to the alien entrepreneur even though the alien entrepreneur only invested a portion of the total capital. The regulations define full-time employment as 35 hours per week, except that job sharing is permitted. For purposes of meeting this requirement, independent contractors are not considered "employees."[253] Only U.S. citizens, legal permanent residents, conditional permanent residents, asylees, refugees, or an alien remaining in the U.S. under suspension of deportation are considered U.S. workers. Additionally, the 10 full-time positions cannot be filled by the alien entrepreneur or his or her spouse, sons or daughters, or any nonimmigrant alien.[254]

However, if the business is a "troubled business", the metric for measuring employment is different. A "troubled business" is one that has existed for at least two years, and has experienced a net loss for accounting purposes of at least 20% of the business' net worth in the 12 or 24 months prior to filing the EB-5 petition.[255] In such instances, the enterprise need not create new, full-time positions, but the alien entrepreneur must provide evidence that the business will maintain the pre-acquisition level of employment.[256] For purposes of determining whether the troubled business has been in existence for two years, successor in interest will be deemed to have been in existence for the same time period as their predecessors.

Under a Regional Center Pilot Program, investments through a "Regional Center" allow for a less restrictive job requirement based upon the creation of "indirect" as well as "direct" jobs. A

---

[252] 8 CFR §204.6(j)(4)(i).

[253] 8 CFR §204.6(e).

[254] Id.

[255] Id.

[256] 8 CFR §204.6(j)(4)(ii); Matter of Soffici, 22 I&N Dec 158 (AAO 1998).

list of Regional Centers can be found on the website of the U.S. Citizenship and Immigration Services.[257] The major problem with using a Regional Center is that the alien entrepreneur will typically become a minority equity owner of a larger business with much fewer legal protections than if the alien entrepreneur made the investment directly in a medium or smaller sized business.

MANAGEMENT BY INVESTOR

The investor must be engaged in the management of the enterprise, either thorough day-to-day managerial control or through policy formation.[258] Being a member of the board of directors, which meets only a few times a year to establish policy, is sufficient to satisfy this requirement. Investors who chose to partner in a pooled investment with other investors, including (but not limited to) prearranged investments through a regional center, will typically have very minimal managerial involvement.

MULTIPLE INVESTORS

The establishment of a new commercial enterprise or the qualifying investments in an existing enterprise may be used as the basis of a petition for EB-5 classification by more than one investor.[259] Multiple investors can include non-qualifying investors (e.g. U.S. citizens).

---

[257] http://www.uscis.gov/portal/site/uscis/menuitem.5af9bb95919f35e66f6 14176543f6d1a/?vgnextoid=d765ee0f4c014210VgnVCM100000082ca60aRCR D&vgnextchannel=facb83453d4a3210VgnVCM100000b92ca60aRCRD
[258] 8 CFR §204.6(j)(5).
[259] 8 CFR §204.6(g).

EVIDENCE REQUIRED BY FILING

To file the petition as an investor pursuant to INA §203(b)(5), Form I-526, Immigrant Petition for Alien Entrepreneur, is submitted along with the following:

1) Enterprise: Articles of Incorporation or business organization documents; or evidence of authorization to do business in a state or municipality to establish the "new commercial enterprise."[260]

2) Capital: Documents establishing investment which may include bank statements; evidence of purchased assets; evidence of property transferred from abroad; stock certificates given for investment; or loan or mortgage agreements to establish required amount of investment.[261]

3) Lawful Means: Foreign business registration records; corporate, partnership and personal tax returns filed within 5 years; evidence identifying other sources of capital; certified copies of any judgments or evidence of all pending governmental civil or criminal actions, administrative actions, and any private civil actions involving monetary judgments within the past 15 years to establish the origin of the capital "through lawful means."[262]

4) Ten Full-time Positions: Copies of I-9s and tax records if employees already hired, including proof that they were working full-time; or a comprehensive business plan demonstrating where and when the 10 employees will be hired within a two-year period to establish creation of at least 10 "full-time positions" for "qualifying employees."[263]

5) Management: Title and description of petitioner's duties on a day-to-day basis; evidence that the alien entrepreneur is a corporate officer and director; or if a partnership, the partners' management or policy making activities consistent with the rights, powers and duties normally granted to limited partners

---

[260] 8 CFR §204.6(j)(1).

[261] *Id.*

[262] 8 CFR §204.6(j)(3).

[263] 8 CFR §204.6(j)(4).

under the Uniform Limited Partnership Act to establish actual "management" of the investor.[264]

FILING FOR PERMANENT RESIDENCE

Upon approval of the I-526, the entrepreneur and dependents (spouse and children under 21) can file for permanent residence ("green card") status. Each applicant files a Form I-485, Application to Register Permanent Residence or Adjust Status.[265] The filing is accompanied by a copy of the I-526 Approval Notice, passport-style photographs of the applicant, copies of certain biographical documentation, and sealed results of a medical exam performed by a Designated USCIS Civil Surgeon.

After the Form I-485 is approved, each applicant will receive a Welcome Notice as well as a permanent resident card in the mail. The permanent resident card will be marked as "conditional" and will be valid for two years.

FILING THE APPLICATION TO REMOVE CONDITIONS ON PERMANENT RESIDENCE

Within 90 days of the expiration of the conditional residence, the entrepreneur must file Form I-829, Petition for Entrepreneur to Remove Conditions.[266] Timely filing the Form I-829 automatically extends conditional permanent residence for a six-month period. Failure to file the Form I-829 results in the automatic loss of

---

[264] 8 CFR §204.6(j)(5).

[265] If the applicant is not already residing in the United States, he or she will file a DS-230, Application for Immigrant Visa and Alien Registration with the Department of State to obtain an EB-5 immigrant visa for admission to the United States.

[266] 8 CFR §216.6(a)(1).

permanent residence status upon expiration of the conditional permanent residence card.[267]

The Form I-829 is submitted along with a copy of the entrepreneur's conditional permanent resident card and additional evidence relating to the commercial enterprise:

1) Evidence of the Commercial Enterprise: This includes documentation that the commercial enterprise was established and still exists,[268] evidence that the required amount of capital has been invested in the enterprise[269] and evidence that the enterprise has been sustained throughout the period of conditional permanent residence.[270]

2) Evidence of the Number of Full-Time Employees: This consists of payroll records, relevant tax documents, and I-9s.[271] In the case of a "troubled business," the investor must show that the number of pre-investment employees has been maintained.

BECOMING A U.S. CITIZEN

To become a U.S. citizen (a process known as "naturalization"), each applicant must file Form N-400, Application for Naturalization. An applicant for naturalization must be 18 years old,[272] a lawful permanent resident[273] and of good moral character.[274] The applicant must have maintained continuous residency in the United States for at least five years as a permanent

---

[267] 8 CFR §216.6(a)(5).

[268] 8 CFR §216.6(a)(4)(i).

[269] 8 CFR §216.6(a)(4)(ii).

[270] 8 CFR §216.6(a)(4)(iii).

[271] 8 CFR §216.6(a)(4)(iv).

[272] 8 CFR §316.2(a)(1).

[273] 8 CFR §316.2(a)(2).

[274] 8 CFR §316.2(a)(7).

resident.[275] The applicant must also have been physically present in the United States for at least 30 of the 60 months preceding the filing of the naturalization application.[276]

Continuity of residence is disrupted for naturalization purposes in several situations; the most common issues relate to extended absences or improper filing of tax returns. An absence of more than 6 months but less than 12 months creates a rebuttable presumption of lack of continuity of residence.[277] An absence of 1 year or more destroys the continuity of the residence.[278] Filing income taxes as a "nonresident alien" (or failure to file federal or state income tax returns) raises a rebuttable presumption of abandonment of permanent residence.[279]

After the application is filed, the applicant will be scheduled for an interview at the local USCIS Sub-Office. During this interview, the applicant will be tested for basic English proficiency (basic speaking, reading and writing) as well as U.S. Civics. USCIS offers free study materials for this test online.[280]

After the interview, USCIS completes adjudication of the naturalization application. Upon approval, the applicant is scheduled for an oath ceremony. Once the applicant takes the oath of naturalization, that individual becomes a U.S. citizen. Instructions on voter registration and how to apply for a U.S. passport are provided at the end of the ceremony.

---

[275] 8 CFR §316.2(a)(3). "Residence" is defined as the domicile and actual dwelling place. 8 CFR §316.5(a).

[276] 8 CFR §316.2(a)(4).

[277] 8 CFR §316.5(c)(1)(i).

[278] 8 CFR §316.5(c)(1)(ii).

[279] 8 CFR §316.5(c)(2).

[280] http://www.uscis.gov/portal/site/uscis/menuitem.eb1d4c2a3e5b9ac8-9243c6a7543f6d1a/?vgnextoid=dd7ffe9dd4aa3210VgnVCM100000b92ca60aR CRD&vgnextchannel=dd7ffe9dd4aa3210VgnVCM100000b92ca60aRCRD

XEROX AND FUJI XEROX
(Harvard Law School Case Study)

We are committed to strengthening the strategic and functional coordination of Xerox and Fuji Xerox so that we will compete effectively against strong and unified global competitors.
- Paul Allaire, President and CEO of Xerox Corporation
- Yotaro Kobayashi, President and CEO of Fuji Xerox

Fuji Xerox, the joint venture between Xerox and Fuji Photo Film, was at a pivotal point in its 28-year history in 1990. Many considered it the most successful joint venture in history between an American and a Japanese company. Originally a sales organization for Xerox products in Japan, Fuji Xerox had evolved into a fully integrated operation with strong research, development, and manufacturing capabilities. As its sales and capabilities evolved, so did its importance within the Xerox Group: its 1989 revenues of $3.6 billion represented 22% of the Xerox Group's worldwide revenue.[281] Furthermore, Fuji Xerox supplied the rest of the Xerox Group with low - to mid-range copiers. In Japan, the home country

---

[281] Copyright©1991,1992 by the President and Fellows of Harvard College. Reprinted with the permission of Harvard Business School.HBS case (391 -156). Research Associate Krista McQuade and Professor Benjamin Gomes-Casseres prepared this case as the basis for class discussion rather than to illustrate either effective or ineffective handling of an administrative situation. The Xerox Corporation (XC) is referred to in this case simply as Xerox. The combination of Rank Xerox (RX), Fuji Xerox (FX), and the Xerox Corporation is referred to as the Xerox Group. The revenues of Rank Xerox were consolidated into those of Xerox Corporation, but Fuji

of Xerox's major competitors, Fuji Xerox held 22% of the installed base of copiers and 30% of revenues in the industry.

Yotaro "Tony" Kobayashi, Fuji Xerox's president and CEO, ascribed a good deal of the company's success to the autonomy that the joint venture had enjoyed from the beginning. Fuji Xerox was not "the norm" for joint ventures, he contended, adding that "the degree to which Xerox let us run was very unusual." Yet, paradoxically, as the company grew to represent a larger portion of Xerox's worldwide business (**Exhibit 1**), this situation seemed to be changing. "We have to begin to pay more attention to what our actions mean to Xerox," explained Kobayashi.

Paul Allaire, Xerox's president and CEO, added that Fuji Xerox's autonomy had been an important factor not only in its own success, but also in its growing contribution to the Xerox Group:

The fact that we had this strong company in Japan was of extraordinary importance when other Japanese companies started coming after us. Fuji Xerox was able to see them coming earlier, and understood their development and manufacturing techniques.

We have excellent relationships with Fuji Xerox at the research, development, manufacturing, and managerial levels. Yet, because of this close relationship, there is a greater potential for conflict. If Fuji Xerox were within our organization, it would be easier, but then we would lose certain benefits. They have always had a reasonable amount of autonomy. I can't take that away from them, and I wouldn't want to.

Over the years, Fuji Xerox saw its local competitors grow rapidly through exports. The terms of its technology licensing agreements with Xerox, however, limited Fuji Xerox's sales to Japan

---

Xerox revenues were not. As described below, Xerox Corporation received 66% of RX earnings, which in turn included half of FX earnings."

and certain Far Eastern territories. As Canon, in particular, grew to challenge Xerox worldwide in low-end copiers, laser printers, and color copiers, Fuji Xerox began to feel constrained by the relationship. "Fuji Xerox has aspirations to be a global company in marketing, manufacturing, and research," explained Jeff Kennard, who had managed the relationship between Xerox and Fuji Xerox since 1977. Kobayashi elaborated:

> The goals of Xerox and Fuji Xerox can be described as mostly compatible and partly conflicting. There *are* serious issues facing us. We often compare our situation with that of Canon or Ricoh, companies that have a single management organization in Japan. Are we as efficient and effective in the worldwide management of our business as we could be?

> Some of Fuji Xerox's products, such as facsimile machines, are managed like Canon's — with single-point design and manufacturing. But now there are external conditions in the United States and Europe that call for local manufacturing and development. Rank Xerox and Xerox are able to reach efficient volumes in their marketplaces. If Fuji Xerox manufactures only for Japan and adjacent markets, our volume will be too small, but Xerox is insisting on this. It is a tough challenge that we have to face together.

How should Fuji Xerox's aspirations be managed within the context of the Xerox Group? This was one of the questions facing the Codestiny Task Force commissioned in 1989 to review the capabilities and goals of Xerox and Fuji Xerox. Composed of senior managers from both companies, the task force would seek ways to enhance the strategic relationship between Xerox and Fuji Xerox for the 1990s. This was the third such review; Codestiny I (1982) and Codestiny II (1984) had both resulted in changes in contracts and agreements between the firms. With the basic technology licensing contract between Xerox and Fuji Xerox due to be renegotiated in 1993, participants in Codestiny III knew that their analysis could well lead to a substantial restructuring of the strategic relationship between the companies.

XEROX'S INTERNATIONAL EXPANSION

When Chester Carlson tried to sell the rights to the revolutionary xerographic technology that he invented in 1938, GE, IBM, RCA, and Kodak all turned him down. Instead, the Haloid Corporation—a small photographic paper firm in Rochester, NY—agreed in 1946 to fund further research, and ten years later acquired the full rights to the technology. By the time the company introduced its legendary 914 copier in 1959, xerographic products had come to dominate its business; in 1961 Haloid's name was changed to Xerox Corporation. The 914 was the world's first automatic plain paper copier (PPC), and produced high-quality copies four times faster than any other copier on the market. These advantages, coupled with an innovative machine rental scheme, led Xerox to dominate the industry for nearly 20 years. Company revenues rose from $40 million in 1960 to nearly $549 million in 1965, and to $1.2 billion in 1968, breaking the American record for the fastest company to reach $1 billion in sales. Net income grew from $2.6 million in 1960 to $129 million in 1968. In a mere decade, the name Xerox had become synonymous with copying.

Xerox moved quickly to establish an international network. Lacking the funds to expand alone, it formed a 50/50 joint venture in 1956 with the Rank Organization of Britain. Xerox would be entitled to about 66% of the profits of Rank Xerox. Rank operated a lucrative morion picture business and was seeking opportunities for diversification. Rank Xerox (RX), the new joint venture, was to manufacture xerographic products developed by Xerox and market them exclusively worldwide, except in the United States and Canada. By the early 1960s, Rank Xerox had established subsidiaries in Mexico, Italy, Germany, France, and Australia. In 1964, Xerox bought back the right to market xerographic products in the Western hemisphere.

Japanese firms immediately inquired about obtaining xerography licenses from Rank Xerox, but they were refused on the grounds that the technology was not commercially mature. By 1958, however, RX executives had turned their sights to the

Japanese market. Aware of Japanese government regulations that required foreign firms to sell through local licensees or joint ventures, they sought a strong partner. Twenty-seven Japanese firms jockeyed for the position; Fuji Photo Film (FPF) was the only nonelectronics firm in this group. Still, the company was chosen, partly because of the personal relationship and trust that had developed between RX President Thomas Law and FPF Chairman Setsutaro Kobayashi.

Fuji Photo Film was a manufacturer of photographic film since the early 1930s and second only to Kodak in that field. The company was trying to diversify its business away from silver-based photography, and was convinced that its technical expertise was well suited to the requirements of xerography. Under the direction of Nobuo Shono, the company had already begun experimenting with xerography; by 1958, it had invested six million yen in research and manufacturing facilities for the copiers that it hoped to license from Rank Xerox. As negotiations between the two companies intensified, Rank Xerox insisted on a joint venture instead of simply a license to Fuji Photo Film.

The Establishment of Fuji Xerox

Fuji Xerox, the 50/50 joint venture established by Fuji Photo Film and Rank Xerox in 1962, was originally intended to be a marketing organization to sell xerographic products manufactured by Fuji Photo Film. When the Japanese government refused to approve a joint venture intended solely as a sales company, however, the agreement was revised to give Fuji Xerox manufacturing rights. Fuji Xerox—not Fuji Photo Film—then became the contracting party with Rank Xerox, and received exclusive rights to xerographic patents in Japan. Fuji Xerox, in turn, subcontracted Fuji Photo Film to manufacture the products. As part of its technology licensing agreements with Rank Xerox, Fuji Xerox had exclusive rights to sell the machines in Japan, Indonesia, South Korea, the Philippines, Taiwan, Thailand, and Indochina. In return, Fuji Xerox would pay Rank Xerox a royalty of 5% on revenues from the sale of xerographic products. Rank Xerox would also be entitled to 50% of Fuji Xerox's profits.

Nobuo Shono became Fuji Xerox's first senior managing director, and Setsutaro Kobayashi, its president. Shono and Kobayashi drew their core executive staff, later known as the "Seven Samurai," from the ranks of Fuji Photo Film. A board of directors consisting of representatives from Rank Xerox and Fuji Photo Film was established to decide policy matters, while day-to-day operations were left to the Japanese management. The Xerox Corporation itself was to have no direct relationship with Fuji Xerox, and would participate in the profits of the joint venture only through its share in Rank Xerox.

Although Fuji Xerox adopted a number of business practices from Xerox, including organizational structure and the rental system, it remained distinctly Japanese throughout its history. Hideki Kaihatsu, managing director and chief staff officer at Fuji Xerox, explained:

> Employees are typically rotated through many functions before rising to the level of general management, and compensation and lifetime employment practices are similar to those of other Japanese firms. We emphasize long-term planning, teamwork, and we follow bottom-up decision making, including the "ringi" system. Furthermore, in procuring parts we follow the Japanese practice of qualifying a small group of vendors and working closely with them.

THE DEVELOPMENT OF FUJI XEROX'S CAPABILITIES

Well before negotiations for the joint venture were finalized, engineers at Fuji Photo Film geared up for the production of Xerox copiers. Xerox machines were disassembled and studied to determine the equipment and supplies necessary for production. Three FPF engineers spent 2 months touring Xerox and Rank Xerox production facilities. At the establishment of the joint venture, a specific schedule was agreed upon, calling first for the sale of imported machines, then the assembly of imported knocked-down kits, and finally the domestic production of copiers. Import restrictions in Japan and government pressure to source locally accelerated this schedule, and the first Japanese-produced Xerox 914 was completed in September 1962; by 1965, 90% of the parts for the 914 came from local suppliers.

Fuji Xerox's first sales plan targeted financial institutions, large manufacturing corporations, and central government agencies. At the time of the introduction of the 914, 85% of the market was held by the inexpensive diazo type of copier. Although these copiers were difficult to operate and produced poor quality copies, they had been enormously successful in Japan, as the large number of characters in the Japanese language made typewriters difficult to use, and made copiers essential even for small offices. Ricoh, Copyer, and Mita had sold diazo copiers since the 1940s. By the early 1960s, Ricoh held an estimated 75% share of the market. A diazo copy was often referred to as a "Ricopy" in Japan.

Though Fuji Xerox had intended to sell the 914 copier outright, at Rank Xerox's insistence it implemented Xerox's trademark rental system. Within a year, the back-order list for the copier was 5 months' long. Output rose fivefold in five years, and Fuji Photo Film soon built a second production facility. In 1967, Fuji Xerox's sales passed those of Rank Xerox's French and German subsidiaries. Fuji Xerox's product line expanded to include other models, including a faster version of the 914, and a smaller, desktop model. The 2400, capable of making 40 copies per minute (cpm)[282], was introduced in 1967. Sales subsidiaries were established throughout Fuji Xerox's licensed territory.

By the late 1960s, Fuji Xerox dominated the high-volume segment of the Japanese copier market. Ricoh, however, had made great inroads into the middle segment with an electrostatic copier based on an RCA technology, and was squeezing Fuji Xerox's

---

282 The copier market was typically divided into low-, mid-, and high-volume segments. In the 1960s, the 2400 was considered a high-volume model; the original 914 copier made seven copies per minute. In the 1980s, copiers making less than 25 cpm were generally considered low-volume, while those making over 90 cpm were considered high-volume.

market from below. In addition to the threat of substitute technologies, Fuji Xerox faced the end of its monopoly in plain paper copying; some of Xerox's core patents were scheduled to expire between 1968 and 1973. FX managers were already aware of efforts by several Japanese firms to develop plain paper copiers. In response to these pressures, Peter McColough, Xerox's president and CEO at the time, proposed to transfer the manufacture of copiers from Fuji Photo Film to Fuji Xerox, and in this way combine manufacturing and marketing activities under one roof. McColough described the rationale for this decision:

> Fuji Xerox had to develop its own manufacturing capability. It had built up a good marketing organization, but had no assured source of supply. That left the company vulnerable. Fuji Photo Film initially resisted this idea because it would lose manufacturing volume and product revenues. They realized in the end that the issue went to the heart of the joint venture. Looking back, that was the most difficult period in our relationship.

In 1971, Fuji Photo Film transferred its copier plants to Fuji Xerox. That same year, Fuji Xerox completed the construction of a 160,000 square-foot manufacturing and engineering facility. From then on, Fuji Photo Film had little direct role in Fuji Xerox's operations. Yoichi Ogawa, senior managing director at Fuji Xerox in 1989 and one of the Seven Samurai, explained why Fuji Photo Film remained a passive partner after 1971:

> According to Fuji Photo Film's agreement with Xerox, the company, as a shareholder, could collect information from Fuji Xerox, but it could not use it in its own operations. In addition, a technology agreement between Fuji Xerox and Xerox provided that any technology acquired by Fuji Xerox from outside sources (including from Fuji Photo Film) could be freely passed on to Xerox.

In a separate development, Rank Xerox also lost much of its direct role in Fuji Xerox's operations. In December 1969, Xerox bought an additional 1% share of Rank Xerox from the Rank Organization, giving it 51% control of that joint venture. From then on, Rank Xerox would be managed as a Xerox subsidiary. Moto Sakamoto, an FX resident at Rank Xerox at the time, noticed an immediate change: "Things changed instantly as the Americans started coming in... gone was the old British style of management." Sakamoto was transferred to Xerox's main facility in Rochester, NY, as Fuji Xerox began to deal directly with Xerox. Rank Xerox's ownership share in Fuji Xerox remained at 50%, and the Xerox Corporation continued to receive 66% of Rank Xerox's profits, and therefore 33% of Fuji Xerox's.

Product Development at Fuji Xerox

The transfer of production facilities to Fuji Xerox and the direct relationship established between Fuji Xerox and Xerox contributed to a continued strengthening of FX technical capabilities. Fuji Photo Film engineers had already been making modifications to Xerox designs in order to adapt the copiers to the local market; Japanese offices, for example, used different sized paper than American offices. Nobuo Shono, however, advocated the development of long-term R&D capabilities that would enable the company to develop its own products. In particular, he envisioned a high-performance, inexpensive, compact machine that could copy books. At the time, Xerox's priorities were different. Tony Kobayashi explained:

> We had been insisting that the Xerox Group needed to develop small copiers as an integral part of its worldwide strategy. However, Xerox's attitude was that the low end of the market was not a priority.... On the other hand, we were seeing rising demand for small copiers in Japan.[283]

---

[283] Quoted in "Fuji Xerox Company, Ltd." Translation of a case study prepared by the Nomura School of Advanced Management in Tokyo.

Shono's development group produced four experimental copiers, each with projected manufacturing costs approximately half those of Xerox's smallest machine. When they first heard of the effort, engineers at Rank Xerox and Xerox doubted that these models could become commercially viable. Shono persisted, and in 1970 took a working prototype to London, where its performance amazed Rank Xerox executives. The machine was slow (5 cpm), but substantially smaller and lighter than comparable Xerox models. This demonstration immediately boosted Fuji Xerox's technical reputation within the Xerox Group, and for the first time Xerox allowed Fuji Xerox a small budget for R&D. In 1973, the FX2200 — the world's smallest copier — was introduced in Japan with the slogan: "It's small, but it's a Xerox." The speed of the FX2200 was doubled in 1977 by the FX2202, and the basic model was improved further by the FX2300 and the FX2305.

Mushrooming Competition

The FX2200 appeared just in time to face an avalanche of new and serious competition. Canon was the first Japanese company to enter the plain paper copier market, introducing its low end "New Process" copiers in 1970; these machines were developed in-house and did not infringe on any Xerox patent. Ricoh and Konica, Fuji Photo Film's chief Japanese rivals in film, followed with their own technologies. In 1972, Canon made another major move by introducing copiers using liquid instead of dry toner. This technology was later licensed to Saxon, Ricoh, and Copyer. Liquid-toner copiers had the advantage of being smaller and less expensive to manufacture than dry-toner copiers like Xerox's, but they were cumbersome to use. They were introduced as a cheap alternative to Xerox dry copiers. Minolta, Copia, Mita, Sharp, and Toshiba also entered the plain paper copier industry; by 1975, eleven companies competed in the Japanese market.

In addition to developing small machines for its local market, Fuji Xerox tried to stem the competitive onslaught with more aggressive sales strategies. The company began to offer two- and three-year rental contracts as well as its standard one-year contract, and provided price incentives that were tied to contract length. It also began to offer three of its new low-priced copiers for outright sale, as the competition had been doing. Matazo Terada, one of the Seven Samurai, recalled that when the company tried to sell copiers before, Xerox management resisted:

> Xerox insisted on uniform policies—every country had to be managed like the U.S. firm. That was successful only while we were protected from competitors because of our monopoly. If Xerox had been more flexible from the beginning, we might have captured a larger market. That was a lost opportunity.

By 1977, Ricoh accounted for 34% of the number of copiers installed in Japan. Fuji Xerox followed with 25%, Canon with 15%, and Konica with 10%. In terms of copy volume, however, Fuji Xerox led the competition with more than 50% of the market, followed by Ricoh with 20%, and Canon and Konica with 10% each. In the low end of the market, Ricoh accounted for 50% of copy volume, compared to 10% for Fuji Xerox.

Fuji Xerox's TQC Movement

Partly as a response to the new competition of the 1970s, as well as the oil shock and recession of 1973-1975, Fuji Xerox launched a Total Quality Control (TQC) program. Fuji Photo Film had operated a successful statistical quality control program, and in 1956 won the prestigious Deming Prize, awarded to companies that had shown outstanding quality management throughout their organization. Fuji Xerox's New Xerox Movement had three primary aims: to speed up the development of products that matched customer needs; to reduce costs and eliminate waste; and to adopt aggressively the latest technologies.

The focal point of the campaign was the development of "dantotsu," roughly translated as the "Absolute No. 1 Product." Company executives challenged the marketing and engineering departments to develop a product fitting this description in less time and at a lower cost than the competition. For 6 months, project proposals were turned down until the basic concept for the new product emerged in 1976: a compact, 40 cpm machine manufactured for half the price of any comparable machine, with half the number of parts of previous models, and developed in two years, compared to Xerox's typical four. Setsutaro's son, Tony Kobayashi, who became FX president in 1978 after his father died, explained:

> This was the first time Fuji Xerox had developed a copier based on our own design concept. The FX2200 copier we previously developed was an improved adaptation of a model developed in the United States. The American system of development was well established in our company. However, the U.S. way of developing new products on a step-by-step basis was too time consuming for our dynamic environment. The competition in the Japanese market required us to study the development systems of our rivals. . . . We found that we had been spending too much time in development. That is why we formulated the design concept for the new model and committed the entire company's resources to its development within a very limited timetable.[284]

The FX3500 was indeed introduced two years later, and by 1979, it had broken the Japanese record for the number of copiers sold in one year. Ricoh and Canon rushed to develop copiers that could compete in the FX3500's market segment. Largely because of Fuji Xerox's effort to develop the FX3500, the company won the Deming Prize in 1980. In addition, the FX3500 firmly established Fuji Xerox as a technologically competent member of the Xerox Group. David Kearns, who would become Xerox's president in 1977, was amazed when he first saw a demonstration of the FX3500 prototype, and spontaneously broke out in applause.

Later, some observers labeled the FX3500 Fuji Xerox's "declaration of independence." The FX3500 project came after Xerox canceled a series of low- to mid-volume copiers on which Fuji Xerox was depending. Code-named SAM, Moses, Mohawk, Elf,

---

[284] Quoted in "Fuji Xerox Company, Ltd."

Peter, Paul, and Mary, they were each canceled in mid-development, even though Fuji Xerox had gaps in its product range in the Japanese market. Jeff Kennard remembered that when Tony Kobayashi was told about the cancellation of Moses, he was also asked to stop work on the FX3500 project. "Tony refused," Kennard recalled, adding that Kobayashi said, in effect, "As long as I am responsible for the survival of this company, I can no longer be totally dependent on you for developing products. We are going to have to develop our own."

XEROX'S LOST DECADE

During the 1970s, competition in the U.S. and European copier markets changed radically. Prior to that period, Xerox had had a virtual monopoly because of its xerography patents. But beginning in 1970, one competitor after another entered the industry, often with new and improved PPC technologies. The Xerox Group share of worldwide PPC revenues fell from 93% in 1971 to 60% in 1975, and 40% in 1985 (**Exhibit 2**). This was Xerox's "lost decade"—an era of increasing competition, stagnating product development, and costly litigation.

New Competition High and Low

The proliferation of PPC vendors that started in Japan in the early 1970s soon appeared in the United States and Europe. By 1975, approximately 20 PPC manufacturers operated worldwide, including reprographic companies (Xerox, Ricoh, Mita, Copyer, A.B. Dick, AM, and 3M), paper companies (Dennison, Nashua, and Saxon), office equipment companies (IBM, SCM, Litton, and Pitney Bowes), photographic equipment companies (Canon, Konica, Kodak, and Minolta), and consumer electronics companies (Sharp and Toshiba).

Canon's New Process copiers were the first to hit the U.S. market, followed by a wave of liquid-toner copiers. The new

Japanese machines were priced aggressively, and sold outright through independent dealers. On average, these machines broke down half as often as Xerox copiers. Canon sold under its own brand name, taking advantage of its reputation for quality photographic products, and supported its dealers through extensive financing, and sales and service training. Ricoh sold its machines through Savin Business Machines and the Nashua Corporation. Savin, primarily a marketing company, had funded the Stanford Research Institute's development of a liquid-toner copier, and subsequently had licensed Ricoh to manufacture the machines. The first Ricoh machines using this new technology were introduced in 1975 and were an instant success. Konica, Toshiba, Sharp, and Minolta, entered the U.S. market through OEM relationships, as well as with their own brands.

Despite the entrance of so many Japanese competitors into the U.S. market, Xerox initially did little to respond to them. These competitors targeted the low end of the market, leaving Xerox's most important segments seemingly unaffected. Furthermore, Xerox continued to dominate the world copier market, with revenues that rose each year by more than Savin's total copier sales. Xerox executives were more concerned by the entrance of IBM and Eastman Kodak into the copier industry, as these companies targeted the mid- and high-volume segments. (See **Exhibit 3**.)

IBM's introduction of its Copier I in 1970 signaled the end of Xerox's monopoly in its home market. Although IBM's first model was not successful because of a combination of high price and performance problems, the Copier II, introduced in 1972, began to take market share away from Xerox. These machines were marketed by IBM's office products sales force on a rental basis, supported by heavy advertising. IBM introduced the Copier II in Europe and Japan in 1975, and by 1976 had installed 80,000 copiers worldwide, against Xerox's estimated 926,000. IBM's high-volume Copier III came out in 1976, but was withdrawn because of reliability problems. It was reintroduced as a mid-volume machine early in 1978, but IBM's copier business suffered permanently from the setback.

Eastman Kodak's main facilities were located across town from Xerox's in Rochester, NY. Kodak's success as a high-technology, chemistry-based, American firm had been a model for Xerox's founders and early leaders. When Kodak introduced the high-end Ektaprint 100 copier in 1975, however, admiration quickly turned to intense rivalry. Unlike the IBM Copier I, Kodak's first machine was extremely innovative. In particular, it featured a microcomputer that monitored the performance of the copier and alerted operators to problems through a digital display. A central computer at Kodak monitored the trouble signals and dispatched service people to a machine before breakdown. The machines were also capable of excellent reproduction. The Ektaprint series was well accepted in the marketplace, and quickly gained a reputation for the highest-quality image reproduction in the field.

Xerox's Stagnation

In its first competitive actions against IBM, Kodak, and the Japanese entrants, Xerox could not come up with a winning strategy. It focused R&D on developing a super high-speed copier and field-tested its first color copier in 1971; neither became a commercial success. Xerox's mid-volume 4000 and 3100 series, introduced in the early 1970s, suffered from reliability problems and were also commercial failures. Even when the price of the 3100 was slashed from $12,000 to $4,400, it did not sell well. Ricoh/Savin became the top seller in the U.S. market in 1976, and Xerox's market share in the United States continued to fall. However, the seriousness of Xerox's situation was slow to sink in, according to David Kearns:

> . . . we dominated the industry we had created. We were convinced that we were providing the world with high-quality machines, and our convictions were reinforced by the broad acceptance of Xerox products by our customers. We had always been successful, and we assumed that we would

continue to be successful. Our success was so overwhelming that we became complacent.[285]

About 1978, Fuji Xerox offered to sell its FX2202 copier to Xerox and Rank Xerox to help them counter Japanese competition in the United States and Europe. Rank Xerox purchased 25,000 of the machines, but Xerox Corporation refused to buy any.[286] Bill Glavin, the managing director at Rank Xerox at that time, noted:

> We had never placed such a large order before and expected to sell them in 12 months. Two thousand machines per month was an incredible rate of sales, but we did it. For Tony Kobayashi, that order must have represented a substantial part of his production that year. We worked closely with them, and they gave us top-notch support.

This first successful cooperation led Rank Xerox to import more of the FX machines. In addition, Kodak had delayed its entry into Europe by two years, giving Rank Xerox time to formulate a defensive marketing strategy for the high end. As for IBM, its excellent distribution network and reputation in Europe could not make up for a generally inferior product. As Wayland Hicks, the general manager of Rank Xerox's U.K. operating company in the late 1970s, noted, "If IBM had Kodak's product, Xerox would have been dead." Rank Xerox was able to defend its market share while Xerox's U.S. share continued to decline.

In 1979, largely because of Rank Xerox's success with the FX product, Xerox began to import the FX2202, and later the FX2300 and the FX2350. Typically, in the year that the products were introduced in the U.S. market, the machines were assembled by Fuji Xerox before export. Then, acceding to union demands in the United States, Fuji Xerox exported them as knock-down units to

---

[285] David T. Kearns, "Leadership Through Quality," *Academy of Management Executive,* vol. 4 (1990): 86-89.

[286] Although Xerox had acquired control of Rank Xerox in 1969, the line operations of the two firms were not integrated until 1978. Rank Xerox could thus make this decision in relative autonomy.

be assembled at Xerox. "Some of our people had been reluctant to import FX machines," recalled Peter McColough. "Our engineers felt that they had developed xerography, and that the first FX machines weren't good enough."

Courtroom Battles

Xerox became involved in the 1970s in a series of courtroom battles. Immediately after IBM came out with its Copier I in 1970, Xerox sued for patent infringement, and IBM countersued. The companies argued 12 separate counts in the United States and Canada. Xerox won some of these suits and the rest were settled in 1978, when the firms agreed to an exchange of patents covering all information-handling products and to a $25 million payment to Xerox. Two other American firms, the SCM Corporation and Van Dyk Research, sued Xerox for alleged antitrust violations in 1973 and 1975, respectively, each claiming $1.5 billion in damages. Both lost their suits in 1978-1979.

More damaging still, the Federal Trade Commission (FTC) initiated action against Xerox in 1973, charging that the firm controlled 95% of the plain paper copier industry, and that its pricing, leasing, and patent-licensing practices violated the Sherman Antitrust Act. The FTC demanded that Xerox offer unrestricted, royalty-free licenses on all its copier patents, that it divest itself of Rank Xerox and Fuji Xerox, and that it allow third parties to service, maintain, and repair copiers leased from Xerox. In 1975, Xerox settled out of court by signing a consent decree with the FTC, in which it agreed to license more than 1,700 past and future patents for a period of 10 years. Competitors were permitted to license up to three patents free of royalties, to pay 0.5% of revenues on the next three, and to license additional patents royalty free. Xerox also agreed to forgive past patent infringements, to cease offering package-pricing plans on machines and supplies, and to begin outright sales of machines.

Kodak, IBM, Canon, Ricoh, and other Japanese firms were among the firms to secure Xerox licenses under this arrangement.

At this point, the Japanese firms that had entered the market with liquid-toner copiers switched to Xerox's dry-toner process.

ADJUSTING THE RELATIONSHIP BETWEEN XEROX AND FUJI XEROX

As Fuji Xerox's business grew and Xerox's came under increasing pressure at home, the relationship between the two companies changed. The original joint venture and technology assistance agreements of the early 1960s were updated in 1976 and in 1983, and numerous interim agreements were signed to adjust policies on such issues as procurement and relations to third parties (**Exhibit 4**). Bob Meredith, a lawyer by training and Xerox's resident director in Tokyo, described the role of these contracts:

> The legal contracts are flexible. We don't follow an adversarial, arm's-length approach, where you might try to gain short-term advantage or act opportunistically. The equity commitment focuses our relationship on one main objective: What is the profit-maximizing thing to do?

Technology agreements and other contracts between Xerox and Fuji Xerox provided guidelines for the relationship. In addition, the contracts specified royalties and transfer pricing procedures. In 1976, a Technology Assistance Contract (TAC) had been signed by Xerox and Fuji Xerox, which maintained the 5% royalty that Xerox received from Fuji Xerox's xerographic sales, and that was to last 10 years. During the Codestiny I discussions, however, the royalty structure of the contract was revised. The 1983 TAA established a basic royalty on Fuji Xerox's total sales, representing Fuji Xerox's right to use the Xerox tradename and technology in its licensed territory. The royalty on xerographic sales, however, was set to decline annually between 1983 and 1993. In addition, for the first time Fuji Xerox would begin receiving a manufacturing license fee (MLF), designed to compensate it for its development and manufacturing investments. In particular, an MLF of up to 20% could be added to the unit costs of FX machines exported in knocked-down form and assembled and sold by Xerox.

These and other subtle changes in the relationship between the two firms tended to reinforce Fuji Xerox's autonomy. David Kearns recalled how he worked to "unfetter" Fuji Xerox in the late 1970s:

> Xerox was attempting to control so many aspects of Fuji Xerox's operations. We were reviewing their marketing strategies, what products they were going to develop, and so on. But it didn't make sense to me to try to run the business from thousands of miles away. So, I encouraged them to pursue their own strategies and develop their own products. Of course, they were moving in that direction anyway.

TURNING AROUND XEROX

In 1979, Xerox began to formalize a strategy based on the reality of its declining position in the copier industry. Kearns recalled the initial shock of the necessity to do so:

> The Japanese were selling products in the United States for what it cost us to *make* them. We were losing market share rapidly, but didn't have the cost structure to do anything about it. I was not sure if Xerox would make it out of the 1980s.

One of Xerox's strategies was to diversify out of copiers by acquiring a number of financial services companies between 1983 and 1988. Financial services, Kearns believed, would provide "an anchor in a nonmanufacturing business, and one in which Japanese companies were not active overseas." Before the financial services industry went sour at the end of the decade, this line of business was a steady source of earnings for Xerox, providing more than $2 billion in profits in five years. In 1989, however, financial services' earnings declined significantly and substantial assets were written off.

Kearns also began to take a closer look at the strategies of Fuji Xerox and other Japanese companies. Upon importing the first FX products, Xerox engineers had been amazed by a reject rate for parts that was a mere fraction of the American rate, and by substantially lower manufacturing costs. Visits to FX facilities introduced Xerox executives to the practice of "benchmarking," or systematically tracking costs and performance in all areas of operations against those of the best in the field. The findings from Xerox's own benchmarking efforts helped fuel Kearns's efforts to infuse his organization with new vision and determination.

In 1981, Kearns announced a companywide initiative for "business effectiveness," and two years later formally launched Xerox's Leadership Through Quality program. Xerox's program was based on the experience of Fuji Xerox, and throughout the effort, Kearns called upon Kobayashi and others at Fuji Xerox for help. Xerox hired Japanese consultants recommended by Fuji Xerox, and some 200 high-level Xerox and Rank Xerox managers visited Fuji Xerox in later years to learn first-hand about its TQC management and philosophy. The Leadership Through Quality program emphasized high employee involvement in attaining five major goals: (1) increased market research and competitive benchmarking; (2) just-in-time manufacturing to decrease costs; (3) faster product development; (4) development of state-of-the-art technology; and (5) a devotion to quality in all areas.

The rallying point for Xerox's quality movement was the development of the 10 Series, a new family of copiers. Wayland Hicks, in charge of this development effort, stated: "The Xerox turnaround started on September 22, 1982, at the announcement of the 1075 in New York." Led by this mid-volume machine, the 10 Series became the most successful line of copiers in Xerox history, and served to restore the company's finances and morale. The series—dubbed the "Marathon" family of copiers—represented a new generation of machines aimed primarily at the mid-volume segment of the market. Altogether, some fourteen models were introduced between 1982 and 1986, six of which were still sold in

1990. Fuji Xerox designed and produced the low end models in the 10 Series — the 1020, 1035, and the 1055, the latter drawing on basic technologies developed for the FX3500. The 1075 became the first American-made product to win Japan's Grand Prize for Good Design. Because at that time Xerox's Japanese competitors were not strong in mid-volume copiers, the 10 Series forestalled their move into that segment of the market and helped Xerox win back market share. The company regained 2-3 percentage points in 1983, and 12 points in 1984. By the end of 1985, more than 750,000 10 Series machines had been rented or sold, accounting for nearly 38% of Xerox's worldwide installed base.

Throughout the 1980s, Xerox continued to change the way it did business. For example, over 100,000 employees went through 3 days of off-site training to unite the entire organization behind the quality effort. The program achieved significant improvements in Xerox operations. After reducing its supplier base, the company reduced its purchased parts' costs by 45% and their quality was improved dramatically. Xerox's average manufacturing costs were reduced by 20% and the time-to-market for new products was cut by 60%. Xerox's progress was recognized by the U.S. Commerce Department in 1989, when the company's Business Products and Systems division received the Malcolm Baldrige National Quality Award for its "preeminent quality leadership." (Xerox's 1980s financial results are in **Exhibit 5**.)

XEROX AND FUJI XEROX IN THE 1990S

The Canon Challenge

A number of factors were expected to continue to draw Fuji Xerox and Xerox closer to each other in the 1990s. One was the continuously rising capabilities of the Xerox Group's competitors, particularly Canon. While Xerox's precipitous decline in the 1970s had been stemmed and many of the competitors from that decade had faded away, Canon's copier business continued to expand. From 1980 to 1989, Canon's total sales grew from $2.9

billion to $9.4 billion, a growth rate of 14% per year. Canon's R&D spending grew even more rapidly at 24% per year, from $77 million to $525 million. By 1989, Canon was no longer primarily a camera company — 40% of its revenues came from copiers, and 20% from laser printers.

In the second half of the 1980s, Canon developed a dominating presence in the low end laser printers that were becoming ubiquitous companions to microcomputers. Laser printing technology was closely related to plain paper copying technology, and as digital copying systems were introduced, the importance of laser printing in the PPC market was bound to increase. Canon's laser printing engines were the core of the highly successful Hewlett-Packard Laserprinter series, which accounted for about 50% of laser printer sales in the United States. This OEM business was thought to yield Canon some $1 billion in revenues. In the rest of the world, Canon sold printers under its own brand name.

In copiers, Canon was strong in the low end of the market, and had recently developed a growing business in color copiers, where it held 50% of the market by 1989. Analysts pointed out that Canon was introducing twice as many products as the Xerox Group, although it spent less than $600 million on R&D annually, compared to Xerox's $800 million and Fuji Xerox's $300 million. Canon's goal was to become a $70 billion company by the year 2000, implying a 22% annual growth rate in the 1990s. A significant portion of this growth was projected to come from Xerox's heartland — high- and mid-volume copiers and printers.

Xerox, however, was determined to be aggressive in its response. Hicks, who in 1989 had become the executive vice president for worldwide marketing at Xerox, hung a framed blow-up of a 1984 *Fortune* article on Canon in his office. It was entitled "And Then We Will Attack;" below it Hicks hung a sign that read: "And Then They Will Lose."

Xerox Group strategists saw the relationship between Xerox and Fuji Xerox as a critical element in competing worldwide against Canon. Canon had a strong presence in all major world markets, as did the Xerox companies (**Exhibit 6**). But Xerox CEO Paul Allaire highlighted a major difference in the two firms' global networks: "When we negotiate with Fuji Xerox, we can't just represent ourselves. We need to find what is fair and equitable to essentially three partners. Canon is 100% owned by one company."

The Fuji Xerox Challenge

Another trend drawing Fuji Xerox and Xerox closer was the growth of Fuji Xerox itself (**Exhibit 7**). Fuji Xerox's dollar revenues grew faster than Xerox's in the 1980s, and represented a more significant portion of the Xerox Group's worldwide revenues than it had previously. Fuji Xerox's financial contribution to Xerox's net earnings in the form of royalties and profits had also grown sharply — from 5% in 1981 to 22% in 1988. And throughout the decade, Fuji Xerox had been an important source of low end copiers for Xerox. Between 1980 and 1988, Fuji Xerox's sales to Xerox and Rank Xerox grew from $32 million to $620 million (**Exhibit 8**). "Fuji Xerox is a critical asset of Xerox," concluded Allaire.

Fuji Xerox developed its technological capabilities further in the 1980s, investing heavily in R&D (**Exhibit 9**). While it continued to rely on Xerox for basic research on new technologies, by the late 1980s very few of the models sold by Fuji Xerox in Japan had been designed by Xerox (**Exhibit 10**). For the most part, they were high-end models, working at speeds of above 120 cpm. Heavy investment by Fuji Xerox during the late 1980s had produced many low-end models, and even a few in the 60-90 cpm range. Many of these were exported to or manufactured by Xerox and Rank Xerox. In 1980, 70% of the low-volume units sold by Xerox and Rank Xerox were of their own design, and 30% were of Fuji Xerox design; by 1987, 94% were of Fuji Xerox design. Even in 1989, however, all of Xerox and Rank Xerox's mid- and high-volume copiers were of their own design.

All these factors led Fuji Xerox and Xerox to intensify their cooperation on research, product development, manufacturing, and planning in the 1980s. Bill Glavin and Jeff Kennard worked together to launch "strategy summits." Glavin described why:

We needed the senior management of research, engineering, manufacturing, and planning from both companies to come together, and begin discussing the issues that affected them jointly. The talks included people from all product lines —- copiers, printers, and systems. We tried to agree on common strategies and allocate who should do what.

These top management summits were held about twice a year during the 1980s, and led to further meetings between the functional organizations on each side. Fuji Xerox's organization mirrored Xerox's: a corporate research group did basic and applied research; machines were designed and built by the development and manufacturing organization; and products were sold and serviced by the marketing organization. Collaboration between Xerox and Fuji Xerox seemed to be most successful in research, and harder to implement in development and manufacturing; there was no coordination at all between marketing groups, as each had a different licensed territory. Of course, there was some tendency to protect traditional turfs. "On both sides you cannot totally dismiss the NIH syndrome," commented Tony Kobayashi. "It is another form of parochialism." Still, where the incentives for collaboration were high, the companies launched joint projects, agreeing on who would take "lead" and "support" roles and eliminating overlapping activities. Bill Spencer, Xerox vice president of technology at the time, described the rationale behind one of these joint research projects:

> It is an attempt to combine American ingenuity with the manufacturing skills of the Japanese. Xerox has excellent basic research and software capabilities, and Fuji Xerox is good at development and hardware design. Together, we should be able to develop better products quicker than alone.

The functional collaboration between the companies was reinforced by exchanges of personnel and by an evolving communication process. Since the 1970s, personnel from Fuji Xerox had spent time as residents at Xerox and engineers from both companies had frequently crossed the Pacific to provide on-the-spot assistance. These personnel exchanges had, in fact, been an important channel for the transfer of technology from Xerox to Fuji Xerox. By 1989, an estimated 1000 young, high-potential FX employees had spent three years each as residents at Xerox, and some 150 Xerox people had done this at Fuji Xerox. These residents were directly involved in the work of their host companies. Every year there were also some 1000 shorter visits by engineers and managers. These exchanges and the summit meetings contributed to a constructive relationship. "Whenever a problem came up, we established a process to manage it," explained Jeff Kennard. "The trust built up between the companies has been a key factor in the success of this relationship. It enables one to take on short-term costs in the interest of long-term gains for the group."

By the mid-1980s, most Xerox managers also had mixed feelings of challenge and admiration toward Fuji Xerox, which were echoed by Kennard:

> It seems that every time Xerox blinks and retracts, Fuji Xerox forges ahead. Fuji Xerox continues to be the agent for change. They have great corporate vision and they target what is strategically important. Then they take tough decisions and make the needed investment.

The Management Challenge

In this context, Allaire and Kobayashi commissioned the Codesriny III Task Force, charging it with developing a framework for cooperation between the two companies in the 1990s. The task force consisted of top planners in each company and was to report to the two CEOs within a year of its formation. Roger Levien, Xerox's vice president for strategy and head of the Codesriny III talks, described the motivation for the project:

Fuji Xerox had certain issues they wanted to discuss, and we agreed to do so in the Codesriny process. One of their desires was to get the worldwide market for the low end. They also wanted to develop a more symmetric relationship with us. We wanted to spell everything out, identify all of the alternatives, and leave the final decision to top management.

One of the issues to be addressed by the Codesriny team was Fuji Xerox's aspirations to expand its markets in Asia. Under the existing technology licensing contracts, Fuji Xerox had the right to sell in Indonesia, South Korea, the Philippines, Taiwan, and Thailand (total GDP in 1989: $570 billion), and it had indeed established sales subsidiaries in each of these markets. But Rank Xerox in London was responsible for managing sales in what it called the South Pacific Operations — Australia (1989 GDP: $280 billion), New Zealand ($45 billion), Singapore ($28 billion), Malaysia ($37 billion), China ($420 billion), and Hong Kong ($63 billion). Since the early 1980s, Fuji Xerox had argued that this arrangement led to inefficiencies in serving the South Pacific markets. At that time, knock-down kits were sometimes shipped from Fuji Xerox to Britain for assembly, and then shipped back to Asia for sale. Furthermore, Rank Xerox followed a very different marketing strategy in these markets than Fuji Xerox did in its neighboring Asian markets. Rank Xerox emphasized high profit margins and sales of high-end machines, whereas Fuji Xerox put greater emphasis on market share and low end products. As a result, when Fuji Xerox urged Rank Xerox in the late 1970s to adopt a more aggressive sales strategy in Australia before Canon entered that market, Rank Xerox refused. Although Rank Xerox managed the South Pacific countries out of a regional office in Hong Kong, Fuji Xerox's sales subsidiaries were usually joint ventures with local partners, and so drew more on local management talent.

Another key issue for the Codestiny team was how the Xerox Group should manage the low-end laser printer business in the United States. This market segment was receiving renewed attention in 1989, following the appointment of Bill Lowe as Xerox's executive vice president for development and manufacturing.

Lowe came to Xerox from IBM, where he had been in charge of the personal computer business. Soon after arriving at Xerox, he began to focus on the problems in the low-end copier and printer businesses, where Fuji Xerox typically developed and manufactured products sold by Xerox.

> Both companies were trying to get full profit out of it, even though the margins were slim. Fuji Xerox's policy was to mark up costs; Xerox's was to get an acceptable gross profit. Furthermore, each product had a different mark-up scheme, and many sideline deals confounded the issues. This fostered sharp dealings between the partners. So, most of our energy was focused on each other, not on Canon. We were pointing fingers and frustrating ourselves.

The Codestiny team analyzed these specific issues within a broad framework, and began by outlining the various options available for cooperation in marketing, research, and development and manufacturing (**Exhibit 11**). The team considered the advantages and disadvantages of each of these options and began to develop possible strategies for the South Pacific Operations and for the low-end printer business in the United States.

But there was much more at stake than decisions in these two areas. The central question facing Xerox and Fuji Xerox was: How should the relationship between the two companies be structured and managed in the new global environment of the 1990s?

Exhibit 1   Growth of Xerox Corporation and Fuji Xerox, 1968-1989

Xerox and Fuji Xerox Revenues

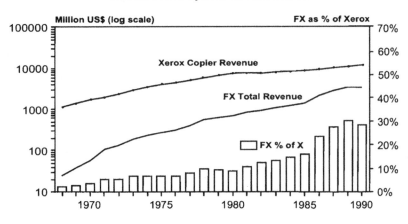

Xerox and Fuji Xerox Earnings

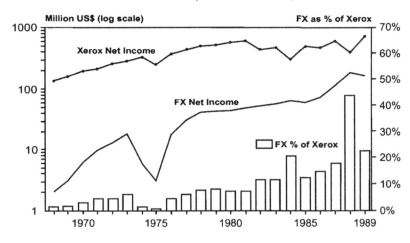

Source: Xerox and Fuji Xerox annual reports

Notes: Top: The Xerox revenues shown include Rank Xerox but not Fuji Xerox.
         Bottom: Xerox earnings include 33% of FX earnings.

Exhibit 2   Copier Sales of Leading Vendors Worldwide, 1975-1985
(in millions of US$)

	1975	1980	1985
Xerox Group	$3,967	$7,409	$8,903
U.S. and Americas	2,340	3,866	4,770
Rank Xerox	1,350	2,856	2,400
Fuji Xerox	277	687	1,733
Canon	87	732	2,178
Ricoh	290	1,092	1,926
Kodak	1	300	900
IBM	310	680	700
Minolta	25	387	743
3M	380	575	400
Oce	178	680	600
Savin	52	430	448
Konishiroku	85	302	470
Nashua	155	401	278
Agfa	115	268	200
Pitney Bowes	52	129	204
A.B. Dick	35	55	60
Saxon	56	127	20
AM International	59	23	10
Other Japanese	155	1,220	2,846
Other	596	792	1,115
Total	**$6,598**	**$15,602**	**$22,001**
Shares of Leading Firms in World Total			
Xerox Group	60%	47%	40%
Americas	35	25	22
Rank Xerox	20	18	11
Fuji Xerox	4	4	8
Canon	1	5	10
Ricoh	4	7	9
Kodak	0	2	4
IBM	5	4	3
Minolta	0	2	3

Source: Donaldson, Lufkin & Jenrette, Inc.

Exhibit 3　Copier Unit Placements of Xerox and Major Competitors

	Thousands of units placed by market segment (net)[a]					Share of net placements in each market segment				
	PCs	Low	Mid	High	Total	PCs	Low	Mid	High	Total
In the United States:										
Xerox										
1975	--	9	-8[b]	1	2	--	29%	--	100%	6%
1980	--	34	6	6	46	--	11%	22%	52%	13%
1985	--	66	27	15	108	0%	10%	21%	53%	10%
1989	12	101	53	13	179	5%	14%	27%	45%	15%
Kodak and IBM										
1975	--	--	10	--	10	--	0%	213%	0%	27%
1980	--	--	5	5	11	--	0%	20%	48%	3%
1985	--	--	2	13	14	0%	0%	2%	46%	1%
1989	--	--	5	9	13	0%	0%	2%	31%	1%
Canon										
1975	--	3	--	--	3	--	10%	0%	0%	8%
1980	--	46	4	--	50	--	15%	14%	0%	14%
1985	176	107	17	--	300	86%	16%	13%	0%	29%
1989	141	106	19	4	270	62%	15%	10%	13%	23%
Others										
1975	--	19	3	--	22	--	61%	55%	0%	59%
1980	--	237	12	--	249	--	75%	44%	0%	70%
1985	30	514	81	--	625	14%	75%	64%	0%	60%
1989	75	513	123	3	714	33%	71%	61%	11%	61%
Total for All Vendors										
1975	--	31	5	1	37					
1980	--	317	27	11	355					
1985	206	687	126	28	1,047					
1989	227	710	200	29	1,176					
In Western Europe:										
Rank Xerox										
1980	--	40	4	4	48	--	11%	22%	100%	13%
1984	--	54	19	9	82	0%	9%	25%	74%	10%
1989	18	73	49	4	144	7%	10%	29%	34%	12%
Kodak										
1980	--	--	4	--	4	--	0%	22%	0%	1%
1984	--	--	--	3	3	0%	0%	0%	26%	0%
1989	--	--	2	2	3	0%	0%	1%	13%	0%
Canon										
1980	--	36	4	--	40	--	10%	21%	0%	11%
1984	115	81	8	--	204	90%	15%	10%	0%	26%
1989	130	110	25	3	268	49%	15%	15%	26%	22%
Total for All Vendors										
1980	--	351	19	4	374					
1984	128	578	76	12	794					
1989	268	752	168	11	1,199					

Exhibit 3   (continued)

	Thousands of units placed by market segment (net)[a]					Share of net placements in each market segment[a]				
	PCs	Low	Mid	High	Total	PCs	Low	Mid	High	Total
In Japan:										
Fuji Xerox										
1986					112					20%
1989					142					21%
Canon										
1986					138					25%
1989					195					28%
Others[c]										
1986					311					55%
1989					354					51%
Total for All Vendors										

Source: Dataquest Incorporated

[a]"Net Placements" are sales and new rentals minus old rentals returned to the vendor. Volume segments are defined as follows:

    PC = less than 12 cpm (average price about $1,000)
    Low = 12 to 30 cpm (average price about $3,000)
    Mid = 31 to 69 cpm (average price about $8,500)
    High = over 70 cpm (average price about $55,000)

[b]Indicates that, on balance, 8,000 rental units were returned

[c]Ricoh was particularly strong in Japan, with a 32% share in 1989

Exhibit 4   Major Agreements Between Xerox and Fuji Xerox

1960 Joint Enterprise Contract and Articles of Incorporation (1962)

- Established equal ownership of FX by Rank Xerox and Fuji Photo Film
- Defined FX's exclusive license to Xerography in its territory:
  - Japan, Taiwan, Philippines, the Koreas, Indonesia, Indochina
- FX nonexclusive license to nonxerographic products in territory
- Specifies terms of technology assistance
  - Royalty due Rank Xerox: 5% of net sales of xerographic products

1976 Joint Enterprise Contract (JEC)

- Agreement between Rank Xerox and Fuji Photo Film, updating 1960 JEC
- Specified Board of Directors composition
- FX Management to be appointed by Fuji Photo Film
- Agreements on technology transfer, royalties, and transfer pricing
- Identified matters requiring Xerox concurrence, including:
  - Financial policy, including major capital expenditures
  - Business and operating plans
  - Relations with third parties
  - Sales outside of FX licensed territory

1976 Technological Assistance Contract (TAC)

- 10-year agreement between Xerox and Fuji Xerox
- Revised technology assistance agreements of 1960, 1968, and 1971
- Maintained 5% royalty on xerographic products

1978 R&D Reimbursement Agreement

- Defines reimbursement to FX for R&D on FX products marketed by Xerox
  - 100% to 120% of design cost

1983 Technology Assistance Agreement (TAA)

- 10-year agreement between Xerox and Fuji Xerox
- Replaced 1976 technology transfer agreements
- Revised royalty rates:
  - Basic Royalty on **total** FX revenue, plus
  - Royalty on **xerographic** revenues to decline annually from 1983 to 1993

1983 Product Acquisition Policy

- Provided guidelines for intercompany transfer pricing
- Established concept of reciprocal Manufacturing License Fee (MLF), designed to reimburse FX for development and manufacturing costs:
  - Up to 25% mark-up on assembled machines supplied by FX
  - Up to 20% mark-up on unit cost for FX machines assembled by XC
  - Specific designs and services required by Xerox reimbursed 100%

1985 Procurement Policy

- Provided guidelines for Xerox procurement in FX licensed territory:
  - FX right to bid first
  - Procurement from third party to be coordinated with FX

1986 Arrangements Strategy Agreement

- Defined parameters for negotiating alliances with third parties

Source: Compiled from Xerox Corporation documents

Exhibit 5 Key Financial Data for Xerox and Fuji Photo Film (in millions of US$)

	1971	1976	1981	1982	1983	1984	1985	1986	1987	1988	1989
XEROX CORPORATION											
Total revenues	1,954	4,515	8,180	8,073	10,463	11,400	11,994	13,287	15,108	16,441	17,635
Document processing			8,013	7,895	8,223	8,714	9,068	9,744	10,834	11,668	12,431
Financial services			167	178	2,240	2,686	2,926	3,543	4,274	4,753	5,204
Operating income	785	1,486	2,071	1,654	1,444	1,557	1,502	1,327	1,376	2,154	2,031
Net income	213	365	598	424	466	291	475	465	578	388	704
Total assets	2,250	4,959	7,674	7,668	14,064	15,154	16,838	19,050	22,450	26,441	30,088
Long-term debt	425	1,000	870	850	1,461	1,614	1,583	1,730	1,539	5,379	7,511
Stockholders' equity	1,052	2,179	3,728	3,724	4,664	4,543	4,828	5,129	5,547	5,667	6,116
R&D expenses	96	226	511	541	529	555	597	650	722	794	809
Employees (millions)	66	100	112	103	108	111	113	112	112	113	111
Earnings/Share ($)	2.85	4.35	6.25	4.06	4.5	3.26	3.42	4.48	5.3	3.49	6.56
Dividend/Share ($)	0.80	1.10	3.00	3.00	3.00	3.00	3.00	3.00	3.00	3.00	3.00
Document processing revenues as share of total	*	*	98%	98%	79%	76%	76%	73%	72%	71%	70%
Operating income/Revenue	40%	33%	25%	20%	14%	14%	13%	10%	9%	13%	12%
Operating income/Assets	35	30	27	22	10	10	9	7	6	8	7
Operating income/Equity	75	68	56	44	31	34	31	26	25	38	33
Net income/Revenue	10.9%	8.1%	7.3%	5.3%	4.5%	2.6%	4.0%	3.5%	3.8%	2.4%	4.0%
Net income/Assets	9.5	7.4	7.8	5.5	3.3	1.9	2.8	2.4	2.6	1.5	2.3
Net income/Equity	20.2	16.8	16.0	11.4	10.0	6.4	9.8	9.1	10.4	6.8	11.5
R&D expense/Revenue	4.9%	5.0%	6.2%	6.7%	5.1%	4.9%	5.0%	4.9%	4.8%	4.8%	4.6%
Long-term debt/Assets	19%	20%	11%	11%	10%	11%	9%	9%	7%	20%	25%
Equity/Assets	47	44	49	49	33	30	29	27	25	21	20
Dividends/Earnings	28	25	48	74	67	92	88	67	57	86	46
FUJI PHOTO FILM											
Total revenue							3,136	4,504	5,636	6,833	6,732
Net income							600	801	1,030	1,217	1,210
Dividends							21	30	35	41	36
Net income/Revenue							19%	18%	18%	18%	18%
Dividends/Earnings							3.5%	3.7%	3.4%	3.4%	3.0%

Source: Company annual reports

*Practically 100%

Exhibit 6 Global Configuration of Xerox Group and Canon in 1989

	UNITED STATES	JAPAN	WESTERN EUROPE	OTHER
Share of world GNP	26%	14%	21% (4 largest countries)	39%
Share of world PPC market (units)	33%	20%	34%	14%

XEROX GROUP

	UNITED STATES	JAPAN	EUROPE	AMERICAS
Revenues	$6.6 billion	$3.5 billion	$4.0 billion	$1.7 billion
Employees	54,000	19,600	29,000	16,000
Production				
PPC	149,000	180,000	176,400	39,100
Printers	15,000	60,000	15,700	--
Systems	8,000	18,000	1,900	--
Faxes	--	95,000	--	--
% of Market (units)				
PPCs	15%	22%	12%	
R&D centers	2	1	1	1
Alliances	--	Fuji Photo Film	Rank Organization	

CANON

	NORTH AMERICA	JAPAN	EUROPE	OTHER
Revenues	$2.9 billion	$2.9 billion	$2.9 billion	
Employees	4,500	27,500	6,500	
Production:				
PPC	60,000	700,000	370,000	
Other	Laser printers and engines	Cameras, printers		Cameras in China
% of market (units)				
PPCs	23%	26%	23%	
Laserprinting	70			
Color PPCs	50			
R&D centers	0	1	0	
Alliances	HP ($1B OEM) Kodak, NeXT	-	Olivetti	

Source: Xerox and industry sources

2012 Foreign Investment Industrial Guidance Catalogue of the People's Republic of China

Catalogue for the Guidance of Foreign Investment Industries (Amended in 2011) Jointly Promulgated by the National Development and Reform Commission and the Ministry of Commerce of the People's Republic of China
Decree of the National Development and Reform Commission, the Ministry of Commerce of the People's Republic of China
No. 12

The Catalogue for the Guidance of Foreign Investment Industries (Amended in 2011), which has been approved by the State Council, is hereby promulgated and shall come into force as of January 30, 2012. The Catalogue for the Guidance of Foreign Investment Industries (Amended in 2007) as promulgated by the National Development Planning Commission and the Ministry of Commerce on October 31, 2007 shall be annulled at the same time.

Attachment: Catalogue for the Guidance of Foreign Investment Industries (Amended in 2011)

Zhang Ping, Director of the National Development and Reform Commission

Chen Deming, Minister of the Ministry of Commerce
December 24, 2011

Catalogue for the Guidance of Foreign Investment Industries
(Amended in 2011)

Catalogue of Encouraged Foreign Investment Industries

I. Farming, Forestry, Animal Husbandry and Fishery Industries

(1)Planting, development and production of woody edible oil, ingredient and industrial raw material

(2)Development of planting technology of green and organic vegetables (including edible fungus and melon-watermelon), dried fruits, teas and production of these products

(3)Development and production of new technology of sugar-yielding crops, fruit trees, forage grass, etc.

(4)Production of flowers and plants, and construction and operation of nursery base

(5)Planting of rubber, oil palm, sisals and coffee

(6)Planting and cultivation of traditional Chinese medicines (limited to equity joint ventures or contractual joint ventures)

(7)Reusing in fields and comprehensive utilization of straws and stalks of crop, development and production of resources of organic fertilizers

(8)Planting of forest trees (including bamboo) and cultivation of fine strains of forest trees, and cultivation of new breed varieties of polyploid trees

(9)Breeding of aquatic offspring (except precious quality varieties peculiar to China)

(10)Construction and operation of ecological environment protection projects preventing and treating desertification and soil erosion such as planting trees and grasses, etc.

(11)Breeding of aquatic products, cage culture in deep water, large-scale breeding of aquatic products, breeding and proliferation of eco-ocean products.

II. Mining and Quarrying Industries

(1)Prospecting, exploitation and utilization of coal-bed gas (limited to equity joint ventures or contractual joint ventures)

(2)Venture prospecting and exploitation of petroleum, natural gas (limited to equity joint ventures or contractual joint ventures)

(3)Exploitation of oil and gas deposits (fields) with low osmosis (limited to equity joint ventures or contractual joint ventures)

(4)Development and application of new technologies that can increase the recovery factor of crude oil (limited to equity joint ventures or contractual joint ventures)

(5)Development and application of new technologies for prospecting and exploitation of petroleum, such as geophysical prospecting, well drilling, well-logging and downhole operation, etc. (limited to equity joint ventures or contractual joint ventures)

(6)Prospecting and exploitation of such unconventional oil resources as oil shale, oil sand, heavy oil and super heavy oil (limited to equity joint ventures or contractual joint ventures)

(7)Prospecting, exploitation, and beneficiation of iron ores and manganese ores

(8)Development and application of new technologies for improving the utilization of tailings and the comprehensive utilization of recovery technology of the mine ecology

(9)Prospecting and exploitation of such unconventional national gas resources as shale gas and submarine natural gas hydrate (limited to equity joint ventures or contractual joint ventures)

III. Manufacturing Industries
1. Farm Products Processing Industry
(1)Development and production of biology feeds, straws and stalks feeds and aquatic feeds

(2)Aquatic products processing, seashell products cleansing and processing, and development of health food made from seaweed

(3)Processing of vegetables, dried fruits, fowl and livestock products

2.Food Manufacturing Industry
(1)Development and production of food for babies and agedness, as well as health-care food

(2)Development and production of forest food

(3)Production of natural addictive for foodstuff and food ingredients

3.Drinks Manufacturing Industry

(1)Development and production of drinks of fruits, vegetables, albumen, tea, coffee and vegetables

4.Tobacco Processing Industry

(1)Production of secondary cellulose acetate and processing of tows (limited to equity joint ventures or contractual joint ventures)

5.Textile Industry

(1)Production of multi-functional industrial textile characterized by lightness, high tenacity, high/low-temperature resistance, and chemical and light resistance with the non-weaving, machine-waving and knitting and the composite technology

(2)Weaving and dyeing as well as post dressing of high-grade loomage face fabric with advanced energy-saving and emission reduction technology and equipment

(3)Processing of special natural fiber products satisfying the requirement of comprehensive utilization of ecology and resources and environment protection (including special animal fiber such as cashmere, fibrilia, bamboo fiber, mulberry silk and colored cotton)

(4)Production of clothes with computer integrated manufacturing system

(5)Production of functional, green and environmentally-friendly and special clothing

(6)Production of top-grade carpet, embroider and drawnwork product

6. Leather, Coat and Feather (Down and Feather) Products Industry

(1)Cleaning processing of leather and fur

(2)Post ornament and processing of leather with new technology

(3)Processing of top-grade leather

(4)Comprehensive utilization of feather waste

7.Lumber Processing Industry and Wood, Bamboo, Vine, Palm, Grass Products Industry

(1)Development and production of new technology and products for the comprehensive utilization of three remainder of forestry, "sub-quality, small wood and fuel wood" and bamboo in the forest area

8.Paper Making and Paper Products Industry

(1)Project mainly utilizing overseas timber resources with an annual production capacity of over 300 thousand tons of chemical wood pulp or an annual production capacity of over 100 thousand tons of chemical mechanical wood pulp in the single production line and synchronized construction of top-grade paper and paper plate production (limited to equity joint ventures or contractual joint ventures)

9.Petroleum Refining, Coking and Nuclear Fuel Processing Industry

(1) Deep processing of needle coke and coal tar

10.Chemical Raw Material and Products Manufacturing Industry

(1) Development and production of new type down-stream products of sodium-process bleaching powder, polrvinyl chloride and organic silicon

(2) Production of supporting raw materials for synthetic materials: hydrogen peroxide propylene oxide-method propylene oxide, NDC and 1,4-CHDM

(3) Production of synthetic fiber raw materials: caprolactam, nylon 66 salt, meltspun spandex resin and 1,3-propylene glycol

(4) Production of synthetic rubber: solution butadiene styrene rubber (excluding thermoplastic butadiene styrene rubber), cri-rich butadiene rubber, butyl rubber, isoprene rubber, polyester rubber, acrylic rubber, chlorohydrin rubber, ethylene propylene rubber and the special rubbers of fluorous rubber and silicon rubber

(5) Production of engineering plastics and plastic alloy: non phosgene-method PC with an annual production of 60,000 or more tons, POM, polyamide (nylon 6, 66, 11 and 12), EVA, polyphenylene sulfide, polyether-ether-ketone, polyimide, polysulfone, polyethersulfone, PAR, liquid crystal polymeride and other products.

(6) Fine chemistry: new products and technologies of catalyst, commercialization processing technology of dying (pigment) materials, electric chemicals and papermaking chemicals, food additives, feed additive, leather chemicals (except N-N DMF), oil additives, surface active agent, water treatment agent, adhesives, inorfil, inorganic nano materials production, and deep-processing of pigment diolame

(7) Production of environmentally-friendly printing ink, and aromatic hydrocarbon

(8) Production of natural perfume material, synthetic perfume and isolate perfume

(9) Production of high-performance coating, hydrophobic automotive paint and supporting waterborne resin

(10) Production of HCFCs substitute

(11) Production of high-performance fluoro resin, fluorous membrane materials, medical fluoro midbody, environmentally-friendly refrigeration agent and cleaning agent

(12) Production of fluorine recycling from phosphorus chemical and aluminum smelting

(13) Development and production of new technology and products of forestry chemicals

(14) Development and production of environmentally-friendly inorganic, organic and biological membrane

(15) Development and production of new fertilizers: bio-fertilizer, high-density potash fertilizer, compound fertilizer, controlled-releasing fertilizer, compound microorganism inoculant, composite microorganism fertilizer, straw and waste decomposing agent and special-function microorganism agent

(16) Development and production of new varieties of effective, safe and environmentally-friendly pesticides, new formulations, special-purpose midbody and addition agents as well as development and application of related cleaning technology (methane-method acetochlor, amine cyanogen-method paraquat and aqueous phase-method chlorpyrifos technology, glyphosate recycling chloromethane technology, stereospecific synthesis-method chirality and stereochemical

structure pesticide production and synthetic technique of ethyl chloride)

(17) Development and production of biopesticide and bio-control products: microbial insecticide, microbial fungicide, agricultural antibiotic, insect pheromone, enemy insect and microbial herbicide

(18) Comprehensive utilization and disposal of exhaust gas, discharge liquid and waste residue

(19) Production of organic polymer material: covering film for plane, rare-earth cerium sulphide red dye, lead-free in electronic packages, serials of special sizing agent by photoetching for color Plasma Display Panel, small-diameter and large specific surface area superfine fiber, high precision fuel filter paper, and Li-ion battery membrane

11.Medical and Pharmaceutical Products Industry

(1)Production of new type compound medication or active composition medication (including bulk drug and preparation)

(2)Production of amino acids: tryptophan, histidine, and methionine for feed with fermentation method

(3)Production of new anti cancer medication, new cardio-cerebrovascular medication and new nervous system using medication

(4)Production of new drugs with bio-engineering technology

(5)Production of new type bacterin for AIDS, HCV and contraception as well as cervical carcinoma, malaria and hand-foot-and-mouth disease

(6)Production of biology bacterin

(7)Exploitation and production of marine drug

(8)Drug preparation: production of new formulation using new technologies of sustained-release, release, targeting and percutaneous absorption

(9) Exploitation and production of new type of pharmaceutical adjuvant

(10) Production of antibacterial raw material drug for animal use (including antibiotics and synthetic chemicals)

(11)Production of new products of antibacterial drug, insect repellent, pesticide, anticoccidial drug for animal use and new formulation

(12)Production of new diagnosis reagent

12.Manufacturing Industry of Chemical Fiber

(1) Production of hi-tech chemical fiber (except viscose) of differential chemical fiber, aramid, carbon fiber, polyethylene of high-strength and high-mode, polyphenylene sulfide (PPS) and so on

(2) Production of new style of fiber and non-fiber polyester: PTT, PEN, PCT and PETG

(3) Production of biopolymer fiber with new type renewable resources and green environmentally-friendly technology, including new solution-method Lyocell, regenerated cellulose fiber with bamboo and fiber as raw materials, PLA, chitosan fiber, PHA and plant and animal protein fiber

(4) Production of polyamide, with a single line daily production capacity of 150 or more tons

(5) Production of meridian tyre aramid fiber and tyre cord

13.Industry of Plastic Products

(1)Development and production of new type photo-ecology multi-functional broad width agricultural film

(2)Digestion and recycle of waste plastics

(3)Exploitation and production of new technology and new production of soft plastic package (high barrier, multi-function film and raw material)

14.Non-metal Mineral Products Processing Industry

(1) Development and production of energy-saving, environmentally-friendly, waste recycling, light and strong, high-performance and multi-functional building materials

(2) Production of using plastic to replace steel and wood, energy-saving and high-efficient chemical architecture materials

(3) Production of not less than 10,000,000sq.m. elastomer, plastic changeable asphaltum waterproof coiled materials, EPDM waterproof coiled materials with width (of not less than 2 meters) and matched materials, PVC coiled material with

width (of not less than 2 meters), and TPO waterproof coiled materials

(4) Development and production of functional glass with new technology: screen electromagnetic wave glass, micro-electronics glass base plate, penetrating infrared non-lead glass, electron grade large spec quartz glass products (pipe, plate, crucible and instrument vessels), optical property high-quality multi-functional windshield glass, extreme materials and products for information technology (including waveguide-level high-precise optical fiber pre-fabricating quartz glass sleeve and ceramic baseplate), and refining and processing of crystal raw materials with high purity of (99.998% or above) and super-purity of (99.999% or above).

(5) Production of film battery conductive glass and solar light-concentration glass

(6) Production of glass fiber products and special glass fibers: dielectric glass fiber, quartz glass fiber, high silica glass fiber, strong and flexible glass fiber, ceramic fiber and products

(7) Production of optical fiber and products: coherent fiber bundle and laser medical optic fiber, super-second generation and third generation microchannel plate, optical fiber surface plate, image inverter and optical glass cone

(8) Standardized refining of ceramic material and production of high-level decorative materials used for ceramics

(9) Production of environmentally-friendly refractory material (without chromizing) used in furnaces for cement kiln, electronic glasses, ceramics and porous carbon bricks

(10) Production of AIN ceramic base piece, and multiple-hole ceramics

(11))Production of inorganic, non-metal materials and products: complex materials, special kind of ceramics, special kind of airproof materials (including quick oil sealed materials), special friction materials (including quick friction braking products), special cementation materials, special type latex materials, water rubber materials and nano materials

(12) Production of organic-inorganic composite foam insulation materials

(13))Production of high-tech compound materials: sequential fiber increasing thermoplasticity compound materials and prepreg, endure heat > 300℃ colophony compound material moulding craftwork assistant materials, colophony compound material (including top grade sports articles and light and strong transport tool parts), special function compound materials and products (including deep water and diving compound material products and medical and healing use compound material products), carbon/carbon compound materials, high-performance ceramic compound materials and products, metal and glass compound materials and products, and pressure≥320MPa super-high-pressure compound rubber pipes, air bus aviation tyres

(14) Production of precise high-performance ceramics materials: carborundum super-minute powder(purity > 99%, average granule diameter < 1μm), Si3N4 super-minute powder(purity > 99%, average granule diameter < 1μm), high pure and super-minute alumina powder(purity > 99%, average granule diameter < 0.5μm), low temperature sintered zirconia (ZrO2) powder (sintered temperature < 1350℃), high pure AlN powder(purity > 99%, average granule diameter < 1μm), rutile TiO2 powder(purity > 98.5%), white char black(average granule diameter < 100nm=, barium titanate (purity > 99%, average granule diameter < 1μm=)

(15) Development and production of top grade artificial crystal and crystal film products: top-grade artificial synthetical crystal (piezo crystal and ultraviolet crystal), super-hard crystal (cubic boron nitride crystal), high temperature resistant and strong insulation artificially synthetic insulation crystal (artificially synthetic mica), new type electric-optic crystal, large power laser crystal and large-sized glittering crystal, and diamond film tools, super-thin artificial diamond saw piece with thickness of 0.3mm or less

(16) Deep processing of non-metal mineral products (super-thin comminution, high level pure, fine production, modification)

(17) Production of super high power black lead electrode.

(18) Production of pearlite mica (granule diameter: 3-150μm)

(19) Production of multiple dimension and multiple direction integer weaving fabric and profile modeling fabric.

(20) Using new dry cement kiln to innocuously dispose of solid waste

(21) Recycling of building waste

(22) Comprehensive utilization of industrial byproduct gypsum

(23) Development and application of new technology for the comprehensive utilization of non-metal mining tailings as well as ecological recovery of mining

15. Non-Ferrous Metallurgical Smelting and Rolling Processing Industry

(1) Production of silicon single crystal with the diameter of more than 200mm and polishing piece

(2) Production of high-tech non-ferrous metallurgical materials: compound semiconductor materials(gallium arsenide, gallium phoshpide, gallium Reexplanation, gallium nitride), high temperature superconduct materials, memory alloy materials (titanium nickel, copper and iron memory alloy materials), super minute (nanometer) calcium carbide and super minute (nanometer) crystal hard ally, super-hard compound materials, noble metal compound materials, aluminum foil used for radiator, middle and high pressure cathode capacitance aluminum foil, special large aluminum alloy materials, aluminum alloy precise model forge product, electrified railway built on stilts leads, super-thin copper strip, erosion proof heat exchanger copper alloy material, high-performance copper nickel, copper and iron alloy strip, beryllium copper strip, thread, tube and stick process material, high temperature bearable tungsten filament, magnesium alloy cast, non-lead solder, magnesium alloy and its applicable products, bubble aluminum, titanium alloy strip materials and titanium jointing pipes, atomic energy grade sponge zirconium, tungsten and deep-processing products of molybdenum

16. Metal Products Industry

(1)Development and production of aviation, aerospace, lightened car, automobile and environmentally-friendly new materials (special-purpose aluminum board, aluminum magnesium alloy materials, automobile aluminum alloy frame and so on).

(2)Development and production of hardware for construction, hot-water heating equipment and hardware parts

(3)Production and processing (including painting and processing inner and outer surface of the products) of metal packing products (thickness < 0.3mm) used to pack all kinds of grain, oil and food, fruits, vegetables, beverages, daily using materials and such contents

(4)Production of section nickel stainless steel products

17. General Machine-building Industry

(1)Manufacturing of numerically controlled machine tools of high level and key spare parts: numerically controlled machine tools which exceed quintuple linkage, digital control coordinate spindle processing center, digital control system which exceeds quintuple linkage and servomechanism installations, high-speed and super-strong knifes for exact digital control manufacturing.

(2)Manufacturing of multi-station forging forming machine of 1,000 or more tons

(3)Manufacturing of equipments for breaking up and smashing retired cars and post-processing sorting equipment

(4)Manufacturing of soft FTL product line

(5)Manufacturing of vertical articulated industrial robots, welding robots and welding equipments thereof

(6)Manufacturing of special processing machines: complete sets of laser cutting and welding equipments, exact processing laser equipments, digital-control and low-speed wire-cuts, submicron cracker

(7)Manufacturing of wheel or crawler crane of 400 or more tons (limited to equity joint ventures or contractual joint ventures)

(8)Designing and manufacturing of high pressure plunger pumps of working pressure of 35MPa or above and engine, designing and manufacturing of low-speed big torquey engine of working pressure of ≥35MPa or above

(9)Manufacturing of electro-hydraulic proportion servo elements of the integral hydraulic multi-channel valves with the working pressure of 25MPa or above

(10)Designing and manufacturing of valve terminal, pneumatic solenoid valves of less than 0.35W and high-frequency electrical control valves of more than 200Hz

(11)Designing and manufacturing of hydrostatic drive device

(12) Development and manufacturing of non-contacting gas film seal of pressure of more than 10MPa, dry gas seal of pressure of more than 10MPa (including experience device)

(13) Development and manufacturing of macromolecule material device for automobiles (rub piece, changed phenol aldehyde plunger, non-metal liquid pressure mother pump and so on)

(14) Manufacturing of car boss axletree of 3 and 4 generation (function elements of boss axletree of flange and transducer inside or outside of the axletree, digital control machine tool or processing centre axletree of high or mid class (the processing center shall have more than three axis interlocking function and 3-4µm repeated precision), high-speed wire or board rolling mill axletree(assistant axletree and roller axletree of single-wire rolling mill of not less than 120m/s and of thin-board rolling mill of not less than 2mm), high-speed railway axletree(with speed of more than 200km/h), low-noise axletree of vibration of less than Z4(Z4, Z4P, V4, V4P), level P4, P2 axletree of various axletree, bearings of wind power generators (mainshaft bearing, speed-up machine bearing and generator bearing of wind generating set of more than 2MW) and aviation bearing (mainshaft bearing of aircraft engine, landing gear bearing, transmission system bearing and handling system bearing)

(15) Manufacturing of high-density, high-precision and shape-complicated powder metallurgy parts as well as chains for vehicles and engineering machinery

(16) Manufacturing of gear transmissions for wind power and high-speed trains, propeller-controllable transmission system for vessels and large-size and heavy-load gear boxes

(17) Production of high temperature resistant and insulation material (with F, H insulation class), as well as insulation shaped parts

(18) Development and manufacturing of accumulator capsule and fluid pressure rubber sealing

(19) Manufacturing of high-precision and high-intensity (above 12.9-level), dysmorphism and combination fasteners

(20) Manufacturing of micro precise transmission coupling parts (clutches)

(21) Manufacturing of coupling shaft for heavy mill

(22) Remanufacturing of mechanical equipment such as machine tools, engineering machinery and railway locomotive equipment as well as auto parts

18. Special Equipment Manufacturing

(1) Manufacturing of mine trolley mining, loading and transporting device: mechanical drive tipper for mine of 200 or more tons, mobile crusher, wheeled digger of 5,000m3/h or above, loading machine for mine of 8 or more m3, electric driving mining machine of 2,500 kw or above and so on

(2) Manufacturing of geophysical, logging equipment: MEME geophone, digital telemetry seismograph, digital imaging, computerized logging system, horizontal wells, directional wells, drilling rig equipment and apparatus, MWD logging while drilling

(3) Manufacturing of oil exploration, drilling, gathering and transportation equipment: floating drilling systems and floating production systems which will work in water with depth of more than 1,500 meters, and supporting equipment for undersea oil production, collection and transportation

(4) Manufacturing of large digging drilling with caliber of 2 or more meters and depth of 30 or more meters, manufacturing of push bench with diameter of 1.2 or more meters, manufacturing of large complete non-digging pipeline laying device with pulling power of 300 or more tons, and manufacturing of diaphragm wall drilling machine

(5) Designing and manufacturing of large soil shifter of 520 hp or above

(6) Designing and manufacturing of purge machine of 100m3/h or above, digging device with digging vessel of 1,000 or more tons

(7) Designing and manufacturing of tuffcrete diosmosing-proof wall for flood control bar

(8) Manufacturing of machines for underwater mass: soil shifter, loader and digger under water with depth of not more than 9 meters

(9) Manufacturing of devices of road bridge maintaining and automatic testing

(10) Manufacturing of devices of road tunnel supervision, winding, disaster control and rescuing system

(11) Designing and manufacturing of maintenance machinery for large-scale construction of railways, railway lines, bridges and tunnels, testing and monitoring equipments and key parts

(12) Manufacturing of (asphalt) shingles equipment, galvanized steel and other metal roof production equipment

(13) Manufacturing of spot spraying polyurethane waterproof thermal insulation system equipment which could protect environment and conserve energy, technology and equipment of polyurethane sealant paste preparation, technology and production equipment of modified silicone sealing paste preparation

(14) Designing and manufacturing of high-precision strip mill (with thickness precision of 10 microns)

(15) Manufacturing of selecting device for multi-element, fine-powder and hard-selecting mine

(16) Manufacturing of key devices of 1,000,000 or more tons/year of oxene complete devices□complicated powder making machine of more than 400,000 tons/year, spiral discharging centrifuge with diagram of 1,000 or more millimeters, and small-flow and high-lift centrifugal pump

(17) Manufacturing of large complete devices of chemical processing of coal (limited to equity joint ventures or contractual joint ventures)

(18) Designing and manufacturing of metal product moulds (such as extrusion moulds of pipe, stick and shape of copper, aluminum, titanium and zirconium)

(19) Designing and manufacturing of punching mould of cover elements of automobile body, large-sized injection molds of fascia and fender-guard, and clamp and testing tools of auto-mobile and motorcycle

(20) Designing and manufacturing of special production equip-ment for car power battery

(21) Designing and manufacturing of precision mold (the preci-sion of punching mould is more than 0.02 millimeter and that of cavity mould is more than 0.05 millimeter)

(22) Designing and manufacturing of non-metal product moulds

(23) Manufacturing of beer filling device of 60,000 bottles /h or above, drink mid or high hot filling device of 50,000 bottles /h, asepticism filling device of 36,000 bottles /h or above

(24) Manufacturing of producing technologies and key equip-ments for aminophenol, enzyme, food additive and so on

(25) Manufacturing of complete feed processing equipment of 10tons/h or above and key parts thereof

(26) Manufacturing of light board and box device of 0.75-milli-meter high or less

(27) Manufacturing of single sheet-fed multi-colored offset print-ing presses (with the breadth of 750 or more millimeters, printing speed of 1,6000 or more sheets per hour in single multi-colored sheet and 1,3000 or more sheets per hour in double multi-colored sheet)

(28) Manufacturing of single roll lithographic printing machine with speed of more than 75,000 pages in folio /h (787×880 millimeters), diprosopia single roll lithographic printing machine with speed of more than 170,000 pages in folio /h (787×880 millimeters) and the commercial roll paper offset press with the printing speed of more than 50,000 pages in folio/h (787x880 millimeters)

(29) Manufacturing of multi-colored breadth flexographic press (with the printing breadth of 1,300 or more millimeters and printing speed of 350 or more meters per second), and the

injection digital printing press (for publishing: printing speed of 150 or more meters per minute and resolution ratio of 600dpi or above; for packaging: printing speed of 30 or more meters per minute and resolution ratio of 1,000dpi or above; for changeable data: printing speed of 100 or more meters per minute and resolution of 300dpi or above)

(30) Manufacturing of computer mass color pre-coordination systems, mass color remote handling systems, mass speed following systems, prints quality automatic testing and following systems, no-axis turning technologies, high-speed automatic splicer with the speed of 75,000 pieces per hour, paper feeder, and high-speed and automatic remote handling paper folding machine, automatic overprinting system, cooling device, silanion putting system, bias-adjusting device and so on

(31) Manufacturing of electronic-gun automatic coating machine

(32) Deep processing technique and equipment manufacturing of plate glass

(33) Manufacturing of complete set of new type of paper (including pulp) making machines

(34) Manufacturing of equipment with new technique for post ornament and processing of leather

(35) Development and Manufacturing of new agriculture processing and storage equipment: new equipment for the processing, storage, preservation, classifying, packing, and drying of food, oil, vegetables, dried fruits and fresh fruits, meat and aqua-products; agricultural product quality testing equipment ; the quality detection equipment of agricultural products' damage; Rheometer; Farinograph; ultrafine pulverization equipment; highly efficient dewatering equipment ; 5-grade plus high efficient fruit juice condensation equipment; equipment for disinfection of powder food in media; aseptic packaging equipment for semi-solid and solid food; disc-type separation centrifuges

(36) Manufacturing of agricultural machinery: facility agriculture equipment (greenhouse automatic irrigation equipment, auto-control configuration and fertilization equipment of

nutritious liquid, efficient vegetable nursery equipment, soil nutrient analysis instruments), tractor and associated farm tools with 120 kilowatts and above matching engine power, low fuel consumption, low noise and low-emission diesel engine, spray machines with residual fog tablets recovery unit matching of large tractor, high-performance rice transplanter, cotton harvesting machine, adapted to a variety of row-spacing self-moving maize reaping machine (hydraulic drive or mechanical drive), rapeseed harvesting machine, cane cutting machine and complete beet harvester

(37) Manufacturing of new technical forestry equipment

(38) Manufacturing of equipment for collecting, bundling and comprehensive utilization of crop straw

(39) Manufacturing of equipment for resource utilization of waste agriculture products and waste fowl and livestock products which are bred in scale

(40) Manufacturing of fertilizer, pesticide, water-saving agricultural technical equipment

(41) Manufacturing of cleaning equipment for electromechanical wells and equipments for laundering drug production

(42) Manufacturing of electronic endoscopes

(43) Manufacturing of fundus cameras

(44) Manufacturing of key components of medical imaging equipments (high magnetic field intensity and superconducting magnetic resonance imaging equipment, X-ray digital tomography imaging equipment, and digital color ultrasonic diagnostic equipment)

(45) Manufacturing of Medical Ultrasonic Transducer (3D)

(46) Manufacturing of boron neutron capture therapy equipments

(47) Manufacturing of image-guiding intensity-modulated radiation treatment system

(48) Manufacturing of Hemodialysis, Blood Filter

(49) Manufacturing of equipment for automatic enzyme immune system (including the functions of application of sample, elisa photo meter, wash plate, incubation, data, post treatment, etc.)

(50) New techniques of quality control of medicine products and new equipment manufacturing

(51) New analytical techniques and extraction technologies, and equipment development and manufacturing for the effective parts of national medicines

(52) Manufacturing of multi-layer co-extrusion water-cooled film mold-blowing equipment for non-PVC infusion bags for medical use

(53) Development and Manufacturing of equipment of new type of knitting machines, key parts and textile testing, laboratory equipment

(54) Manufacturing of computer Jacquard artificial fur machine

(55) Manufacturing of special equipments for solar cell production

(56) Manufacturing of equipment for prevention and treatment of air pollution: equipment for high temperature-resistant and corrosion-resistant filter materials, low NOx combustion equipment, complete equipment for fuel gas denitrification catalysts and denitrification, equipment for industrial organic waste gas purification, equipment for diesel vehicle ventilation purification, and equipment for exhaust treatment of heavy metal

(57) Manufacturing of equipment for prevention and treatment of water pollution: horizontal spiral centrifugal machine, film and film materials, ozone generator of 50kg/h or above, chlorine dioxide generator of 10kg/h or above, ultraviolet disinfection device, small sewage treatment equipment in the rural areas, and treatment equipment for waste water with heavy metal

(58) Manufacturing of equipment for treatment of solid waste: equipment for sludge treatment and resource utilization at the sewage treatment plant, complete equipment for waste incineration with daily treatment of more than 500 tons, technical equipment for landfill leachate treatment, leakage-proof geomembrane at the landfill field, equipment for construction waste and resource utilization, equipment for dangerous waste treatment, methane gas power generation device at the

landfill field, equipment for treatment of iron and steel scrap, and equipment for polluted soil remediation

(59) Development and manufacturing of equipment for comprehensive utilization of red mud in the aluminum industry

(60) Manufacturing of equipment of comprehensive utilization of tailings

(61) Manufacturing of waste plastics, electronics, rubber, battery recycling equipments

(62) Manufacturing of equipment for recycling treatment of waste textiles

(63) Manufacturing of the remanufacturing equipment of used mechanical and electronic products

(64) Manufacturing of equipment for comprehensive utilization of scrap tires

(65) Environmental protection technology and equipment manufacturing of aquatic ecosystem

(66) Manufacturing of movable combination water purification equipment

(67) Unconventional water treatment and repeated utilization equipment and water quality monitoring instrument

(68) Industrial water pipe network and leak-testing equipment and instrument

(69) Development and manufacturing of 100,000 cubic meters and above daily production seawater desalination and recycling cooling technology and complete sets of equipments

(70) Manufacturing of special meteorological observation and analysis equipments

(71) Development of seismic station, seismic network, and mobile seismological observation technology system, and manufacturing of equipments

(72) Manufacturing of three-drum radial tire building machines

(73) Manufacturing of rolling resistance testing machine and tire noise lab

(74) Manufacturing of new heating measurement and temperature control device technical equipments

(75) Manufacturing of preparation, storage and transportation equipment and inspection systems of hydrogen energy

(76) Manufacturing of new heavy residue gasification atomization nozzle, steam leakage rate of 0.5 percent and below efficient steam traps, 1,000 ° C and above high-temperature ceramic heat exchanger manufacturer

(77) Manufacturing of equipment for marine oil-spilling recovery

(78) Manufacturing of low-density coal gas and ventilation air utilization device

19. Communication and Transportation Equipment Industries

(1) Manufacturing of automobile engine, and construction of engine research and development organization: gasoline motor with output per liter not lower than 70 kw, diesel motor with output per liter not lower than 50 kw and discharge capacity below 3 liters, diesel motor with output per liter not lower than 40 kw and discharge capacity above 3 liters, motor driven by such new resources as fuel cells and compound fuel

(2) Manufacturing of key auto parts and development of key technology: DCT, AMT, gasoline engine turbocharger, viscous even shaft device (for four-wheel drive), automatic transmission actuator (magnetic valve), hydrodynamic retarder, eddy current brake, gas generator for SRS, common rail fuel injection technology (with maximum injection pressure of more than 2,000pa), VGT, VNT, engine emission control device up to the standard for the V stage of China, ITM and coupler assembly, steer-by-wire system, diesel particles trap, special vehicle bridge for large low-floor passenger cars, absorption steering system, large-and-medium frequency air condition system for passenger cars, special rubber parts for vehicles, as well as key parts and components of the above-mentioned parts

(3) Production as well as research and development of automobile electronic devices: engine and under-chassis control system as well as key spare parts, in-vehicle electronic technology (automobile information system and navigation system), automobile electronic network technology (limited to equity joint ventures), components for the input (sensor and sampling system) and the output (actuator) of electronic control system, EPS electronic controller (limited to equity joint

ventures), embedded electronic integration system (limited to equity joint ventures or contractual joint ventures), electronic-controlled air suspension, ECS, electronic valve system equipment, EIC, ABS/TCS/ESP system, BBW, TCU, TPMS, OBD, IMMO, ABICAS, and testing system for testing and maintenance of autos and motorbikes

(4) Manufacturing of key parts and components for new energy vehicles: energy power battery (energy density of 110Wh/ kg or above, cycle life of 2,000 or more times, and foreign investment proportion of not more than 50%), positive materials of battery (specific capacity of 150mAh/g or above, and cycle life of 2,000 times takes up not less than 80% of the initial discharging capacity), battery separator (with thickness of 15-40µm and porosity of 40%-60%); battery management system, motor management system, electronic integration of electric cars; drive motor for electric cars (peak power density of 2.5kW/kg or above, high efficient area: 65%, and working efficiency of 80% or above), DC/DC for vehicles (input voltage of 100V-400V),high power electronics (IGBT, voltage level of 600V or above and current of 300A or above); and plug-in hybrid electromechanical coupling drive system.

(5) Manufacturing of key parts and components for high-emission motorcycles (with emission of more than 250ml): technology of electrical control fuel injection for motorcycle (limited to equity joint ventures or contractual joint ventures), and engine discharging device complying with motorcycle discharging criteria stage Ⅲ of China

(6) Equipment for railway transportation (limited to equity joint ventures or contractual joint ventures): research and development, design as well as manufacturing of complete train and key spare parts (drive system, control system, brake system) of rapid transit railway, railway of passenger special line, intercity railway, trunk railway and equipment for urban railway transportation; research and development, design as well as manufacturing of passenger service facilities and equipment for rapid transit railway, railway of passenger special line, intercity railway and urban railway transportation,

design as well as research and development of related information system in the process of construction of information age; research and development, design as well as manufacturing of railway and bridge facilities and equipments for rapid transit railway, railway of passenger special line, intercity railway, manufacturing of equipment and fixtures for electrical railway, research and development of technologies for controlling railway noise and vibrating, manufacturing of discharging equipment for trains, manufacturing of safety monitoring equipment for railway transportation

(7) Design, manufacturing and maintaining of civil plane: those of trunk and branch lines (Chinese part shall hold the majority of shares), general ones (limited to equity joint ventures or contractual joint ventures)

(8) Production and maintaining of spares parts for civil planes

(9) Designing and manufacturing of civil helicopters: those of three or more tons (Chinese part shall hold the majority of shares), those of less then three tons (limited to equity joint ventures or contractual joint ventures)

(10) Production of spares parts for civil helicopters

(11) Manufacturing of ground and water effect plane (Chinese part shall hold the majority of shares)

(12) Designing and manufacturing of no-people plane and aerostat (Chinese part shall hold the majority of shares)

(13) Design, manufacturing and maintaining of plan engines and spare parts as well as air assistant power systems (limited to equity joint ventures or contractual joint ventures)

(14) Designing and manufacturing of civil air-borne equipment (limited to equity joint ventures or contractual joint ventures)

(15) Manufacturing of flight ground equipments: civil airfield facilities, support equipment for civil airfield work, ground equipment for flight test, equipment for flight simulation and practice, equipment for aeronautic testing and measuring, equipment for aeronautic ground testing, comprehensive testing equipment for machines, special equipment for aeronautic manufacturing, equipment for pilot manufacturing aeronautic materials, ground receiving and applying equipment for

civil aircraft, ground testing equipment for rocket launcher, equipment for dynamic and environmental experience for rocket launcher

(16) Manufacturing of mechanical and electrical products for aircrafts, temperature control products for aircrafts, test equipment for planet products and structure and organization products for aircrafts

(17) Manufacturing of light gas-turbine engine

(18) Designing of luxury cruise and deep-water (more than 3,000 meters deep) marine engineering equipment of luxury cruise (limited to equity joint ventures or contractual joint ventures)

(19) Manufacturing and maintenance of marine engineering equipment (including modules) (Chinese part shall hold the majority of shares)

(20) Designing of low-and-medium-speed diesels and their parts for vessels (limited to equity joint ventures or contractual joint ventures)

(21) Manufacturing of crankshafts of low and mid speed for diesel engine for vessels (Chinese part shall hold the majority of shares)

(22) Designing and manufacturing of stateroom machine for vessels (Chinese part shall hold the relative majority of shares)

(23) Designing and manufacturing of communication and directing systems for vessels: communication systems, electronic directing equipment, vessel radar, electric compass automatic pilot, public broadcasting systems inside vessels and so on

(24) Designing and manufacturing of cabin cruiser (limited to equity joint ventures or contractual joint ventures)

20. Electric Machinery and Equipment Industries

(1) Manufacturing of pivotal equipment of super-critical units of over 1,000, 000KW of fire and electricity set (limited to equity joint ventures and cooperative joint ventures): safety valve and adjustment valve

(2) Manufacturing of the denitration technical equipment for sintering machine at the coal-burning power plant and the steel industry

(3) Designing and manufacturing of equipment of fire-electricity airproof
(4) Manufacturing of heavy casting and forging equipment for coal-burning power plant and hydroelectric power station
(5) Manufacturing of key auxiliary equipment for hydro-power generating units
(6) Manufacturing of power transmitting and transforming equipment (limited to equity joint ventures and cooperative joint ventures): amorphous alloy transformer, operational mechanism for the switch of 500KV or above, arc control device, large tube insulator (more than 1000KV and 50 KA), outlet device for transformer of more than 500 KV, sleeve (alternating current of 500, 750 and 1000KV, and direct current of 14 size), tap changer (alternating current 500, 750 and 1,000 KV on-load and offload tap changer), dry PKG for the transmission of direct current, converter valve for the transmission of direct current of ±800KV (water-cooled equipment and direct current field equipment), electrical contactor materials in line with EU RoHS instructions and welding materials with Pb and Cd.
(7) Manufacturing of new energy electricity-power complete equipment or key equipment: photovoltaic power, geothermal power generation, tidal power generation, wave power generation, rubbish power generation, methane power generation, wind power generation equipment of over 2.5MW
(8) Manufacturing of large pumped-storage aggregate with the nominal power of 350MW or above (limited to equity joint ventures and cooperative joint ventures): pump turbine and speed controller, large speed-variable reversible pump turbines, generator motor and such accessory equipment as excitation and starting device
(9) Manufacturing of Stirling generating set
(10) Development and manufacturing of straight linear and planar motor and drive system
(11) Manufacturing of hi-tech green battery: lithium battery power, zinc nickel storage battery, zinc-silver accumulator,

lithium ion battery, solar battery, fuel cell and so on (except energy power battery for new energy vehicles)

(12) Manufacturing of refrigeration air conditioning compressor with motor adopting DC variable frequency technology, refrigeration air conditioning compressor adopting CO_2 natural medium and refrigeration air conditioning equipment with renewable energy (air, water and ground source)

(13) Manufacturing of solar air conditioning, heating system, solar dryer

(14) Manufacturing of biomass drying pyrolysis system, biomass, gasification unit

(15) Manufacturing of ac-fm voltage regulation drawbar

21. Communication Equipment, Computer and Other Electronic Equipment Manufacturing

(1) Manufacturing of Hd camcorders and digital sound-playing equipment

(2) Manufacturing of flat panel display such as TFT-LCD, PDP and OLED and the material of flat panel display (except TFT-LCD glass base plate of the sixth-generation or below)

(3) Manufacturing of such parts as optical engine, light source, projection screen, high-resolution projection tube and LCOS module used in large screen color projection display

(4) Manufacturing of digital audio and visual coding or decoding equipment, digital broadcasting TV studio equipment, digital cable TV system equipment, digital audio broadcast transmission equipment, digital television converter, digital television broadcasting Single Frequency Network (SFN), satellite digital TV up-linking station, front-end equipment manufacturing of SMATV

(5) Designing of integrate circuit, and manufacturing of large digital integrate circuit with its wire width of not more than 0.18 micron, manufacturing of simulated and digital analogy integrate circuit of not more than 0.8 micron and the encapsulation, manufacturing of MEMS and compound semiconductor integrated circuit and test of such advanced equipment as BGA, PGA, CSP, MCM

(6) Large and medium-sized computer, high-performance computer with its operation of 100 trillion times, portable micro computer, high-rank server with its operation of not less than 1 trillion times per second, large-scale simulated system, large industrial controller and the manufacturing of controller

(7) Manufacturing of computer digital signal process system and board card

(8) Manufacturing of figure and image recognition process system

(9) Development and manufacturing of large-capability optical and disk driver

(10) Manufacturing of high-speed storage system and intelligent storage equipment with its capability of not less than 100 TB

(11) Manufacturing of Computer Assistance Design (three-dimensional CAD), Computer Assisted Testing (CAT), Computer Aided Manufacture (CAM), Computer Aided Engineering (CAE) and other computer application system

(12) Development and manufacturing of software product

(13) Development and manufacturing of specialized electronic material (except the development and manufacturing of optical fiber perform rod)

(14) Manufacturing of specialized equipment, testing equipment, tools and moulds

(15) Manufacturing of new type electronic components and parts :slice components, sensitive components and sensors, frequency monitoring and selecting components, mix integrated circuit, electrical and electronic components, photoelectric components, new type components for machinery and electronics, polymer solid electrolytic capacitor, super-capacitors, integrated passive components, high-density interlinked build-up board, multilayer flexible board, flexible printing circuit board and packaging substrate

(16) Manufacturing of touch-control system (touch screen and touch components)

(17) High-brightness LBD with its luminous efficiency of more than 1001m/W, epitaxial slice LBD (blue) with its luminous efficiency of more than 1001m/W, white luminous tube with

luminous efficiency of more than 1001m/W and its power of more than 200mW

(18) Development and manufacturing of key components and parts used in high-precision digital CD drive

(19) Reproduction of read-only compact disk and manufacturing of recordable compact disk

(20) Design and manufacturing of civil satellites (Chinese partner shall hold the majority of shares)

(21) Manufacturing of civil satellites effective payload (Chinese partner shall hold the majority of shares)

(22) Manufacturing of spare pans for civil satellites

(23) Manufacturing of telecommunication system equipment for satellites

(24) Manufacturing of receiving equipment of satellite navigation and key components

(25) Manufacturing of optical communication measurement and instrument and light transceiver with its speed of not less than 10Gb/s

(26) Ultra Broad Band (UWB) communication equipment manufacture

(27) Manufacturing of wireless Local Area Network (including supporting WAPI0 and Wide Area Network

(28) Manufacturing of TDM of 40Gbps or above, DWDM, broad band passive network equipment (including EPON, GPON and WDM-PON), next generation DSL chip and equipment, 16OXC, ASON, and optical fiber transmission equipment of 40G/sSDH or above

(29) Development and manufacturing of system equipment, terminal equipment, test equipment, software and chips on the basis of the next-generation internet equipment of IPv6

(30) Development and manufacturing of the third-generation and following-up mobile communication cell pones, base station, core network equipment and network testing equipment

(31) Development and manufacturing of high-end router, and network switcher of more than 1 kilomega

(32) Manufacturing of air traffic control system equipment (limited to joint venture and cooperation)

22 .Machinery Industries for Instrument and Meter, Culture and Office

(1) Manufacturing of automatic control system and device in the industrial process: FCS, PLC, two phase flow meter, solid flow meter, new sensors and field measurement instrument

(2) Development and manufacturing of large-scale sophisticated instruments: electron microscope, laser scanning microscope, scanning tunneling microscope, electronic probe, large metallurgical microscope, photo-electric direct reading spectrometer, Raman spectrometer, mass spectrograph, GC/MS spectrometer, nuclear magnetic resonance spectrometer, energy dispersive analysis system, X-ray fluorescence spectrometer, diffraction analysis system, industrial CT, 450KV industrial X -Ray defect defector, large-scale balance measuring machine, automatic testing system of on-line mechanical quality, three coordinate measuring machine, laser comparator, electrical prospecting instrument, airborne electrical prospecting and gamma-ray spectrometry measuring instrument of more than 500 m, borehole gravimeter and 3-dimensional magnetograph, high-precision microgal and aviation gravity gradiometer, aviation gravity gradient measurement instrument, linear scale and coder

(3) Manufacturing of high-precision digital voltmeter, current meter (with measuring range of seven bit and a half and above)

(4) Wattless power manufacturing of automatic compensation equipment

(5) Manufacturing of new equipment for safe production

(6) VXI bus-type automatic test system (in accordance with IEEE1155 international standards)

(7) Development and manufacture comprehensive management system for under-mine monitoring and disaster-forecasting apparatus and coal safety measurement

(8) Manufacturing of the equipment for engineering measurement and global geographical observation equipment: digital triangle surveying system, Digital programmed system for three-dimensional topography model (acreage>1000×1000mm,

horizontal error<1mm, altitude error <0.5mm), ultra wide-band seismograph($\square$ < 5cm, frequency band0.01-50HZ, equivalent quaking speed noise<10-9m/s), integrated earthquake data processing system, extensive under-well earthquake and auspice observation apparatus, sophisticated controllable epicenter system, engineering velocity measuring system, high-precision GPS receiver (precision 1mm + 1ppmm), INSAR graphics receiving and processing system, absolute gravimeter with the precision of less than 1 microgal, satellite gravimeter, Doppler weather radar adopting coherent technology or double polarization technology, visibility measuring apparatus, meteorological sensor, (including temperature, pressure, humidity, wind, precipitation, cloud, visibility, radiation, frozen earth, depth of snow), anti lightning stroke system, multilevel soot and dust sampler, three-dimension supersonic anemoscope, high-precision intelligent total station machine, three-dimensional laser scanner, high-performance diamond bit used for drilling, laser rangefinder without cooperative target, wind profiler(affixed with RASS), GPS electronic probe system, CO_2/H_2O general observation system, boundary layer laser doppler radar, granule chromatography, (3nm-20μm), high-performance data collector, and under-water glider

(9) Manufacturing of environment motoring apparatus: SO_2 automatic sampler and calcimeter, NOX, NO_2 automatic sampler and calcimeter, O_3 automatic monitor, CO automatic monitor, automatic sampler and calcimeter for soot and Pm2.5 dust, portable calcimeter for harmful and toxic gas, automatic analyzer for organic pollutants in the air, COD automatic online monitor, BOD automatic online monitor, automatic online monitor for turbidity, DO automatic online monitor, TOC automatic online monitor, automatic online monitor for ammonia nitrogen, radiation dose monitor, ray analyzer, online monitoring equipment of heavy metal, water quality pre-warning monitoring equipment of online bio-toxicity

(10) Manufacturing of instrument and equipment for hydrological data collecting, processing, transmitting and flood warning

(11) Manufacturing of ocean exploring apparatus and equipment: deep-sea underwater video camera and underwater camera, multi-beam explorer, shallow and deeper subbottom profiler, navigation warm-salt profiler, fluxgate compass, hydraulic wire line winch, underwater airproof electronic connector, energy recycle device used in filtration-proof seawater desalinization with its efficiency of higher than 90%, Marine ecosystem inspection buoy, section probing buoy, disposable measuring instrument of electrical conductivity, temperature and depth (XCTD), on-the-spot water quality measuring apparatus, intelligent chemical transducer for measuring the water quality of the ocean (continues work for 3-6 months), electromagnetic current meter sensor, navigating acoustic Doppler current profiler(self-contained, direct-read, used-in-ship), electricity conductivity rate deep-section profiler, acoustic responding emancipator(set deep into the ocean)

(12) Manufacturing of digital camera of 1,000 super HAD CCD or above

(13) Manufacturing of office machines: multi-functional integrated office equipment (copy, print, fax and scanning) and color-printing equipment, color-printing head and photosensitive drum with high resolution and precision of 2,400dpi and above

(14) Manufacturing of motion picture machinery: 2k and 4k digital film projector, digital movie camera, digital image manufacture and edit equipment

23. Handicraft and Other Manufacturing Industries

(1) Development and utilization of clean-coal technical product (coal gasification, coal liquefaction, water-coal, industrial lump-coal)

(2) Coal ore dressing by washing and comprehensive utilization of powered coal (including desulphurized plaster), coal gangue

(3) Production of all biodegradable material

(4) Recovery processing of waste electrical and electronic products, autos, electromechanical devices, rubber, metal and batteries

IV. Production and Supply of Power, Gas and Water

1. Construction and operation of electricity power by employing the clean fuel technology of integral gasification combined circulation (IGCC), circulating fluidized bed of not less than 0.3 million kw, Pressurized Fluidized Bed Combustion Combined Cycle (PFBC) of not less than 0.1 million kw
2. Construction and operation of back pressure combined and heat power
3. Construction and management of hydropower stations with the main purpose of power generating
4. Construction and management of nuclear-power plants (Chinese partner shall hold the majority of shares)
5. Construction and management of new energy power plants (including solar energy, wind energy, magnetic energy, geothermal energy, tide energy and biological mass energy, etc.)
6. Utilization of sea water (direct use of sea water, and seawater desalinization)
7. Construction and operation of urban water-supply plant
8. Construction and operation of renewable water plant
9. Construction and operation of charging stations of motor vehicles and battery replacement stations

V. Communication and Transportation, Storage, Post and Telecommunication Services

1. Construction and management of grid of national trunk railways (Chinese partner shall hold the majority of shares)
2. Construction and management of feeder railways, local railways and related bridges, tunnels and ferry facilities (limited to equity joint ventures or contractual joint ventures)
3. Comprehensive maintenance of infrastructure of high-speed railway, special railway line, intercity (Chinese partner shall hold the majority of shares)
4. Construction and management of highways, independent bridges and tunnels
5. Road freight transportation companies
6. Construction and management of public dock facilities of ports
7. Construction and management of civil airports (the Chinese party shall hold the relative majority of shares)

8. Air transportation companies (Chinese partner shall hold the majority of shares)
9. General aviation companies for agriculture, forest and fishery (limited to equity joint ventures or contractual joint ventures)
10. International liner and tramp maritime transportation business (the Chinese party shall hold the relative majority of shares)
11. International containers inter-model transportation
12. Construction and management of oil (gas) pipelines, oil (gas) depots and petroleum wharf
13. Construction and management of the facilities of coal delivery pipelines
14. Construction and management of automatic elevated three-dimensional storage facilities and storage facilities relating to transportation services

VI. Wholesale and Retail Trade Industry
1. Joint distribution of general goods and modern fresh agricultural logistics and related technical services of low-temperature distribution
2. Chain distribution in rural areas
3. Construction and operation of stock and container unit sharing system

VII .Rent and Business Service
1. Accounting and auditing (limited to equity joint ventures or contractual joint ventures)
2. Information consulting service of international economy, science and technology, environmental protection and logistics
3. Engaged in such information technology and business flow outsourcing services as system application management and maintenance, information technology supportive management, bank background service, financial settlement, human resource service, software development, offshore call center, data processing by means of accepting service outsourcing
4. Venture investment enterprise.
5. Intellectual property services
6. Domestic service

VIII. Scientific Research, Technology Service and Geological Exploration

1. Biological engineering technique and bio-medical engineering technique

2. Isotope, irradiation and laser technique

3. Sea development and sea energy development technology, comprehensive technology of sea chemical resources, development of the relevant products and deep-processing technology, sea medicine and biochemical product development technology

4. Sea surveying technology (sea tidal wave, meteorology, environmental monitoring) sea bed probing, exploration and evaluation technology of ocean resource

5. Comprehensively use of high chemical additional value technology to distill chemical potassium, bromine, magnesium from dense sea water after desalinization and its deep procession

6. Technology of marine oil pollution clearing and ecological restoration, and development of related products, prevention and treatment technology of eutrophication of sea water, prevention and treatment technology of marine biological explosive growth disasters, and restoration technology of ecological environmental in the coastal zone

7. Development and service of energy-saving technology

8. Technology for recycling and comprehensive utilization of resource, development and application of the recycling technology of the waste dispelled by enterprises

9. Technology for environment pollution treatment and monitoring

10. Energy-saving and consumption-reduction in chemical fiber production and printing and dyeing and the new technology to deal with polluted air, water and solid waste

11. Technology for preventing from desertification and desert improvement

12. Comprehensive management technology for balancing grass and domestic animal

13. Application technique of civil satellite

14. Research and development centers
15. Incubator for hi-tech, new products developing, and incubation of enterprises

IX. Water, Environment and Public Facility Management Industry

1. Construction and management of key water control projects for comprehensive utilization (the Chinese party shall hold the relative majority of shares)
2. Construction and management of urban access-controlled roads
3. Construction and management of metro and city light rail (Chinese partner shall hold the majority of shares)
4. Construction and management of treatment plants for sewage, garbage, the dangerous wastes (incineration and landfill), and the facilities of environment pollution treatment

X. Education

1. Advanced educational institution (only limited to joint venture or cooperative)
2. Vocational skills training

XI. Public Health, Social Security and Social Welfare

1. Service agencies for the elderly, the handicapped and children

XII. Culture, Sports and Entertainment

1. Operation of the performance site (the Chinese party shall hold the relative majority of shares)
2. Operation of the gymnasium, body-fitting, competition performance, sports training and agency service

Catalogue of Restricted Foreign Investment Industries

1. Farming, Forestry, Animal Husbandry and Fishery Industries

1. Breeding and seeds developing production of new train crop breed (Chinese party shall hold the majority of shares)
2. Processing of the logs of precious varieties of trees (limited to equity joint ventures or contractual joint ventures)
3. Cotton (raw cotton) processing

II. Mining Industries

1. Exploring and mining of special and scarce coals exploration (Chinese partner shall hold the majority of shares)
2. Exploring and mining of barite (limited to equity joint ventures or contractual joint ventures)

3. Exploring and mining of precious metals (gold, silver, platinum families)

4. Exploring and mining of important nonmetallic ores of diamond, high aluminum refractory clay, wollastonite and plumbago

5. Exploring and cradling of phosphorite, lithium and iron pyrite, and extraction of brine resource in salt lakes

6. Mining of szaibelyite and szaibelyite iron ores

7. Mining of Celestine

8. Mining of Ocean Manganese Nodule (Chinese partner shall hold the majority of shares)

III. Manufacturing Industries

1. Farming Subsidiary Foodstuff Industry

(1)Processing of edible oil of soybean, rapeseed, peanut, cottonseed, tea seed, sunflower seed and palm (Chinese partner shall hold the majority of shares), processing of rice and flour, and deep-processing of corn

(2)Manufacturing of biology liquid fuel (fuel ethanol and biodiesel) (Chinese partner shall hold the majority of shares)

2. Beverage Manufacturing Industries

(1)Manufacturing of rice wine and quality liquor (Chinese partner shall hold the majority of shares)

3. Tobacco Industries

(1)Manufacturing of threshing and curl tobacco leaf

4. Printing and Copy of Recording Vehicle

(1)Print of publication (Chinese partner shall hold the majority of shares)

5. Petroleum Processing, Coking and nuclear fuel processing Industries

(1) Oil refining of not more than 10 million tons per year under the normal pressure, catalytic cracking of not more than 1.50 million tons per year, continuous reforming of not more than 1 million tons per year (including aromatics extraction) and hydrocracking manufacturing of not more than 1.5 million tons per year

6. Chemical Raw Material Products Manufacturing Industry

(1)Manufacturing of sodium carbonate and caustic soda as well as sulfuric acid, hydrogen acid and potash below the designated size or with the backward technology
(2)Production of sensitive materials
(3)Production of benzidine
(4)Production of chemical products from which narcotics are easily made (ephedrine, 3, 4-idene dihydro phenyl-2-acctonc, phenylacetic acid, 1-phenyl-2-acetone, heliotropin, safrole, isosafrole, acetic oxide)
(5)Manufacturing of low-end HCFC of hydrogen fluoride
(6)Production of divinyl rubber (except cis-rich poly butadiener rubber), emulsion polymerization buna S, thermoplastics buna S
(7)Production of PVC with the acetylene method, ethene below the designated scale and post-processing products
(8)Production of paints and coatings with harmful matter and backward technology and below the designated scale
(9)Processing of ludwigite
(10)Production of inorganic salt characterized by large occupation of resource, serious environmental pollution and application of backward technology
7. Medical and Pharmaceutical Products Industry
(1)Production of chloramphenicol, penicillin G, lincomycin, gentamicin, dihydrostreptomycin, amikacin, tetracycline hydrochloride, oxytetracycline, medemycin, kitasamycin, ilotyin, ciprofloxacin and ofloxacin
(2)Production of analgin, paracetamol, Vitamin B1, Vitamin B2, Vitamin C, Vitamin E
(3)Production of vaccine varieties included in the state immunization program
(4)Production of material medicines for addiction narcotic and A class psychoactive drug (Chinese partner shall hold the majority of shares)
(5)Production of blood products
8. Chemical Fiber Production Industry
(1)Production of chemical fiber drawnwork of conventional chipper

(2)Production of rayon staple viscose fiber

9. Non-Ferrous Metal Smelting and Rolling Processing Industry

(1)Non-ferrous metal refining of tungsten, molybdenum, stannum (except tin compounds), antimony (including antimony oxide and antimony sulphide)

(2)Non-ferrous metal refining of electrolytic aluminium, copper, lead, zinc and another non-ferrous metal

(3)Smelting and separation of rare earth metal (limited to equity joint ventures or contractual joint ventures)

10. Common Purpose Equipment Manufacturing Industry

(1)Manufacturing of all kinds of general (p0) axletree and accessory (steel ball, cage), rough

(2)Manufacturing of wheeled model, crawler crane of less than 400 tons (limited to equity joint ventures or contractual joint ventures)

11. Special Purpose Equipment Manufacturing Industry

(1)Manufacturing of equipment for producing long Dacron thread and short fiber

(2)Manufacturing of crawler dozers of not more than 320 horsepower, hydraulic excavator of not more than 30 tons, wheel loader of not more than 6tons, grader of not more than 220 horsepower, road roller, fork-lift truck, electric-driving non-calzada dumper truck at the level of 135 tons or below, hydromechanical transmission non-calzada dumper truck at the level of 60 tons or below, asphalt concrete stirring and paving equipment and aerial work machinery, garden machine and tools, production of commodity concrete machinery (pump, agitating lorry, mixing plant, and pump vehicle)

12. Manufacturing of transport and communication facilities

(1)Repairing, designing and manufacturing of ship (including subsection) (Chinese partner shall hold the majority of shares)

13. Manufacturing of Communication Apparatus, Computers and another Electric Installation

(1)Production of satellite television receivers and key parts

IV. Production and Supply of Power, Gas and Water

1.Construction and management of conventional coal-fired power of condensing steam plants whose unit installed capacity is 300,000kW or below, and coal-fired power of condensing-extracted steam plants with dual use unit cogeneration whose unit capacity is 100,000kW within the small power grid

2.Construction and management of power network (Chinese partner shall hold the majority of shares)

3.Construction and management of urban gas, heating power and water supply and drainage pipe network with a population of 500,000 or more (Chinese partner shall hold the majority of shares)

V. Communication and Transportation, Storage, Post and Telecommunication Services

1.Railway freight transportation companies

2.Railway passenger transportation companies (Chinese partner shall hold the majority of shares)

3.Corporate of highway passenger transport

4.Corporate of enter-leave country fleet operation

5.Corporate of water transportation (Chinese partner shall hold the majority of shares)

6.General aviation companies engaging in photographing, prospecting and industry (Chinese partner shall hold the majority of shares)

Tele communication companies: telecommunication increment service (the foreign capital shall not exceed 50 percent), basic telecom business (the foreign capital shall not exceed 49 percent)

VI. Wholesale and Retail Trade Industries

1. Commodity direct selling, mail order selling, and on-line selling

2. Purchase of grain, and wholesale, retail and logistic distribution of grain, cotton, vegetable oil, sugar, medicines, tobaccos, automobiles, crude oil, capital goods for agricultural production (Chinese should hold the majority of shares of the multiple shops which have more than 30 branch stores and sell different kinds and brands of commodities from multi-suppliers)

3. Construction and operation of large wholesale market of agricultural products

4. Distributing and selling of audiovisual products (except movies) (limited to joint ventures)

5. Ship agent (Chinese should hold the majority of shares), tally for foreign vessels (limited to equity joint ventures or contractual joint ventures)

6. Wholesaling product oil and construction and operation of gasoline stations (Chinese should hold the majority of shares of the multiple shops which have more than 30 branch stores and sale different kinds and brands of commodities from multi-suppliers)

VII. Banking and Insurance Industries

1.Banks, finance companies, trust investment companies, currency brokerage companies

2.Insurance companies (the share of life-insurance companies shall not exceed 50%)

3.Security companies (confined to A share consignment-in, B share, H share and government and company bonds consignment-in and transaction, the foreign-capital shall not exceed one-third), security investment fund management companies (the foreign-capital shall not exceed 49%)

4.Insurance brokerage companies

5.Futures companies (Chinese should hold the majority of shares)

VIII. Real Estate Industry

1.Development of pieces of land (limited to equity joint ventures or contractual joint ventures)

2.Construction and operation of high-ranking hotels, high-class office buildings and international exhibition centers

3.Real estate transaction in second-grade market and medium and brokerage companies

IX. Leasing and Commercial Service Industry

1.Legal consulting

2.Market Research (limited to equity joint ventures or contractual joint ventures)

3.Status enquiry and grade service companies

X. Scientific Research and technical Services Industries, Geological Prospecting

1. Mapping companies (Chinese partner shall hold the majority of shares)
2. Inspection, verification and attestation companies for imported and exported goods
3. Photography service (including trick photography like air photograph, except mapping aerial photography, limited to equity joint ventures)

XI. Education
1. Common high school education mechanism (limited to contractual joint ventures)

XII. Art, Sports and Entertainment Industries
1. Production and publication of broadcasting and TV programs and film-making (limited to contractual joint ventures)
2. Construction and operation of cinemas (Chinese partner shall hold the majority of shares)
3. Construction and operation of large theme park
4. Brokering agency of stage performances
5. Operation of entertainment occupancies (limited to equity joint ventures or contractual joint ventures)

XIII. Other industries restricted by the State or international treaties that China has concluded or taken part in

Catalogue of Prohibited Foreign Investment Industries

I. Farming, Forestry, Animal Husbandry and Fishery Industries
1. Research, development, cultivation and growth of China's rare and unique precious breeds, and production of related propagating materials (including tine genes in plants industry, husbandry and aquatic products industry)
2. Research and development of genetically modified organisms, and production of genetically modified plants' seeds, stud stock birds and aquaculture
3. Fishing in the sea area under the jurisdiction of China and in in-land water of China.

II. Mining and Quarrying Industries
1. Exploring and mining of tungsten, molybdenum, tin, antimony, fluorite
2. Exploring, mining and dressing of rare earth metal
3. Exploring, mining and dressing of radioactive mineral products

III. Manufacturing Industry

1.Beverage manufacturing Industry

(1)Processing of green lea and special tea with China's traditional handicraft (famous tea, dark tea, etc.)

2.Medical and Pharmaceutical Products Industry

(1)Processing of traditional Chinese medicines that have been listed as the Regulations on Conservation and Management of Wild Chinese Medicinal Material Resources and Rare and Endangered Plants in China

(2)Application of preparing technique of traditional Chinese medicines in small pieces ready for decoction, like steam, frying, moxibustion, calcining, and production of the products of secret recipe of traditional Chinese patent medicines

3.Non-Ferrous Metal Smelting and Rolling Processing Industry

(1) Smelting and processing of radioactive mineral products.

4.Special Equipment Manufacture Industry

(1)Manufacturing of Weapons and Ammunition

5.Electric Machinery and Equipment Manufacture Industry

(1)Manufacturing of open-lead-acid (namely, acid fog direct outside-release) cells, mercury button-type silver oxide cells, mercury button type alkaline zinc-manganese dioxide cells, paste dioxide-zinc battery, and nickel cadmium cells

6.Industry Products and Other Manufacturing Industries

(1)Ivory carving

(2)Tiger-hone processing

(3)Production of bodiless lacquer ware

(4)Production of enamel products

(5)Production of Xuan-paper (rice paper) and ingot-shaped tablets of Chinese ink

(6)Production of carcinogenic, teratogenic, mutagenesis and persistent organic pollutant products

IV. Production and Supply of Power, Gas and Water

1. Construction and management of conventional coal-fired power of condensing steam plants whose unit capacity is not more than 300,000kW, within the small power grid, and the coal-fired power of condensing-extraction steam plants with

dual use unit cogeneration with unit capacity of not more than 100,000KW

V. Communication and Transportation, Storage. Post and Telecommunication Services

1.Companies of air traffic control

2.Companies of postal services, and domestic express delivery of letters

VI. Leasing and Commercial Service Industry

1.Social investigation

VII. Scientific Research and Technical Services Industries, Geological Prospecting

1.Development and application of human stem cells and gene diagnosis therapy technology

2.Geodetic survey, marine charting, mapping aerial photography, administrative region mapping, and compilation of relief map, common map and electronic navigation map

VIII. Irrigation, Environment and Public Utilities Management

1.Construction and management of nature reserve and international signify marshy

2.Development of resources about wild animals and plants be native to domestic protected by nation

IX. Education

1.Institution of compulsory education and special education, like military, policeman, politics and party school

X. Art, Sports and Entertainment Industries

1.News agencies

2.Publication of books, newspaper and periodical

3.Publication and production of audio and visual products and electronic publications

4.Radio stations, TV stations, radio and TV transmission networks at various levels (transmission stations, relaying stations, radio and TV satellites, satellite up-linking stations, satellite receiving stations, microwave stations, monitoring stations, cable broadcasting and TV transmission networks)

5.Companies of publishing and playing of broadcast and TV programs

6.Companies of films making, issuing, business

7.News website, network audiovisual service, Internet service location, internet art management (except music)

8.Construction and management of golf course and villa

9.Gambling industry (including gambling turf)

10.Eroticism

XI. Other Industries

1.Projects that endanger the safety and performance of military facilities

XII. Other industries restricted by the State or international treaties that China has concluded or taken part in

> Notes: 1. CEPA agreement between the Mainland and Hong Kong and supplemental agreement, CEPA agreement between the Mainland and Macao and supplemental agreement, Cross-strait Economic Cooperation Framework Agreement and supplemental agreement and free trade agreement signed by China and other related countries shall prevail if there are any separate regulations
>
> 2. If otherwise provided in the special regulations of the State Council or industrial policies, such regulations or policies shall prevail.

Development and Reform Commission, Ministry of Commerce
2011-12-24

Appendix 3

Joint Venture Agreement Between A U.S. Company and a Chinese Company

[The Joint Venture Agreement below is a publicly available joint venture agreement but is not intended as a model for a cross-border joint venture agreement since it omits some major provisions.]

Exhibit 10.1

JOINT VENTURE AGREEMENT

ANHUI MEINENG STORE ENERGY CO., LTD.

BY AND BETWEEN

ZBB POWERSAV HOLDINGS LIMITED

AND

ANHUI XINDONG INVESTMENT MANAGEMENT CO., LTD.

_____, 2011

TABLE OF CONTENTS

ANHUI MEINENG STORE ENERGY CO., LTD.
JOINT VENTURE AGREEMENT

This JOINT VENTURE AGREEMENT (this "**Agreement**") is made and entered into as of August 17, 2011 (the "**Effective Date**"), by and between (i) ZBB POWERSAV HOLDINGS LIMITED, a Hong Kong limited liability company ("**Hong Kong Holdco**") and (ii) ANHUI XINDONG INVESTMENT MANAGEMENT CO., LTD. (Chinese name: 安徽鑫东投资管理有限公司), a Chinese limited liability company ("**China JV**") . Hong Kong Holdco and the China JV are sometimes referred to collectively herein as the "**Parties**" and individually as a "**Party** ."

STATEMENT OF PURPOSE

WHEREAS, ZBB Cayman Corporation, a Cayman Islands exempted company ("**ZBB Energy**"), and PowerSav Inc., a Cayman Islands exempted company ("**PowerSav**"), formed Hong Kong Holdco for the purposes of forming and investing in a Sino – foreign equity joint venture company (the "**Company**"), the name of which is temporarily Anhui Meineng Store Energy Co., Ltd. (Chinese name: 安徽美能储能有限公司) and subsequently shall be what is verified on the Name Verification Notification by the Approval Authority as defined below.

WHEREAS, AnHui Xinlong Electrical Co., Ltd. a Chinese corporation ("**AnHui Xinlong**"), and Wuhu Huarui Power Transmission & Transformation Engineering Co., Ltd. a Chinese corporation ("**Wuhu Huarui**"), formed the China JV for the purposes of forming and investing in the Company.

WHEREAS, the Parties desire to form the Company to (i) source, market and distribute (A) certain advanced energy storage and power control technology product families (the "**ZBB Products**") of ZBB Energy's Affiliates and (B) certain new products that may be developed by the Company (the "**Company**

Products, " and together with the ZBB Products, the "**Products**"), (ii) integrate the Products into other technologies and (iii) render other services in support of such Products (the "**Services**"), as applicable, all as more fully described on **Exhibit B** hereto.

WHEREAS, the Parties intend for the Company to bring the Products into large-scale production in the People's Republic of China (excluding Hong Kong, Macau and Taiwan) ("**Mainland China**"), for distribution in Mainland China, Hong Kong, Macau and Taiwan (collectively, the "**Territory**"), in accordance with the terms and conditions of the License Agreement (as defined below).

WHEREAS, the Parties intend for the Company upon its establishment to enter into the following agreements: (i) that certain License Agreement by and between the Company and ZBB Energy Corporation, Inc., a Wisconsin corporation ("**ZBB Corp.**"), in the form attached hereto as **Exhibit C** (the "**License Agreement**"); (ii) that certain Management Services Agreement by and between the Company and Hong Kong Holdco, in the form attached hereto as **Exhibit D** (the "**Management Services Agreement**") and (iii) that certain Research and Development Agreement by and between the Company and ZBB Corp. in the form attached hereto as **Exhibit E** (the "**R&D Agreement** ", collectively with the License Agreement and the Management Services Agreement, the "**Related Agreements**").

WHEREAS, the Parties desire to enter into this Agreement for the purpose of setting forth the rights and obligations of the Parties (including their rights and obligations as JV Investors, as defined below) with respect to the Company.

NOW THEREFORE, in consideration of the aforesaid Statement of Purpose, the mutual terms, provisions, covenants and agreements set forth herein, and other good and valuable consideration, the receipt and sufficiency of which are hereby acknowledged, the Parties hereby agree as follows:

AGREEMENT

1. <u>DEFINITIONS</u>.

1.1 Certain Definitions. For the purposes of this Agreement, the following capitalized terms have the respective meanings set forth below:

"**Accounting Principles** "means, collectively, the China Accounting Principles and the U.S. Accounting Principles.

"**Affiliate**" means, as to any Person, any other Person that directly, or indirectly through one or more intermediaries, (i) Controls, (ii) is Controlled by or (iii) is under common Control with such Person.

"**Applicable Law**" means, as to any Person, any statute, law, rule, regulation, directive, treaty, judgment, order, decree or injunction of any Governmental Authority that is applicable to or binding upon such Person.

"**Approval Authority** "means the Ministry of Commerce of the People's Republic of China (or its local branch office with competent authority and jurisdiction) and the Wuhu City, Anhui Province government (and its relevant departments).

"**Board** "means the Board of Directors of the Company.

"**Business Day**" means a day on which commercial banks in Shanghai, China generally are open to conduct their regular banking business.

"**Business Plans**" means, collectively, (i) the Initial Business Plan and (ii) any subsequent business plan of the Company, as approved by the Board pursuant to the terms of this Agreement, and in effect from time to time.

"**China Accounting Principles** "means generally accepted accounting principles in the People's Republic of China (or any other country which the JV Investors may agree to in writing) as set forth in pronouncements of the Chinese Institute of Certified Public Accountants, as consistently applied.

- 2 -

"**China JV Change of Control** "means any one, or a series of any one, of the following: (i) a merger, consolidation, security exchange, issuance or sale of equity securities or other reorganization of, or involving, the China JV pursuant to which the China JV's interest holders (determined immediately prior to the time at which such transaction is effected) collectively have beneficial ownership of less than 51% of the total outstanding ownership interest of the China JV, or comparable equity securities of the surviving entity if the China JV is not the surviving entity, immediately following such transaction; (ii) any sale, lease, exchange or other transfer (in one transaction or a series of related transactions), of all or substantially all of the assets of the China JV; (iii) the interest holders' or board's approval of any plan or proposal for the liquidation or dissolution of the China JV or (iv) the China JV's submission or becoming subject to any bankruptcy proceeding, the appointment of a trustee, custodian or conservator or any other similar voluntary or involuntary creditors' right proceeding.

"**Company Documents** "means this Agreement, the Related Agreements, the Business Plans and the Articles of Association of the Company, as amended from time to time.

"**Control**" means the possession, directly or indirectly, of the power to direct or cause the direction of the management or policies of a Person (whether through the ownership of securities, by contract, or otherwise).

"**Director**" means a member of the Board.

"**Effective Date**" means the date set forth in the first paragraph of this Agreement.

"**Encumbrance** "means any lien, mortgage, deed of trust, pledge, collateral assignment, security interest, hypothecation, option, right of first refusal or other encumbrance.

"**Entity**" means a corporation, partnership, limited liability company, firm or other business association or entity.

"**Fiscal Year**" means the twelve (12) month period ending June 30 of each year, or such other fiscal year as the Board may designate from time to time.

"**Governmental Authority**" means any domestic or foreign government, governmental authority, court, tribunal, agency or other regulatory, administrative or judicial agency, commission or organization, and any subdivision, branch or department of any of the foregoing.

"**Initial Business Plan**" means the initial business plan of the Company, covering the period running from the Effective Date through the end of the fifth full Fiscal Year after the Effective Date, as agreed upon by the JV Investors and adopted by the Board.

"**Interests**" means the equity interests of the Company.

"**IPO** "means an initial public offering on a nationally recognized securities exchange.

- 3 -

"**JV Investor** "means a Person that owns Interests in the Company. A list of the initial JV Investors is set forth on **Exhibit A,** which may be amended from time to time.

"**Party**" and "**Parties**" are defined in the opening paragraph of this Agreement.

"**Percentage Ownership Interest**" means the percentage of Interests of the Company owned by a particular JV Investor, determined based on the following formula: the percentage that corresponds to (i) the quotient of (A) the JV Investor's committed registered capital divided by (B) the aggregate registered capital contributed to the Company by all of the JV Investors.

"**Person**" means a natural individual, Governmental Authority or Entity.

"**Transfer**" means, as a noun, the transfer of legal, beneficial or equitable ownership by sale, exchange, assignment, gift, donation, grant or other transfer of any kind, whether voluntary or involuntary, including transfers by operation of law or legal process. As a verb, the term means the act of making any Transfer.

"**Supervisor** "means a member of the Board of Supervisors.

"**U.S. Accounting Principles**" means generally accepted accounting principles in the United States (or any other country which the JV Investors may agree to in writing) as set forth in pronouncements of the Financial Accounting Standards Board (and its predecessors) and the American Institute of Certified Public Accountants, as consistently applied.

1.2 Other Definitions. Terms not otherwise defined, but used, herein that are defined in any Related Agreement shall have the same meaning as in the Related Agreement when used in this Agreement, unless the context otherwise requires.

2. GENERAL COMPANY INFORMATION

2.1 Company, Generally. The name of the Company is Anhui Meineng Store Energy Co., Ltd. (Chinese name: _____ _____). The Company's principal office shall be located at such location within Wuhu City, Anhui Province, the People's Republic of China (or such other location within the People's Republic of China as may be determined, from time to time, by the Board).

2.2 JV Investors, Generally. **Exhibit A** hereto, which may be amended from time to time by the Board, as required, sets forth the following information pertaining to each of the initial JV Investors: (i) the name of the JV Investor, (ii) the address of the principal office of the JV Investor, (iii) information for the legal representative of the JV Investor, (iv) the committed registered capital of the JV Investor and (v) the Percentage Ownership Interest of the JV Investor.

3. COMPANY STRUCTURE AND STRATEGY

3.1 Business Scope. The Company shall (a) source, market and distribute the Products, (b) integrate the Products into other technologies and (c) render Services to customers within the Territory. A more detailed description of the initial scope of the Company's business, including (i) stages of development of the Company; (ii) the Products to be sourced, marketed and distributed by the Company and (iii) the Services to be provided by the Company, is set forth on **Exhibit B** hereto.

- 4 -

3.2 Structure. The Company shall be formed as a Chinese limited liability company. The liability of any JV Investor with respect to the Company shall be limited to the amount of such JV Investor's respective registered capital contribution made to the Company pursuant to this Agreement and no JV Investor shall have any liability to the Company or any third party in excess of such JV Investor's registered capital contribution. The JV Investors shall share the profits, risks and losses in proportion to their respective registered capital contributions, which are set forth on **Exhibit A** .

3.3 Strategy. The Company will pursue its objectives as set forth in Section 3.1 above only with respect to certain sectors and regions within the Territory, as more fully described in the License Agreement, which is attached hereto as **Exhibit C,** all in accordance with the terms and conditions of the Company Documents.

4. **OWNERSHIP OF THE COMPANY**

4.1 Registered Capital. The initial registered capital of the Company shall be Eighty Seven Million Two Hundred Thousand Renminbi (RMB 87,200,000) ("**Registered Capital**"), which will be contributed by the Parties in the amounts, and forms, as set forth on **Exhibit A** ; provided, however, that if (i) upon an assessment of the initial assets to be contributed by the Parties hereunder, the relevant People's Republic of China Governmental Authority determines under Applicable Law that certain assets do not warrant the valuations set forth on **Exhibit A** and (ii) whereupon, unless the JV Investors contribute such amount of funds as is necessary to maintain the Percentage Ownership Interests of the JV Investors as set forth on **Exhibit A** within ten (10) Business Days of the JV Investors' receipt of notice of the occurrence of (i) hereof, this Agreement shall terminate automatically without any further actions by the Parties and all previous contributions to the Company shall be returned promptly to the relevant JV Investor who made such contribution originally.

4.2 Use of Registered Capital. The registered capital of the Company shall be used (a) for the purchase of production equipment and raw materials and (b) for working capital and other purposes as deemed appropriate by the Board, from time to time.

4.3 Payment Schedule of Initial Registered Capital Contributions. Each of the JV Investors shall contribute to the Company its corresponding portion of the initial registered capital of the Company in two (2) installments:

(a) *First Installment.* The JV Investors shall contribute the respective amounts listed below within thirty (30) days following the issuance of the Business License to the Company by the Approval Authority:
  (i) Hong Kong Holdco shall contribute an aggregate amount of Thirty Six Million Seven Hundred Thousand Renminbi (RMB 36,700,000), of which Ten Million Five Hundred Thousand Renminbi (RMB 10,500,000) will be contributed in cash and Twenty Six Million Two Hundred Thousand Renminbi (RMB 26,200,000) will be credited to Hong Kong Holdco for the intellectual property rights granted to the Company by ZBB Corp., an Affiliate of Hong Kong Holdco member, ZBB Energy; and

- 5 -

  (ii)   the China JV shall contribute an aggregate amount in cash of Twenty Million Renminbi (RMB 20,000,000).

(b) *Second Installment.* The JV Investors shall contribute the respective amounts listed below by June 1, 2012:

    (i)   Hong Kong Holdco shall contribute an aggregate amount in cash of Ten Million Five Hundred Thousand Renminbi (RMB 10,500,000); and

    (ii)   the China JV shall contribute an aggregate amount in cash of Twenty Million Renminbi (RMB 20,000,000).

4.4 Decrease or Increase of Registered Capital. During the Term (as defined below) of this Agreement, the Company may increase or decrease the amount of its registered capital; provided, that any increase or decrease in the registered capital of the Company shall require the unanimous approval of the Board and the approval and registration of the Approval Authority.

4.5 Distribution of Net Profits. Subject to any restrictions imposed by Applicable Law, the Company will distribute the net profits it receives to the JV Investors, on a pro-rata basis, in amounts corresponding to their respective Percentage Ownership Interest. The distribution of net profits, in each instance, will be subject to (a) the approval of the Board, (b) the establishment of reasonable reserves and (c) the payment of any associated fees and taxes.

5. OPERATIVE AGREEMENTS; VOTING AGREEMENT

5.1 Operative Agreements .

(a) *License Agreement.* As of the date of establishment of the Company, the Company and ZBB Corp. shall enter into the License Agreement, as set forth on **Exhibit C** hereto.

(b) *Management Services Agreement.* As of the date of establishment of the Company, the Company and Hong Kong Holdco shall enter into the Management Services Agreement, as set forth on **Exhibit D** hereto.

(c) R&D Agreement. As of the date of establishment of the Company, the Company and ZBB Corp. shall enter into the R&D Agreement, as set forth on **Exhibit E** hereto.

(d) Supply Agreements. Additionally, as promptly as practicable following the date of establishment of the Company, the Company and ZBB Corp. shall enter into supply agreements of a fixed term on an arms-length basis, subject to commercially reasonable terms and conditions, pursuant to which (i) the Company shall purchase from ZBB Corp. certain Products manufactured by ZBB Corp. at a cost equal to One Hundred Twenty Percent (120%) of ZBB Corp.'s fully absorbed costs in manufacturing the same, as calculated in accordance with the terms of such supply agreement and (ii) ZBB Corp. may purchase from the Company certain Products manufactured by the Company, priced in a manner corresponding with the above.

- 6 -

5.2 Voting Agreement; Operation of the Company. Each JV Investor agrees (a) to hold all of the Interests of the Company registered in its name or beneficially owned by such JV Investor as of the Effective Date (and any and all other Interests of the Company legally or beneficially acquired by such JV Investor after the Effective Date) in accordance with the terms and conditions of this Agreement; (b) to vote such Interests in accordance with the provisions of this Agreement and (c) to cause the Directors and Supervisors nominated by such JV Investor, within the bounds of the fiduciary duties of the Directors and Supervisors to the Company under the Company Documents or Applicable Law, to vote to effect the terms hereof.

6. **BOARD OF DIRECTORS**

6.1 Composition of the Board of Directors .

(a) Initial Composition; Term. The Company shall be managed by the Board in accordance with this Agreement, the applicable

provisions of the Company Documents and Applicable Law. The Board shall initially consist of five (5) Directors, of which (i) Hong Kong Holdco shall appoint three (3) Directors and (ii) the China JV shall appoint two (2) Directors. The initial Directors appointed by the Parties are set forth on **Exhibit F.** Any change to the number, or representative composition, of Directors shall require the unanimous vote of the JV Investors, as set forth in Section 8.4. The Directors shall serve for such term, or terms, as the JV Investors shall determine.

(b) Removal; Vacancies. Each Director shall remain in office until such Director's death, disability, retirement resignation or removal. In the event of a vacancy on the Board (as a result of the death, disability, retirement, resignation or removal of the Director, or otherwise), the JV Investor that appointed such Director shall be entitled to appoint a replacement Director. At any time the JV Investors must elect a Director, the JV Investors shall vote all of their respective Interests so as to elect the Director appointed by the applicable JV Investor in accordance herewith.

6.2 Removal; Reappointment of Directors. Any Director may be removed for cause in accordance with the applicable provisions of this Agreement and Applicable Law; provided, however, that any JV Investor proposing to remove any Director for cause shall first consult with the other JV Investors so that the JV Investors may, in good faith, attempt to resolve the matter without a formal vote. In addition, any vote taken to remove any Director elected pursuant to Section 6.1, or to fill any vacancy created by the death, disability, retirement, resignation or removal of a Director elected pursuant to Section 6.1, shall also be subject to the provisions of this Section 6.2. In the event of the death, disability, retirement, resignation or removal of any Director (a "**Former Director**"), and pending the replacement of such Former Director, the remaining members of the Board shall give effect to the vote of the other Directors appointed by the same JV Investor as if the Former Director still served on the Board and had cast such Director's vote in the same way as such other Directors.

- 7 -

6.3 Board Meetings .

(a) Convention of Meetings. Any single Director shall have the authority to convene a meeting of the Board. The Board shall meet at least quarterly and written notice of each Board meeting shall be given no less than thirty (30) Business Days in advance of the proposed meeting (which period may be waived by Directors sufficient to represent a quorum under the terms hereof, either through a written waiver or by actual attendance, without objection, at such Board meeting).

(b) Participation by Other Means. Members of the Board may participate in any meeting of the Board, or any committee of the Board, by any means permitted under Applicable Law, including by videoconference or teleconference.

(c) Conduction of Meetings. Board meetings shall be conducted in English and minutes of each meeting shall be prepared by the Company in English and distributed to each Director promptly following such meeting. Proposals or reports brought before any Board meeting for information or action (including, without limitation, the Company's financial statements) shall be prepared in English.

(d) Chairman of the Board. The Board shall designate a Director to serve as the "Chairman" of the Board, who shall preside over all meetings of the Board. The initial Chairman of the Board is the person so appointed and set forth on **Exhibit F.** The Chairman of the Board shall be the legal representative of the Company and shall represent the Company in accordance with the Applicable Laws of the People's Republic of China

and the Articles of Association of the Company. Acts of the Chairman that are either (i) not authorized by the Board or (ii) beyond the Chairman's authority, as the legal representative, as set forth in the Articles of Association of the Company, shall not bind the Company. If the Chairman of the Board is unable to perform the Chairman's duties, the Chairman of the Board shall appoint, in writing, another Director to fulfill such duties in the absence of the Chairman of the Board. If the Chairman of the Board is unable to appoint a temporary replacement, the Board shall appoint one of the Directors to act as the same.

(e) Reimbursements. Each Director shall be reimbursed by the Company for coach class airfare, hotel and food expenses related to such Director's attendance at Board meetings; provided, that such expenses shall be properly documented, with receipts provided to the Company, and the associated reimbursements for each Director shall not exceed Nineteen Thousand Renminbi (RMB 19,000) per quarter.

6.4 Board Quorum: Resolutions. A quorum shall be deemed to exist for the purposes of Board action as long as at least four (4) of the members of the Board are present, including at least one (1) Director appointed by each JV Investor; provided, that all Directors have received notice of such meeting as is required by Applicable Law and the terms of Section 6.3. Except as provided herein, including in Sections 6.6 and 6.7, any action, determination or resolution of the Board shall require the affirmative vote of a majority of the Directors at a duly constituted meeting of the Board.

- 8 -

6.5 Action by the Board Without a Meeting. Any action required or permitted to be taken at a meeting of the Board may be taken without a meeting, if a proposed written consent, setting forth the action so taken or to be taken (i) is sent to all Directors,

(ii) is signed by the number of Directors needed to approve such action and (iii) once signed, is delivered to the Board. Action taken under this Section shall be effective when all of the Directors needed to approve such action have signed the proposed written consent or counterpart thereof, unless the written consent specifies that it is to be effective as of an earlier or later date and time. Such a written consent shall have the same force and effect as if the subject matter was voted upon at a duly called and constituted meeting of the Board and may be described as such in any document or instrument.

6.6 Board Unanimous Approval Rights. Notwithstanding any other provision of this Agreement or the Company Documents, the affirmative vote of all of the members of the Board shall be required for any of the following Company actions:

(i)   amendment of the Articles of Association of the Company;

(ii)   termination, dissolution or extension of the Term of the Company, except as otherwise provided under Section 16;

(iii)   increase, decrease or transfer of the registered capital;

(iv)   merger of the Company with another Entity; or

(v)   reorganization of the Company into several Entities.

6.7 Board Supermajority Approval Rights. Notwithstanding any other provision of this Agreement or the Company Documents, the affirmative vote of at least four (4) Directors shall be required for any of the following Company actions:

(i) approval of the Company's annual budget or any material changes thereto;

(ii)   entry into any agreement or arrangement by the Company with any Affiliate of any JV Investor;

(iii) the hiring or termination of any employee or consultant with annual compensation in excess of Six Hundred Forty Five Thousand Renminbi (RMB 645,000) or with executive responsibilities, and the adoption of any employee benefit plan;

(iv)   entry into, termination, cancellation or material modification of any contract involving payments to or from the Company in excess of Two Million Renminbi (RMB 2,000,000);

(v)   the introduction of new Products or Services;

- 9 -

(vi)   the Company's entry into a line of business outside of the production, marketing and distribution of Products or the provision of the Services;

(vii) the creation of marketing materials for the Company bearing the logos, names or other intellectual property of ZBB Corp. pursuant to the License Agreement;

(viii)   a change in auditors or Accounting Principles; or

(ix)   the issuance of additional Company Interests.

6.8 Deadlock. In the event that (a) the Board is deadlocked with an equal number of votes in favor and opposed on any matter requiring majority approval, or (b) any action requiring supermajority or unanimous approval of the Board fails to pass and such action is necessary for the immediate continued operation of the Company, then the chief executive officers of Hong Kong Holdco and the China JV shall confer over a thirty (30) day period in an attempt to resolve the deadlock. If such discussions do not resolve the deadlock, then, upon the expiration of the abovementioned thirty (30) day period, the Parties shall submit the dispute for resolution pursuant to the dispute resolution procedures set forth in Section 17.2 below. If within one hundred and thirty (130) days from the expiration of the abovementioned thirty (30) day period, either (i) the dispute is not submitted for resolution pursuant to this Section 6.8; (ii) the HKIAC (as defined in Section 17.2) does not accept the arbitration application; or (iii) the HKIAC does not render an arbitral award, Hong Kong Holdco may elect to exercise its rights pursuant to Section 13 below, and, on the date on which Hong Kong Holdco exercises its rights under Section 13 pursuant to this Section 6.8, Hong Kong Holdco and the China JV shall immediately apply to, and use their best efforts to cause, the arbitral tribunal to terminate the arbitration proceedings immediately. Any arbitral award issued after the date on which Hong Kong Holdco exercises its rights under Section 13 shall be nonbinding against the Parties.

7. **BOARD OF SUPERVISORS**

7.1 Composition of the Board of Supervisors .

(a) Initial Composition; Term. The Board of Supervisors shall oversee the accounting and financial activities of the Company and monitor the conduct of the members of the Board and senior executives, in accordance with the terms of this Agreement, the applicable provisions of the Company Documents and Applicable Law. The Board of Supervisors shall initially consist of three (3) Supervisors, of which (i) Hong Kong Holdco will appoint two (2) Supervisors and (ii) the China JV will appoint one (1) Supervisor. Any change to the number, or representative composition, of Supervisors shall require the unanimous vote of the JV Investors, as set forth in Section 8.4. The Supervisors shall serve for such term, or terms, as the JV Investors shall determine.

(b) Removal; Vacancies. Each Supervisor shall remain in office until such Supervisor's death, disability, retirement resignation or removal. In the event of a vacancy on the Board of Supervisors (as a result of the death, disability, retirement, resignation or removal of the Supervisor, or otherwise), the JV Investor that appointed such Supervisor shall be entitled to appoint a replacement Supervisor. At any time the JV Investors must elect a Supervisor, the JV Investors shall vote all of their respective Interests so as to elect the Supervisor appointed by the applicable JV Investor in accordance herewith.

- 10 -

7.2 Removal; Reappointment of Supervisors. Any Supervisor may be removed for cause in accordance with the applicable provisions of this Agreement and Applicable Law; provided, however, that any JV Investor proposing to remove any Supervisor for cause shall first consult with the other JV Investors so that the JV Investors may, in good faith, attempt to resolve the matter without a formal vote. In addition, any vote taken to remove any Supervisor elected pursuant to Section 7.1, or to fill any vacancy created by the death, disability, retirement, resignation or removal of a Supervisor elected pursuant to Section 7.1, shall also be subject to the provisions of Section 7.1 and this Section 7.2. In the event of the death, disability, retirement, resignation or removal of any Supervisor (a **"Former Supervisor"**), and pending the replacement of such Former Supervisor, the remaining members of the Board of Supervisors shall give effect to the vote of the other Supervisors appointed by the same JV Investor as if the Former Supervisor still served on the Board of Supervisors and had cast his or her vote in the same way as such other Supervisors.

7.3 Meetings of the Board of Supervisors .

(a) Convention of Meetings. Any Supervisor shall have the authority to convene a meeting of the Board of Supervisors. The Board of Supervisors shall meet at least twice a year and written

notice of each meeting of the Board of Supervisors shall be given no less than thirty (30) Business Days in advance of the proposed meeting (which period may be waived by Supervisors sufficient to represent a quorum under the terms hereof, either through a written waiver or by actual attendance, without objection, at such meeting of the Board of Supervisors).

(b) Participation by Other Means. Members of the Board of Supervisors may participate in any meeting of the Board of Supervisors, by any means permitted under Applicable Law, including by videoconference or teleconference.

(c) Conduction of Meetings. Meetings of the Board of Supervisors shall be conducted in English and minutes of each meeting shall be prepared by the Company in English and distributed to each Supervisor promptly following such meeting. Proposals or reports brought before any meeting of the Board of Supervisors for information or action (including, without limitation, the Company's financial statements) shall be prepared in English. The Board of Supervisors shall designate a Supervisor to serve as the "Chairman" of the Board of Supervisors, who shall preside over meetings of the Board of Supervisors. The initial Chairman of the Board of Supervisors is the person so appointed and set forth on **Exhibit F**.

(d) Reimbursements. Each Supervisor shall be reimbursed by the Company for coach class airfare, hotel and food expenses related to such Supervisor's attendance at meetings of the Board of Supervisors; provided, that such expenses shall be properly documented, with receipts provided to the Company, and the associated reimbursements for each Supervisor shall not exceed Nineteen Thousand Renminbi (RMB 19,000) per quarter.

- 11 -

7.4 Quorum: Resolutions. A quorum shall be deemed to exist for the purposes of Board of Supervisors action as long as all members of the Board of Supervisors are present. Except as provided herein, any action, determination or resolution of the Board of Supervisors shall require the unanimous vote of the Supervisors at a duly constituted meeting of the Board of Supervisors.

7.5 Action by the Board of Supervisors without a Meeting. Any action required or permitted to be taken at a meeting of the Board of Supervisors may be taken without a meeting, if a proposed written consent, setting forth the action so taken or to be taken (i) is sent to all Supervisors, (ii) is signed by all Supervisors and (iii) once signed, is delivered to the Board of Supervisors. Action taken under this Section shall be effective when all of the Supervisors needed to approve such action have signed the proposed written consent or counterpart thereof, unless the written consent specifies that it is to be effective as of an earlier or later date and time. Such a written consent shall have the same force and effect as if the subject matter was voted upon at a duly called and constituted meeting of the Board of Supervisors and may be described as such in any document or instrument.

7.6 Deadlock. In the event that any action requiring the approval of the Board of Supervisors fails to pass and such action is necessary for the immediate continued operation of the Company, then the chief executive officers of Hong Kong Holdco and the China JV shall confer over a thirty (30) day period in an attempt to resolve the deadlock. If such discussions do not resolve the deadlock, then, upon the expiration of the abovementioned thirty (30) day period, the Parties shall submit the dispute for resolution pursuant to the dispute resolution procedures set forth in Section 17.2 below. If within one hundred and thirty (130) days from the expiration of the abovementioned thirty (30) day period, either (i) the dispute is not submitted for resolution pursuant to this Section 7.6; (ii) the HKIAC (as defined in Section 17.2) does not accept the arbitration application; or (iii) the HKIAC does not render an arbitral award, Hong Kong Holdco may elect to exercise its rights pursuant to Section 13 below, and, on the date on which Hong Kong Holdco exercises its rights under Section 13 pursuant to this Section 7.6, Hong Kong Holdco and the China JV shall immediately apply to, and use their best efforts to cause, the arbitral tribunal to terminate the arbitration proceedings immediately. Any arbitral award issued after the date on which Hong Kong Holdco exercises its rights under Section 13 shall be non-binding against the Parties.

8. JV INVESTORS

8.1 Meetings .

(a) Convention of Meetings. The Board may call for meetings of the JV Investors at such times as it determines to be necessary or appropriate and shall call a meeting upon the written request of any single JV Investor. A JV Investor requesting a meeting must sign the request, deliver the same to the Board and specify therein the purposes of the proposed meeting. There shall be no requirement that annual or other periodic meetings of the JV Investors be held. The Board shall give all JV Investors notice stating the date, time and place of a meeting of the JV Investors, which date shall not be less than fifteen (15) Business Days after the date such notice is given (which period may be waived by the JV Investors sufficient to represent a quorum under the terms hereof, either through a written waiver or by actual attendance, without objection, at such meeting of the JV Investors).

- 12 -

(b) Participation by Other Means. JV Investors may participate in any meeting of the JV Investors, by any means permitted under Applicable Law, including by videoconference or teleconference.

(c) Conduction of Meetings. Meetings of the JV Investors shall be conducted in English and minutes of each meeting shall be prepared by the Company in English and distributed to each JV Investor and the Board promptly following such meeting. Proposals or reports brought before any meeting of the JV

Investors for information or action (including, without limitation, the Company's financial statements) shall be prepared in English.

8.2 Voting Rights; Actions of JV Investors; Quorum. Each JV Investor shall be entitled to vote, and to cast a number of votes equal to the product of (i) one hundred (100) multiplied by (ii) that JV Investor's Percentage Ownership Interest (for the avoidance of doubt, the JV Investors have an aggregate of one hundred (100) votes) on any matter submitted to a vote of the JV Investors in accordance with applicable provisions of this Agreement and Applicable Law. A quorum shall be deemed to exist for purposes of JV Investor action as long as a majority in interest of the JV Investors are present. Except as provided herein, any action, determination or resolution of the JV Investors shall require the majority vote of the JV Investors at a duly constituted meeting of the JV Investors.

8.3 Action by JV Investors Without a Meeting. Any action required or permitted to be taken at a meeting of the JV Investors may be taken without a meeting, if a proposed written consent, setting forth the action so taken or to be taken (i) is sent to all JV Investors, (ii) is signed by the JV Investors holding the number of Interests needed to approve the action and (iii) once signed, is delivered to the Board. Action taken under this Section shall be effective when all of the JV Investors needed to approve such action have signed the proposed written consent or counterpart thereof, unless the written consent specifies that it is to be effective as of an earlier or later date and time. Such a written consent shall have the same force and effect as if the subject matter was voted upon at a duly called and constituted meeting of the JV Investors and may be described as such in any document or instrument.

8.4 JV Investor Unanimous Approval Rights. Notwithstanding any other provision of this Agreement or the Company Documents, the affirmative vote of all of the Interests held by the JV Investors shall be required for any of the following Company actions:

(i)   Any change to the number (or representative com-
       position) of Directors on the Board of Directors; or

(ii)   Any change to the number (or representative com-
       position) of Supervisors on the Board of Supervisors.

8.5 JV Investor Supermajority Rights. Notwithstanding any
other provision of this Agreement or the Company Documents,
the affirmative vote of JV Investors holding at least eighty (80)
votes (as described in Section 8.2 hereof) shall be required for any
of the following Company actions:

- 13 -

(i)   the borrowing of or the incurrence of any indebt-
       edness by the Company or the granting by the
       Company of any liens (other than those arising by
       the operation of law) or encumbrances on a mate-
       rial amount of its assets;

(ii)   the amendment of the constitutive documents of
       the Company;

(iii) the issuance of additional Interests, or securities
       convertible into shares, in the Company; or

(iv)   the filing of a voluntary winding up petition by, or
       the liquidation or dissolution of, the Company.

8.6 Deadlock. In the event that (a) the JV Investors are deadlocked with an equal number of votes in favor and opposed on
any matter requiring majority approval, or (b) any action requiring supermajority or unanimous approval of the JV Investors
fails to pass and such action is necessary for the immediate continued operation of the Company, then the chief executive officers of Hong Kong Holdco and the China JV shall confer over a
thirty (30) day period in an attempt to resolve the deadlock. If

such discussions do not resolve the deadlock, then, upon the expiration of the abovementioned thirty (30) day period, the Parties shall submit the dispute for resolution pursuant to the dispute resolution procedures set forth in Section 17.2 below. If, within one hundred and thirty (130) days from the expiration of the abovementioned thirty (30) day period, either (i) the dispute is not submitted for resolution pursuant to this Section 8.6; (ii) the HKIAC (as defined in Section 17.2) does not accept the arbitration application; or (iii) the HKIAC does not render an arbitral award, Hong Kong Holdco may elect to exercise its rights pursuant to Section 13 below, and, on the date on which Hong Kong Holdco exercises its rights under Section 13 pursuant to this Section 8.6, Hong Kong Holdco and the China JV shall immediately apply to, and use their best efforts to cause, the arbitral tribunal to terminate the arbitration proceedings immediately. Any arbitral award issued after the date on which Hong Kong Holdco exercises its rights under Section 13 shall be nonbinding against the Parties.

9. OFFICERS

9.1 Appointment and Term of Office. The officers of the Company (a) shall consist of the chief executive officer, chief financial officer and administrative assistant to the Board and (b) may consist of other officers, all as may be appointed from time to time by the Board. Such officers will hold office until the earlier of that officer's death, resignation, retirement, disqualification, or removal from office by the Board and until that officer's successor has been duly elected and qualified. Two or more offices may be held by the same person.

9.2 Removal. Any officer appointed hereunder may be removed from office at any time by the Board, with or without cause. Such removal will be without prejudice to the contract rights, if any, of the person so removed. Election or appointment of an officer will not of itself create contract rights.

9.3 Vacancies. Any vacancy in an officer position shall be filled by the Board.

- 14 -

9.4 Compensation. The compensation of all officers of the Company shall be determined by the Board and may be altered by the Board from time to time, except as otherwise provided by contract, and no officer shall be prevented from receiving such compensation by reason of the fact such officer is also a Director or Supervisor. All officers shall be entitled to be paid or reimbursed for all costs and expenditures incurred in conjunction with carrying out the Company's business.

9.5 Powers and Duties. Officers shall have such powers and duties as are provided herein and as may otherwise be established or delegated to them, from time to time, by the Board. The officers of the Company shall possess such powers and duties as customarily are associated with their respective offices, subject to the general direction and supervision of the Board. Such powers and duties will include the following:

(a) *Chief Executive Officer.* Except as otherwise provided in the Company Documents, the Company's day-to-day operations will be managed by the chief executive officer of the Company. The interim chief executive officer, as appointed by Hong Kong Holdco, is set forth on **Exhibit F.** The interim chief executive officer shall be responsible for initially identifying and recruiting candidates to serve as the chief executive officer, the chief financial officer and the administrative assistant to the Board of the Company, and shall submit such candidates to the Board for approval. The person holding the office of chief executive officer also shall perform, under the direction and subject to the control of the Board, such other duties as may be assigned by the Board, from time to time.

(b) *Chief Financial Officer.* The chief financial officer shall be the principal accounting and financial officer of the Company and will have active control of and shall be responsible for all matters pertaining to the accounts and finances of the Company. The chief financial officer will have charge of Company funds and securities and will keep a record of the property and indebtedness of the Company. The chief financial officer shall be prepared at all times to give information as to the condition of the Company and shall make a detailed annual report of the entire business and financial condition of the Company. The person holding the office of chief financial officer shall also perform, under the direction and subject to the control of the Board, such other duties as may be assigned by the Board, from time to time.

(c) *Administrative Assistant to the Board.* The administrative assistant to the Board shall give notice to, attend, and keep the minutes of all of the proceedings at all meetings of the Board, the Board of Supervisors and the JV Investors and will be the custodian of such minutes and all other legal records of the Company. The administrative assistant to the Board will see that all notices required to be given to the Directors, Supervisors and the JV Investors are duly given in accordance with this Agreement or as required by Applicable Law. It shall also be the duty of the administrative assistant to the Board to keep a ledger, in which shall be correctly recorded, all transactions pertaining to the Interests of the Company. The person holding the office of administrative assistant to the Board also shall perform, under the direction and subject to the control of the Board, such other duties as may be assigned by the Board, from time to time.

(d) *Other Officers.* The Board may appoint such other officers, with such titles, powers, duties and compensation, as they may deem necessary for the conduct of the business of the Company. In addition, the Board may authorize the chief executive officer (or other officers) to appoint such agents or employees as the Board deems necessary for the conduct of the business of the Company.

- 15 -

---

10. BUSINESS PLANS; FINANCIAL AND OTHER RECORDS

10.1 Business Plans. The JV Investors will agree to, and the Board will adopt an Initial Business Plan. The Initial Business Plan and each subsequent Business Plan shall set forth, among other things: (i) the scope of the Company's business; (ii) the growth needs of the Company, including personnel requirements, working capital and investment capital; (iii) marketing plans for the Company; (iv) capital and operational budgets for the transactions and entities contemplated by the Company Documents and (v) plans regarding interacting with the appropriate regulatory authorities in connection with the approval of the Products for production and sale, and the Services for provision, in the Territory. After adoption of the Initial Business Plan, the chief executive officer shall submit a proposed Business Plan to the Board for approval at least sixty (60) days prior to the start of each Fiscal Year. Each such Business Plan shall cover one Fiscal Year of the Company's operations and shall contain the matters set forth in this Section.

10.2 Accounting and Management Information Systems. In the conduct of its business, the Company shall pursue a policy of adopting and maintaining accounting and management information systems that facilitate the Company's compliance with the Reporting Requirements (as defined below), the Accounting Principles and are otherwise consistent with sound business practices and corporate governance in the context of the Company's business and operations. The Company shall engage a reputable, international accounting firm to provide accounting services in conjunction with the Reporting Requirements; the initial accounting firm shall be Deloitte LLP. Two (2) sets of books and records will be kept, one in accordance with China Accounting Principles and one in accordance with U.S. Accounting Principles.

10.3 Financial Statements, Accounting and Other Reports. The Company shall cause (i) two (2) sets of the following financial statements to be prepared (one in accordance with China Accounting Principles and one in accordance with U.S. Accounting Principles) and (ii) such financial statements to be provided to each JV Investor (the following requirements being referred to collectively as the "**Reporting Requirements**"):

(a) Annual Financial Statements. As soon as available, but in any event within forty five (45) days after the end of each Fiscal Year, a copy of the annual financial statements of the Company, including, a balance sheet, income statement, statement of cash flows and statement of the JV Investors' equity as of the end of the Fiscal Year, setting forth in each case in comparative form the figures for the previous year, and audited and certified by the Company's accounting firm.

(b) Quarterly Financial Statements. As soon as available, but in any event within thirty (30) days after the end of each fiscal quarter, a copy of the Company's unaudited financial statements for such fiscal quarter including a balance sheet, income statement, statement of cash flows and statement of the JV Investors' equity as of the end of such quarter, setting forth in comparative form the figures for the corresponding quarter in the previous Fiscal Year, and certified by the chief financial officer of the Company as being fairly stated in all material respects (subject to normal year-end audit adjustments).

- 16 -

(c) Quarterly Management Reports. On a quarterly basis, the Company's management shall report to the Board: (i) the Company's current business objectives and compliance with the Business Plan then in effect, (ii) notice of any new clients, and (iii) such other reasonable information as the Board may request.

10.4 Right of Inspectio n. During the regular office hours at the location of the Company, and upon reasonable notice to the Company, each JV Investor shall have (a) full access to all properties, books of account, and records of the Company, (b) the right to make copies from such books and records at its own expense and (c) the right to discuss with the Company's executive officers the affairs, finances and accounts of the Company. Any information obtained by a JV Investor through exercise of rights granted under this Section shall, to the extent constituting Confidential Information hereunder, be subject to the confidentiality provisions set forth in Section 14. Any JV Investor having rights under this Section shall also have the right to confer, upon reasonable notice and during normal business hours, with the auditors of the Company, and with the accounting firm which has prepared or is preparing any of the financial statements required to be delivered by the Company, as a part of the Reporting Requirements and the Company shall grant, or use commercially reasonable efforts to provide for, any permission requested by such auditors to permit such conferences to take place.

11. <u>INSURANCE; INDEMNIFICATION</u>

11.1 Liability. To the fullest extent permitted by Applicable Law, each Director, Supervisor and officer of the Company shall not be personally liable to the Company or the JV Investors for monetary damages for breach of any duty owed as a Director, Supervisor or officer of the Company, and the Company's Articles of Association shall so provide.

11.2 Indemnification of Directors, Supervisors and Officers .

(a) Generally. Except to the extent limited hereunder, each Director, Supervisor or officer of the Company (each a "**Company Representative**") who is made a party or is threatened to be made a party to or is involved in any proceeding by reason of the fact that such Company Representative, or the legal representative of such Company Representative, is or was a Company Representative, shall be indemnified and held harmless by the

Company to the fullest extent authorized by Applicable Law, as the same exists or may hereafter be amended (but, in case of any such amendment, only to the extent that such amendment permits the Company to provide broader indemnification rights than said law permitted the Company to provide prior to such amendment), against all expense, liability and loss (including attorneys' fees, judgments, fines, excise taxes or penalties and amounts paid or to be paid in settlement) reasonably incurred or suffered by such person in connection therewith and such indemnification shall continue as to a person who has ceased to be a Company Representative, and shall inure to the benefit of such Company Representative's heirs, executors and administrators. The right to indemnification conferred herein shall be a contract right based upon an offer from the Company, which offer shall be deemed to be accepted by such person's service or continued service as a Company Representative. The Company may, by action of the Board, provide indemnification to employees or agents of the Company, to the extent permitted by Applicable Law, with the same scope and effect as the foregoing indemnification of Company Representatives.

- 17 -

(b) Limitations. Notwithstanding the foregoing, the provisions of 11.2(a) shall not eliminate or limit the liability of, or provide indemnity to, a Company Representative for or in connection with any act, inaction or omission of such Company Representative that (i) constitutes a breach by Company Representative of that Company Representative's duties of loyalty or care to the Company or the JV Investors (other than as expressly excepted under this Agreement; (ii) was detrimental to the Company and not in good faith; (iii) involved intentional misconduct or a knowing violation of the law: (iv) clearly was in conflict with the interests of the Company or (v) results in such Company Representative deriving an improper personal benefit. The right to indemnification conferred in this Section 11.2 shall not be exclusive of any other right that a Company Representative may

have or hereafter acquire under law or equity, provision of this Agreement or otherwise.

11.3 Indemnification of JV Investors .

(a) Generally. To the extent permitted by law, the Company will indemnify and hold harmless each JV Investor, the partners, officers and directors of each JV Investor and each person, if any, who Controls such JV Investor (each an "**Indemnified Party**") against all liability, loss, damage, penalty, action, claim, judgment, settlement, cost and expense of any kind or nature whatsoever (including all reasonable attorneys' fees) (collectively referred to as "**Losses**") that arise under applicable securities laws, that in any way relate to, or arise out of, or are alleged to relate to or arise out of any of the following statements, omissions or violations (collectively a "**Violation**") by the Company: (i) any untrue statement or alleged untrue statement of a material fact contained in any registration statement, including any preliminary prospectus or final prospectus contained therein or any amendments or supplements thereto, or otherwise, (ii) the omission or alleged omission to state therein a material fact required to be stated therein or otherwise, or necessary to make the statements therein not misleading, or (iii) any violation or alleged violation by the Company of any applicable securities laws; and the Company will pay to each such Indemnified Party any legal or other expenses reasonably incurred by such Indemnified Party in connection with investigating or defending any such Loss; provided, however, that the indemnity agreement contained in this Section 11.3 shall not apply to amounts paid in settlement of any such Loss if such settlement is effected without the consent of the Company, which consent shall not be unreasonably withheld, nor shall the Company be liable in any such case for any such Loss to the extent that it arises out of or is based upon a Violation which occurs in reliance upon and in conformity with written information furnished expressly for use in connection with any registration of the Company's Interests by such Indemnified Party.

(b) Indemnity Claims. Promptly after receipt by an Indemnified Party under this Section 11.3 of notice of the commencement of any action (including any governmental action), such Indemnified Party will, if a claim in respect thereof is to be made against the Company under this Section 11.3, deliver to the Company a written notice of the commencement thereof and the Company shall have the right to participate in, and, to the extent the Company so desires, to assume the defense thereof with counsel mutually satisfactory to the parties; provided, however, that an Indemnified Party shall have the right to retain its own counsel, with the fees and expenses to be paid by the Company, if representation of such Indemnified Party by the counsel retained by the Company would be inappropriate due to actual or potential differing interests between such Indemnified Party and the Company. The failure to deliver written notice to the Company within a reasonable time of the commencement of any such action, if materially prejudicial to its ability to defend such action, shall relieve the Company of any liability to the Indemnified Party under this Section 11.3, but the omission so to deliver written notice to the Company will not relieve it of any liability that it may have to any Indemnified Party otherwise than under this Section 11.3.

- 18 -

(c) Unavailability of Indemnification. If the indemnification provided for under this Section 11.3 is held by a court of competent jurisdiction or by an arbitral tribunal to which an Indemnified Party has submitted the matter to be unavailable to an Indemnified Party with respect to any Losses referred to herein, the Company, in lieu of indemnifying such Indemnified Party thereunder, shall to the extent permitted by Applicable Law contribute to the amount paid or payable by such Indemnified Party as a result of such Loss in such proportion as is appropriate to reflect the relative fault of the Company on the one hand and of the Indemnified Party on the other in connection with the Violations that resulted in such Loss, as well as any other relevant equitable considerations. The relative fault of the Company

and of the Indemnified Party shall be determined by reference to, among other things, whether the untrue or alleged untrue statement of a material fact or the omission to state a material fact relates to information supplied by the Company or by the Indemnified Party and the parties' relative intent, knowledge, access to information and opportunity to correct or prevent such statement or omission; provided, that in no event shall any contribution by a JV Investor hereunder exceed the registered capital contributed by such JV Investor.

11.4 Advancement. The Company shall reimburse, promptly following request therefor, all reasonable expenses incurred by a Person indemnified by the Company pursuant to Section 11.2 or 11.3 hereof (an "**Indemnitee**") in connection with any threatened, pending or completed action, suit, arbitration, investigation or other proceeding ("**Claim**") arising out of, or relating to the matters identified in this Article 11; provided, however, that prior to such advancement, the Indemnitee shall have agreed in writing (determined to be sufficient by the Board to protect the interests of the Company) to repay such advancement in connection with acts, conduct or omissions as to which it shall be determined by a court of competent jurisdiction or an arbitrator that such Indemnitee engaged in intentional misconduct or in a knowing and culpable violation of the law.

11.5 Insurance. The Company shall obtain and maintain, and will continue to maintain at all times during the terms of this Agreement, the insurance listed below, in commercially reasonable amounts, at its own expense, from an insurer that is A.M. Best Company rated A- or higher. Any such policy shall be endorsed to name specifically each of the Parties and their respective subsidiaries, affiliates, successors and assigns as additional insureds. The Company shall provide any certificate of insurance to the Parties upon request and all such certificates shall indicate that thirty (30) days prior written notice to the Parties of cancellation or non-renewal is required.

(a) General liability insurance;

- 19 -

(b) Product liability insurance;

(c) Errors & omissions insurance; and

(d) Director & officer insurance, to protect the Company and its Directors, Supervisors and officers, against any such expense, liability or loss, whether or not the Company would have the power to indemnify such person against such expense, liability or loss under the Related Agreements.

12. COMPLIANCE WITH LAWS

12.1 General. In the conduct of its business, the Company shall comply with all Applicable Laws and maintaining all franchises, permits, licenses and similar authorities necessary for the conduct of its business; provided further, that the Company shall comply with all statutes, laws, rules, regulations, directives, treaties, judgments, orders, decrees or injunctions of any Governmental Authority that are applicable to ZBB Corp. as a publicly-traded U.S. company, including without limitation relevant provisions of the Securities Exchange Act of 1934, the Sarbanes-Oxley Act of 2002 and the Dodd–Frank Wall Street Reform and Consumer Protection Act, to the extent reasonably requested by Hong Kong Holdco.

12.2 Anti-Corruption. Neither the Company, nor any of its Directors, Supervisors, officers, employees, agents or other Person associated with or acting for or on behalf of the Company, will take any action that would cause the Company to be in violation of the Foreign Corrupt Practices Act of 1977, as amended, or any similar state or local Applicable Law, the Anti-Kickback Act of 1986 or any state or local/municipality anti-kickback Applicable Law, Applicable Laws restricting the payment of contingent fee arrangements, or any Applicable Laws of similar effect.

13. TRANSFERS AND SALES OF INTERESTS

13.1 Transfers of Interests .

(a) General Restriction on Transfers. Except to the extent otherwise provided in this Section 13, no JV Investor shall Transfer (or create or suffer to exist any Encumbrance against) all or any portion of that JV Investor's Interest, except with the advance approval of all JV Investors. Such approval may specify the rights and obligations the transferee shall have, including whether the proposed transferee is to be admitted as a full substituted JV Investor. The grant or denial of a JV Investor's approval for a proposed Transfer or Encumbrance may be made in such JV Investor's sole and absolute discretion.

(b) Rights and Obligations of Substituted JV Investor. A substituted JV Investor shall have all the rights and powers, and shall be subject to all the restrictions and liabilities, of the Transferring JV Investor (as defined below), relative to such transferred Interest.

(c) Continuing Obligations of Transferor. Any Transferring JV Investor (as defined below) who Transfers all of such JV Investor's Interest shall cease to be a JV Investor; provided, however, that such Transfer, without more, shall not release the Transferring JV Investor from any liability with respect to the transferred Interest or any other obligation that such Transferring JV Investor may have to the Company.

- 20 -

13.2 Unauthorized Transfers   Any purported Transfer or Encumbrance of an Interest of any JV Investor that does not comply with the conditions set forth in this Section 13 shall be null, void and of no effect.

13.3 *Withdrawal of a JV Investor.* A JV Investor shall have no right to withdraw, dissociate or withdraw such JV Investor's registered capital from the Company.

13.4 Transfers Pursuant to a Bona Fide Offer; Rights of First Refusal.

(a) Notice of Bona Fide Offer. Notwithstanding the general restrictions on Transfers in Section 13.1, if a JV Investor desires to Transfer all or any portion of that JV Investor's Interest pursuant to a Bona Fide Offer (as defined below) made to that JV Investor by a third-party, and such JV Investor is unable to obtain the approval of the other JV Investors to such Transfer, as provided in Section 13.1(a) above, then such JV Investor desiring to so transfer (a "**Transferring JV Investor**") shall give written notice thereof (which shall include a copy of such bona fide offer) to the other JV Investors (the "**Receiving JV Investors**"). As used herein, the term "**Bona Fide Offer**"means a legally binding offer made in good faith (in writing) by a third party, who the Transferring JV Investor reasonably believes has the financial means to consummate the proposed Transfer, which offer includes (i) the Interests to be transferred; (ii) the name and address of the proposed transferee; (iii) in the case of a proposed transferee that is an entity (i.e., not a natural Person), the identity of all direct and indirect owners of the proposed transferee; (iv) the proposed consideration for the Transfer and (v) the other terms of the proposed Transfer.

(b) Receiving JV Investors' Right of First Refusal. The Receiving JV Investors shall have the right to purchase all, but not less than all, of the subject Interest from the Transferring JV Investor on the terms and conditions contained in the Bona Fide Offer.

(c) Exercise of Right of First Refusal; Closing. The Receiving JV Investors shall have sixty (60) calendar days from the date of receipt of the notice referenced in Section 13.4(a) (the "**Election Period**") to elect to exercise their purchase rights by sending

written notice thereof to the Transferring JV Investor. Those Receiving JV Investors exercising said purchase right (the "**Electing JV Investors**") may divide the Interests to be purchased by them in any amounts or proportions that they may mutually agree upon. In the event that they cannot or do not agree upon the Interests to be purchased by each, then each such Electing JV Investor shall purchase that percentage of the subject Interests proportionate to that Electing JV Investor's respective Interest relative to the aggregate Interests of all Electing JV Investors. The Electing JV Investors must purchase all of the Interests described in the Bona Fide Offer. The closing of such a purchase shall occur at a date, time and place determined by the Electing JV Investors, which date shall be no later than thirty (30) days following the end of the Election Period.

(d)   Transfer to Third-Party Transferee.   If the Receiving JV Investors do not elect to purchase all of the Interests within the Election Period, then the Receiving JV Investors shall have no right to purchase any of the Interests, and the Transferring JV Investor may Transfer, within a period of thirty (30) calendar days beginning at the end of the Election Period, all of the Interests described in the Bona Fide Offer to the proposed third-party transferee on the terms and conditions contained in the Bona Fide Offer; provided, however, that the proposed third-party transferee must have delivered to the Company, prior to such Transfer, an agreement, in form and substance reasonably satisfactory to the JV Investors, duly executed by the proposed third-party transferee, under the terms of which such third-party transferee joins in the execution of this Agreement, becomes a substituted JV Investor and agrees to be bound by all of the terms and provisions of this Agreement. If the Transferring JV Investor does not Transfer such Interests by the end of such thirty (30) day period, the subject Interests, and the Interest represented thereby, shall again become subject to the restrictions of this Agreement, as though they had never been so offered.

- 21 -

13.5 Acknowledgment of Liquidity. The JV Investors (a) acknowledge and agree that the provisions of this Agreement provide reasonable methods of exiting the Company and an adequate means for obtaining liquidity with respect to their investment in the Company and (b) agree not to assert any claim in any legal proceeding that the provisions of this Section 13 are unreasonable, unlawful or unenforceable.

13.6 Buy/Sell Provisions .

(a) *Hong Kong Holdco Call Right.* Notwithstanding the foregoing, Hong Kong Holdco shall have the right to require the China JV to sell the China JV's Interests in the Company to Hong Kong Holdco at any time following any of the circumstances listed below, upon written notice to the China JV:

> (i)   in the event of a deadlock by the Company's Board that cannot be resolved or a failure to approve an action requiring a unanimous or supermajority vote of the Directors, in any case with respect to a matter that seriously impairs the Company's operations;

> (ii)   in the event that the Board of Supervisors fails to approve an action requiring a unanimous vote, in any case with respect to a matter that seriously impairs the Company's operations;

> (iii)   in the event of a deadlock on a JV Investor vote that cannot be resolved or a failure to approve an action requiring a supermajority or unanimous vote of the JV Investors, in any case with respect to a matter that seriously impairs the Company's operations;

(iv)   a private equity fund or other financial sponsor acquires an equity interest in, or loans money to, the China JV (a "**China JV Change in Structure**");

(v)   a China JV Change of Control; or

(vi)   a material breach or default of this Agreement by the China JV (a "**China JV Breach**").

- 22 -

(b) Hong Kong Holdco Put Right. Notwithstanding the foregoing, Hong Kong Holdco shall have the right to require the China JV to purchase Hong Kong Holdco's Interests in the Company at any time following any of the circumstances listed below, upon written notice to the China JV:

(i)   in the event of a deadlock by the Company's Board that cannot be resolved or a failure to approve an action requiring a unanimous or supermajority vote of the Directors, in any case with respect to a matter that seriously impairs the Company's operations;

(ii)   in the event that the Board of Supervisors fails to approve an action requiring a unanimous vote, in any case with respect to a matter that seriously impairs the Company's operations;

(iii)   in the event of a deadlock on a JV Investor vote that cannot be resolved or a failure to approve an action requiring a supermajority or unanimous vote of the JV Investors, in any case with respect to a matter that seriously impairs the Company's operations;

(iv)   a China JV Change in Structure;

(v)   a China JV Change of Control; or

(vi)   a China JV Breach.

(c) China JV Call Right.   Notwithstanding the foregoing, the China JV shall have the right to require Hong Kong Holdco to sell Hong Kong Holdco's Interests in the Company to the China JV at any time following a material breach or default of this Agreement by Hong Kong Holdco (a "**Hong Kong Holdco Breach**"), upon written notice to Hong Kong Holdco.

(d) China JV Put Right.   Notwithstanding the foregoing, the China JV shall have the right to require Hong Kong Holdco to purchase the China JV's Interests in the Company at any time following a Hong Kong Holdco Breach, upon written notice to Hong Kong Holdco.

(e) Buy/Sell Arrangements.   The value of the Interests in the Company being purchased under this Section 13.6 shall be determined as follows:

(i)   In the event that either Hong Kong Holdco or the China JV exercises its put right due to a China JV Breach or a Hong Kong Holdco Breach, respectively, an amount equal to (i) 1.15 multiplied by (ii) the Interest Value (as defined below);

(ii)   In the event that either Hong Kong Holdco or the China JV exercises its call right due to a China JV Breach or a Hong Kong Holdco Breach, respectively, an amount equal to (i) .85 multiplied by (ii) the Interest Value (as defined below); or

---

(iii)   In all other cases (for example, if Hong Kong Holdco exercises its put right due to a China JV Change in Control), an amount equal to the Interest Value. For purposes hereof, the **"Interest Value"** shall mean the amount equal to the appraised value of the Company, as determined by an independent third party mutually selected by the Parties, multiplied by a fraction equal to the percentage of equity interest represented by the Interest being sold.

The closing of any purchase or sale pursuant to this Section 13.6 shall occur at a date, time and place determined by the JV Investor initiating the same, which date shall be no later than thirty (30) days following the determination of the Interest Value.

13.7 Sale of the Company. In the event that all of the Interests of the Company are sold to a third party, Hong Kong Holdco shall work with the buyer of those Interests to transfer cell stack manufacturing knowledge to the purchaser's chosen location in a manner mutually agreed by such purchaser and Hong Kong Holdco.

14. CONFIDENTIALITY

Each Party (the **"Receiving Party"**) undertakes to retain in confidence the terms of this Agreement and all other non-public information, technology, materials and know-how of the other Party (**"Disclosing Party"**) disclosed or acquired by the Receiving Party pursuant to or in connection with this Agreement that is either designated as proprietary and/or confidential or, by the nature of the circumstances surrounding disclosure, ought in good faith to be treated as proprietary and/or confidential

("**Confidential Information**"); provided, that each Party may disclose the terms and conditions of this Agreement to its immediate legal and financial consultants in the ordinary course of its business. Neither Party may use any Confidential Information with respect to which it is the Receiving Party for any purpose other than to carry out the activities contemplated by this Agreement. Each Party agrees to use commercially reasonable efforts to protect Confidential Information of the other Party, and in any event, to take precautions at least as great as those taken to protect its own confidential information of a similar nature. Each Party will also notify the other promptly in writing if such Party learns of any unauthorized use or disclosure of any Confidential Information that it has received from the other Party, and will cooperate in good faith to remedy the occurrence to the extent reasonably possible. The restrictions set forth in this Section do not apply to any information that: (a) was known by the Receiving Party without obligation of confidentiality prior to disclosure thereof by the other Party; (b) was in or entered the public domain through no fault of the Receiving Party; (c) is disclosed to the Receiving Party by a third party legally entitled to make the disclosure without violation of any obligation of confidentiality; (d) is required to be disclosed by applicable laws or regulations (but in that event, only to the extent required to be disclosed, and provided that the Disclosing Party is given the opportunity to review and redact the Agreement prior to disclosure); or (e) is independently developed by the Receiving Party without reference to any Confidential Information of the other Party. Upon request of the Disclosing Party, the Receiving Party will return to the Disclosing Party all materials, in any medium, that contain or reveal all or any part of any Confidential Information of the Disclosing Party. Each Party acknowledges that breach of this provision by it would result in irreparable harm to the other Party, for which money damages would be an insufficient remedy, and therefore that the other Party will be entitled to seek injunctive relief to enforce the provisions of this Section.

- 24 -

15. REPRESENTATIONS AND WARRANTIES OF THE JV INVESTORS

15.1 Warranties of the JV Investors. Each of the JV Investors hereby represents and warrants that, as of the date of the execution and delivery hereof, the following statements are true and correct:

(a) Organization; Good Standing. The JV Investor is a legal entity, organized and validly existing under the laws of the applicable jurisdiction, with full power to own its assets and conduct its business as conducted and as proposed to be conducted. The JV Investor is registered or qualified to do business and in good standing in each jurisdiction in which it owns or leases property or transacts business and where the failure to be so qualified would have a material adverse effect on the ability of the JV Investor or the Company to consummate the transactions contemplated by this Agreement or the Related Agreements, and no proceeding has been instituted in any such jurisdiction, revoking, limiting or curtailing, or seeking to revoke, limit or curtail, such power and authority or qualification. Each of the JV Investors will provide, upon request of any other JV Investor, a copy of its formation and governing documents, as are then currently in effect.

(b) Authorization. The JV Investor has all requisite corporate power and authority to execute and deliver this Agreement, to perform fully its obligations hereunder and to consummate the transactions contemplated by this Agreement or the Related Agreements. All corporate action on the part of the JV Investor necessary for the authorization, execution and delivery of this Agreement and for the performance of all of its obligations hereunder has been taken, and this Agreement when fully executed

and delivered shall constitute a valid, legally binding and enforce-able obligation of the JV Investor (except as the enforceability thereof may be limited by any laws affecting creditors' rights generally, by general principles of equity, regardless of whether such enforceability is considered in equity or at law).

(c) Government and Other Consents. No consent, authorization, license, permit, registration or approval of, or exemption or other action by, any Governmental Authority, or any other Person, is required in connection with the JV Investor's execution, deliv-ery and performance of this Agreement, or if any such consent is required, the JV Investor has satisfied the applicable require-ment, except for any matters that would not have a material adverse effect on the ability of the JV Investor or the Company to consummate the transactions contemplated by this Agreement or the Related Agreements.

(d) Effect of Agreement. The JV Investor's execution, delivery and performance of this Agreement, and the consummation of the transactions contemplated hereby will not result in a breach or violation of any of the terms, conditions or provisions of, or constitute a default (or with notice or lapse of time or both con-stitute) or require the consent of any other Person under (i) any indenture, mortgage, agreement or other instrument or arrange-ment to which the JV Investor is a party; (ii) any of the terms or provisions of the formation or governing documents of the JV Investor or any provision of Applicable Law; (iii) any judgment, order, writ, injunction or decree applicable to the JV Investor; or (iv) or have any effect on the compliance by the JV Investor with, any applicable licenses, permits or authorizations, except in each case under clauses (i), (ii), (iii) or (iv) where such breach, violation or default would not have a material adverse effect on the ability of the JV Investor or the Company to consummate the transactions contemplated by this Agreement or the Related Agreements.

- 25 -

(e) Proceedings. There is no action, suit or proceeding at law or in equity or otherwise in, before or by any Governmental Authority or, to the JV Investor's knowledge, threatened by or against the JV Investor which question the validity of, or which question the JV Investor's right to enter into or perform this Agreement, or which would prevent or restrict its ability to enter into and perform its obligations under this Agreement, except where such action, suit or proceeding could not reasonably be expected to have a material adverse effect on the ability of the JV Investor or the Company to consummate the transactions contemplated by this Agreement or the Related Agreements.

(f) Anti-Corruption. Neither the JV Investor, nor any of its directors, supervisors, officers, employees, agents or other Person associated with or acting for or on behalf of the JV Investor, has taken, or will take, any action that would cause the JV Investor or the Company to be in violation of the Foreign Corrupt Practices Act of 1977, as amended, or any similar state or local Applicable Law, the Anti-Kickback Act of 1986 or any state or local/municipality anti-kickback Applicable Law, Applicable Laws restricting the payment of contingent fee arrangements, or any Applicable Laws of similar effect.

16. **TERM AND TERMINATION**

16.1 Term. This Agreement shall be effective as of the Effective Date and shall continue in effect until the earlier of (a) the expiration of the Agreement on the tenth (10 th) anniversary of the Effective Date or (b) upon the date of termination of this Agreement pursuant to Section 16.2 (the "**Term**").

16.2 Termination. This Agreement shall terminate:

> (i)   Upon the mutual written agreement of the JV Investors;

(ii)   Upon the material breach (or default in the performance of the terms) of this Agreement by any JV Investor;

(iii)   As to any JV Investor, upon the permitted Transfer of all Interests of the Company held by such JV Investor;

(iv)   Upon either Party's exercise of its buy/sell options under Section 13.6 of this Agreement; or

(v)   Upon the occurrence of an IPO or purchase by a third party of all of the Interests of the Company.

16.3 Survival. The rights and obligations of the Parties under Section 14 (Confidentiality), Section 16.4 (Continuing Liability), Section 17 (Governing Law and Dispute Resolution) and Section 18 (General Provisions) (except for Section 18.5 (Further Assurances)) shall survive any termination of this Agreement.

- 26 -

16.4 Continuing Liability. Termination of this Agreement for any reason shall not release a Party from any liability or obligation which has already accrued as of the effective date of such termination, and shall not constitute a waiver or release of, or otherwise be deemed to prejudice or adversely affect, any rights, remedies or claims, whether for damages or otherwise, which a Party may have hereunder, at law, equity or otherwise or which may arise out of or in connection with such termination.

17. GOVERNING LAW; DISPUTE RESOLUTION

17.1 Governing Law. The validity, construction and enforceability of this Agreement shall be governed by and construed in accordance with the laws of the People's Republic of China.

17.2 Discussions and Arbitration. The Parties will discuss and finally settle all disputes between them, and among them and the Company, arising out of this Agreement (including with respect to this Section 17), in accordance with the Domestic Arbitration Rules of Hong Kong International Arbitration Centre ("**HKIAC**"). The Company and the Parties shall at all times maintain authorized agents in each of the United States and Wuhu City, Anhui Province, the People's Republic of China to receive, for and on its behalf service of any summons, complaint or other legal process.

18. <u>GENERAL PROVISIONS</u>

18.1 Non-Competition; Business Opportunities .

(a) Non-Competition. The JV Investors agree that, as applicable, they will not (and will cause the Company and their respective members, including AnHui Xinlong and Wuhu Huarui, not to) compete, either directly or indirectly, with ZBB Energy or its Affiliates, or with the Company, as applicable, with respect to the sourcing, production, marketing and distribution of any products sourced, produced, marketed or distributed by ZBB Energy or its Affiliates or the Company, as applicable, during the Term of this Agreement and for five (5) years thereafter, anywhere in the world, except as explicitly provided herein or in the Company Documents.

(b) Business Opportunities. The JV Investors agree that they will cause the Company, and the Directors, Supervisors and officers of the Company, to refer any new business opportunities within the scope of this Agreement to the JV Investors for determination as to whether those opportunities are best explored in the Company or through one or more of the JV Investors or their respective Affiliates.

- 27 -

(c) Opportunities Outside the Agreement. The fact that a JV Investor or Affiliate takes advantage of an opportunity that

is not within the scope of this Agreement (either alone or with other Persons, including Entities in which such JV Investor or Affiliate has an interest) and does not offer such opportunity to the Company or to the other JV Investors shall not subject such JV Investor or Affiliate to liability to the Company or to the other JV Investors on account of any lost opportunity.

(d) Exceptions. Notwithstanding the foregoing, the Company will renounce, and not accept or be involved in, any interest or expectancy in any business opportunity presented to, or which came to the attention of, any Director or Supervisor who also is an employee or director of ZBB Energy or its Affiliates (other than the Company, the Parties or PowerSav) in the course of performing such Person's official duties for ZBB Energy or its Affiliates.

18.2 Notices and Other Communications. Any and all notices, requests, demands and other communications required by or otherwise contemplated to be made under this Agreement or Applicable Law shall be in writing and in English and shall be provided by one or more of the following means and shall be deemed to have been duly given (a) if delivered personally, when received; (b) if transmitted by facsimile, on the date of transmission with receipt of a transmittal confirmation or (c) if by international courier service, on the fourth (4 th) Business Day following the date of deposit with such courier service, or such earlier delivery date as may be confirmed in writing to the sender by such courier service. All such notices, requests, demands and other communications shall be addressed as follows:

If to the Company :

_____

_____

_____

_____

_____

with a copy (which copy shall not constitute notice) to :

_____
_____
_____
_____
_____

- 28 -

If to Hong Kong Holdco :

_____
_____
_____
_____
_____

with a copy (which copy shall not constitute notice) to :

Mr. Mark Busch and Mr. Eliab Erulkar
K&L Gates LLP
Hearst Tower, 47 th Floor
214 North Tryon Street
Charlotte, North Carolina, USA 28202

If to the China JV :

_____
_____
_____
_____
_____

with a copy (which copy shall not constitute notice) to :

_____
_____

_____
_____
_____
_____

or to such other address or facsimile number as a Party may specify to the other Party from time to time in writing.

18.3 Severability. If any provision in this Agreement shall be found or be held to be invalid or unenforceable then the meaning of said provision shall be construed, to the extent feasible, so as to render the provision enforceable, and if no feasible interpretation would save such provision, it shall be severed from the remainder of this Agreement which shall remain in full force and effect. In such event, the Parties shall use their respective best efforts to negotiate in good faith a substitute, valid and enforceable provision or agreement that most nearly affects the Parties' intent in entering into this Agreement.

- 29 -

18.4 References to this Agreement; Headings. Unless otherwise indicated, references to sections and exhibits herein are to sections of, and exhibits to, this Agreement. Words such as "herein," "hereby," "hereinafter," "hereof," "hereto," and "hereunder" refer to this Agreement as a whole, unless the context otherwise requires. The subject headings of the sections of this Agreement are for reference only, and shall not affect the construction or interpretation of any of the provisions of this Agreement.

18.5 Further Assurances. The Parties shall each perform such acts, execute and deliver such instruments and documents, and do all such other things as may be reasonably necessary to carry out the provisions of this Agreement.

18.6 No Waiver. No waiver of any term or condition of this Agreement shall be valid or binding on a Party unless the same shall have been set forth in a written document, specifically referring to this Agreement and duly signed by the waiving Party. The failure of a Party to enforce at any time any of the provisions of this Agreement, or the failure to require at anytime performance by the other Party of any of the provisions of this Agreement, shall in no way; be construed to be a present or future waiver of such provisions, nor in any way affect the ability of a Party to enforce each and every such provision thereafter.

18.7 Entire Agreement; Amendments. The terms and conditions contained in this Agreement and the Related Agreements (including the exhibits hereto and thereto) constitute the entire agreement between the Parties and supersede all previous agreements and understandings, whether oral or written, between the Parties with respect to the subject matter hereof and thereof. No agreement or understanding amending this Agreement shall be binding upon any Party unless set forth in a written document which expressly refers to this Agreement and which is signed and delivered by duly authorized representatives of each Party.

18.8 Expenses. Except as otherwise described in this Agreement or the Related Agreements, each Party shall bear its own legal and other costs and expenses in connection with this Agreement, and the Related Agreements; provided, however, that upon execution of this Agreement and the issuance of a business license by the Approval Authority, the Company will reimburse each Party for all direct expenses incurred by each Party in connection with this Agreement or the formation of the Company, including without limitation all reasonable travel expenses, legal fees and accounting fees.

18.9 Assignment. No Party shall have the right to assign its rights or obligations under this Agreement except in connection with a transfer of all of a JV Investor's Interests in a manner permitted hereunder, under terms reasonably acceptable to the non-assigning JV Investor and providing for the assignee to be bound by the terms hereof, and for the assigning JV Investor to remain liable for the assignee's performance of its obligations hereunder. Any assignment or purported assignment not made in accordance with this Section and Section 13, as applicable, shall be void and of no force and effect. This Agreement shall inure to the benefit of, and shall be binding upon, the Parties and their respective successors and permitted assigns.

- 30 -

18.10 No Agency. The authority of each Party hereunder is limited to that which explicitly is set forth herein and the Company Documents. Neither Party has, and shall not hold itself out as having, any right, power or authority in any manner, (i) to accept, any offer, proposal or negotiated terms solicited by that Party pursuant to the terms hereof on behalf of the other Party, or otherwise commit or bind the other Party, without the other Party's advance written consent, (ii) to otherwise create any contract or obligation, either express or implied, on behalf of, in the name of, or binding upon the other Party or (iii) to accept legal process on behalf of the other Party.

18.11 No Third Party Beneficiaries. This Agreement is made solely and specifically between and for the benefit of the Parties and their respective successors and assigns, and no other Person, unless express provision is made herein to the contrary, shall have any rights, interests or claims hereunder or be entitled to any benefits under or on account of this Agreement as a third party beneficiary or otherwise.

18.12 Incidental and Consequential Damages. No Party will be liable to any other Party under any contract, negligence, strict liability or other theory for any indirect, incidental or consequential damages (including without limitation lost profits) with respect to a breach of this Agreement.

18.13 Counterparts. This Agreement may be executed in any number of counterparts, and each counterpart shall constitute an original instrument, but all such separate counterparts shall constitute one and the same instrument.

18.14 Execution by the Company. Each of the Parties shall cause (i) the Company to be formed as a Sino-foreign joint venture company and (ii) the Company to enter into this Agreement and other Related Agreements to which it is a party as soon as possible after its formation.

18.15 Approval by the Approval Authority. Notwithstanding any other provision herein, this Joint Venture Agreement shall come into effect upon approval by the Approval Authority.

[*SIGNATURES APPEAR ON NEXT PAGE*]

- 31 -

IN WITNESS WHEREOF, the Parties have executed this Agreement as of the Effective Date

"Hong Kong Holdco "
ZBB PowerSav Holdings Limited

"China JV "
Anhui Xindong Investment Management Co., Ltd.

By: _____

Name:
Title:

By: _____

Name:
Title:

About the Authors

Frederick D. Lipman (lipman@blankrome.com) is a senior partner with the international law firm of Blank Rome LLP, with offices throughout the U.S. and in Hong Kong and Shanghai. He has lectured on business topics in China, appeared on Chinese television, and has also lectured at the United Nations in Geneva, Switzerland, as well as in Bangkok, Thailand and Mumbai, India. He has held faculty positions in the MBA program at the Wharton School of Business and at the University of Pennsylvania Law School for a combined total of thirteen years and at Temple University Law School for five years. A graduate of Harvard Law School, Mr. Lipman has appeared on CNBC, CNN, Fox Business, and Bloomberg television and has been quoted in the Wall Street Journal, the New York Times, USA Today, Forbes, and other business publications. He is an internationally known authority on business law and has authored 14 other books, including *Whistleblowers, Incentives, Disincentives and Protection Strategies* (John Wiley & Sons, Inc. 2012), *Audit Committees* (The Bureau of National Affairs, Inc. 2011), *The Family Business Guide* (Palgrave Macmillan 2010), *International and U.S. IPO Planning* (John Wiley & Sons, Inc. 2009), *Executive Compensation Best Practices* (John Wiley & Sons, Inc. 2008), *Corporate Governance Best Practices* (John Wiley & Sons, Inc. 2006) and *Valuing Your Business: Strategies to Maximize the Sale Price* (John Wiley & Sons, Inc. (2005).

Professor Larry Dongxiao Qiu (larryqiu@hku.hk) is a professor at the School of Economics and Finances and an Associate Dean at The University of Hong Kong. He teaches courses in foreign trade and investment in China and has published a number of academic papers, including a paper entitled "Cross-Border Strategic Alliances and Foreign Market Entry", and co-authored an article entitled "International Mergers: Incentives and Welfare." Dr. Qiu obtained his Bachelor of Science (Math) degree in 1983 from Zhongshan University, China, Master of Arts (Economics) degree in 1989 and PhD (Economics) degree in 1993 from University of British Columbia, Canada. He then joined Hong Kong University of Science and Technology in 1993 as an assistant professor and later became an associate professor and then professor. He moved to The University of Hong Kong in January 2008 as a professor. Dr. Qiu's research covers a wide range of topics, with focuses on industrial organization, international trade and foreign direct investment (FDI). In the field of FDI, he analyzes cross-border M&As, strategic alliances and technology transfer. He has also done some research on China's foreign trade and FDI. He has published extensively in international journals and books. Dr. Qiu has taught a variety of courses at all levels and in many places including China, Hong Kong and Portugal. Examples of his courses include globalization, international trade and finance, China's industry analysis, and foreign trade and investment in China.

Printed in Great Britain
by Amazon

40356402R00189